THE COLLECTOR'S MANUAL

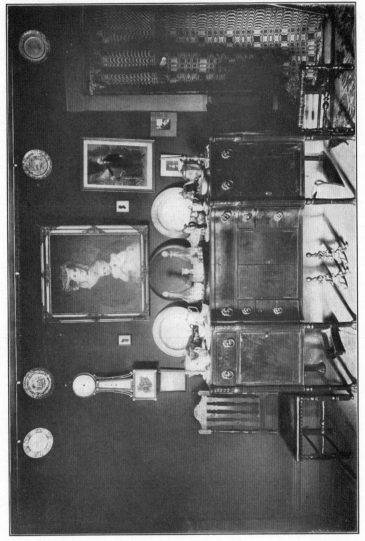

A Dining-Room in Lynn, Mass.

THE
COLLECTOR'S
MANUAL

BY
N. HUDSON MOORE

AUTHOR OF "THE OLD CHINA BOOK," "THE OLD FURNITURE BOOK,"
"OLD PEWTER, BRASS, COPPER, AND SHEFFIELD PLATE,"
"THE LACE BOOK," "FLOWER FABLES
AND FANCIES," ETC.

WITH 336 ENGRAVINGS

*"I love everything that's
old; old friends, old times,
old manners, old books, old
wine."* — GOLDSMITH.

TUDOR PUBLISHING CO.
NEW YORK

692046

PRINTED IN THE UNITED STATES OF AMERICA
BY THE VAN REES PRESS, NEW YORK CITY

CONTENTS

ILLUSTRATIONS

ILLUSTRATIONS

CHAPTER III

ILLUSTRATIONS

CHAPTER IV

ILLUSTRATIONS

CHAPTER V

X

ILLUSTRATIONS

CHAPTER VI

ILLUSTRATIONS

xii

ILLUSTRATIONS

ILLUSTRATIONS

xiv

ILLUSTRATIONS

ILLUSTRATIONS

THE COLLECTOR'S MANUAL

THE
COLLECTOR'S MANUAL.

I — TABLES AND SIDEBOARDS

AT the first glance it would not seem that there was very close connection between these two objects, but the sideboard is the direct outgrowth from the side table. When some enthusiastic furniture collector tells you that he has a sideboard three hundred years old, do not believe him, for there were no sideboards then, no, nor a hundred and fifty years ago, either. The earliest ones are not more than one hundred and twenty-five to thirty years of age, and such antiques as these are few and far between. None of them are to be " picked up."

In order to get a clear idea of the matter, I am going to begin as far back as those days which seem so remote to us, before the Mayflower had begun her perilous voyage across the sea.

The very earliest form of table was a board on trestles. This was used for eating from, and since the small number of dishes and trenchers could be placed on it at once, there was no necessity of any side table. Conveniences increased, elegancies crept in, and the time arrived when it was necessary to have an extra table to place the table furniture upon, and on which to display the plate and cups when not in use. The trestle-table,

1

1

with its bench or form, was early in use in England. It was mentioned in inventories by 1530, and the seats were placed on one side only, the other being unoccupied, so that those at table could be conveniently served.

These trestles and boards are still preserved in some of the old English dwellings, particularly in those which have been held in one family for several centuries. In Berkeley Castle, near the Welsh border, are antiquities of all kinds, for the castle has been in the possession of the Berkeley family since about 1260, with the exception of a few years when it was confiscated by the crown. In the vast dining-room, which is really a hall in size and lofty grandeur, the modern dining-table looks lonely enough. But, when the castle was a feudal stronghold, hundreds have no doubt sat down to meals there, and there are standing against the walls boards and trestles which have come down with the castle, and which are black with age. These are used now when a large company banquets there, for the family pride themselves on their adherence to old-time customs.

Matthew Parker, Archbishop of Canterbury, was born at Norwich, England, in 1504. He was appointed chaplain to Anne Boleyn, that unfortunate wife of Henry VIII, and later held high state at Canterbury, to which bishopric he was appointed in 1559. To give some idea of how these princes of the church lived, I quote the following from " Strype's Life of Parker ":

"In their daily eating this was the custom. The steward, with the servants that were gentlemen of the better rank, sate down at the tables in the hall at the right hand, and the

2

almoner, with the clergy and other servants, sat on the other side. Where there was plenty of all sorts of wholesome food, both for eating and drinking. The daily fragments thereof did suffice to fill the bellies of a great number of poor hungry people, that waited at the gate. And so constant and unfailing was this great supply at my lord's table, that whosoever came in either at dinner or supper, being not above the degree of a knight, might here be entertained worthy of his quality, either at the steward's or at the almoner's table. And moreover it was the Archbishop's command to his servants, that all strangers should be received and treated with all manner of civility and respect, and that their places at the table should be assigned to them according to their dignity and quality, which redounded much to the praise and commendation of the Archbishop. The discourse and conversation at meals was void of all brawling and loud talking; and for the most part consisted in framing men's manners to religion, or in some such honest and seeming subject. There was a monitor of the hall. And if it happened that any spoke too loud, or concerning things less decent, it was presently hushed by one that cried silence."

"Holinshed's Chronicles" (about 1570), which are great sources of information about life at that period in England, Scotland, and Ireland, has this about breakfast:

"Heretofore there has been much more time spent in eating and drinking than commonly is in these days; for whereas of old we had breakfasts in the forenoon, beverages or nuntions after dinner, and thereto rear suppers generally when it was time to go to bed, — now these odd repasts, thanked be God, are very well left, and each one in manner (except here and there some young hungry stomach that cannot fast till dinner time) contenteth himself with dinner and supper only."

3

There is also an ancient manuscript of the Percy family which relates to the family during the sixteenth century, and which gives in detail the bill of fare of the family, throughout the whole year, and shows what appeared on the table-boards of the nobility at that time.

It gives not only the meals for the Earl and Countess, but for the children of the family as well.

" Breakfast for my Lord and Lady, during Lent.

First, a loaf of bread in trenchers, 2 manchets, a quart of beer, a quart of wine, 2 pieces of salt fish, 6 baconn'd herring, 4 white herring, or a dish of sprats.

Breakfast for my Lord Percy and Master Thomas Percy.

Item, half a loaf of household bread, a manchet, a bottle of beer, a dish of butter, and a piece of salt fish, a dish of spratts, or three white herring.

Breakfast for the nursery, for my Lady Margaret and Master Ingeram.

Item a manchet, a quart of beer, a dish of butter, a piece of salt fish, a dish of sprats, or three white herring."

And except for the season of Lent and fish-days, the ordinary allowance for the family was as follows:

" Breakfasts of flesh days daily throughout the year. For my Lord and Lady.

First a loaf of breade in trenchers, 2 manchets, a quart of beer, a quart of wine, half a chine of mutton, or else a chine of beef boiled.

4

Breakfasts for my Lord Percy and Master Thomas Percy.

Item, half a loaf of household bread, a manchet, 1 bottle of beer, a cheeking, or else three mutton bones boiled.

Breakfasts for the nursery.

Item, a manchet, 1 quart of beer, and three mutton bones boiled."

Nothing very dainty, truly, for the nursery or the great hall! "A manchet" was a loaf of fine white bread, which seems something choicer than what is denominated "household bread."

There was nothing known at this period but the trestle-board, and few of them are left even in England, while in our own land, where so few things are kept, except in some conservative old families in New England and the South, the trestle-board was chopped up long ago, and I know of but two really old ones which are still preserved, even though they have been banished to the attic.

Robert White, of Essex, England, had a very long inventory attached to his will, which was filed in 1617. He gives to his son, John White, "the ioyned standinge bedstead w'ch is in the parlour, with the featherbed, flockbed, bolster covering, with other furniture thereunto belonginge. Alsoe the presse cupboard, the cupboard table and my newest chest, all which are in ye parlour, to be delivered him after the death of my said wife Bridgett White, or instead thereof the sum of 20 marks of like lawful moneye."

In a will executed in Devonshire, England, dated

5

July, 1617, is this item: "To my sonne William my tableboard in ye hall. To my daughter Susan my Cribbone in ye hall." I have never yet been able to discover what the latter article was. Among the un-expected kinds of tables which I find inventoried is, "1 old Billyard table, £3," which Francis Hulin, of New York, bequeaths in 1704, showing that these tables had been in use earlier than this, since he classes his as old.

In Figures 1 and 2 are given the second step in table growth, both of these dating to about 1600, the smaller table being the style which was used in private houses, with the joint stool to sit on. The larger one, generally called a "cavalier" table, was in use at the inns, and one can almost see the cavalier himself coming in and throwing down his feathered hat, and crying, "A cup of wine, landlord," just as they do in the play. It would not seem to offer much inducement to linger long over the meal, for a more uncomfortable object than that stool it would be hard to imagine.

The baluster table in Figure 3 was in use about fifty years later, that is, by 1650, and is, like the two preced-ing ones, of oak. The legs of all three are turned, and the carved decoration is of the familiar patterns which we have found on chests of the same period. The baluster table is ten feet long, and the ends may be dropped if a shorter table is desired.

This seems to be the first type of distinctively serving-tables, Figure 1, and Figure 2 as well, being properly dining-tables.

6

Fig. 1 Oak Table and Joint Stool

Fig. 2 Cavalier Table

Fig. 3 Baluster Table

Fig. 4 SIDE-TABLE WITH DRAWERS

Fig. 5 "HUNDRED-LEG" TABLE

Fig. 6 SERVING-TABLE WITH LEAVES

Fig. 7 "EXTENDING DINING-TABLE"

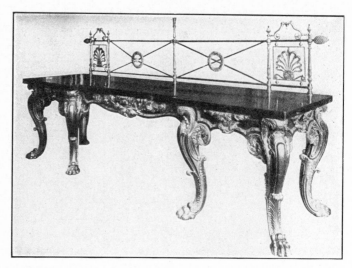

Fig. 8   CHIPPENDALE SIDEBOARD TABLE

Fig. 9   HEPPLEWHITE SIDEBOARD

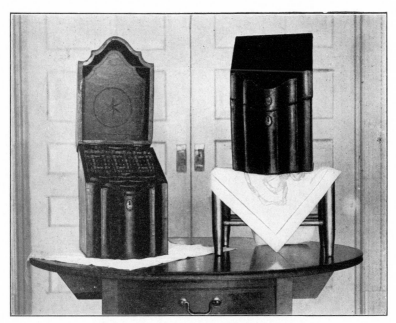

Fig. 10 GENERAL WASHINGTON'S KNIFE-BOXES

Fig. 11 KNIVES AND FORKS, XVIII CENTURY

Fig. 12 SIDEBOARD, KNIFE-BOXES, AND WINE-COOLER

Fig. 13 SIDEBOARD WITH TAMBOUR WORK

Fig. 14 SHERATON SIDEBOARD

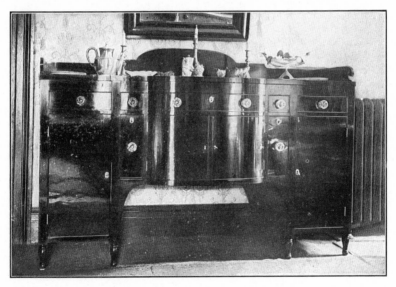

Fig. 15 SIDEBOARD "SHERATON STYLE"

Fig. 16 CORNER SIDEBOARD

Fig. 17 CORNER SIDEBOARD

The one given in Figure 4 is a very early type, and shows that the idea of having a place in which to keep the table linen and other table furniture was taking hold, and that the familiar chest was no longer all-sufficient. The panelling of the drawers of this table, the bail handles, which were fastened in with twisted wire instead of screws, and the turned legs, — all place it in the last of the seventeenth or early in the eighteenth century. The wood is oak, and there are two panels to each drawer, and three styles of ornament are used in these panels. These drawers were used for plate or linen and, as you see, could be locked. With time and wear the wood has grown very black and almost as solid as iron.

Occasionally in an English inventory prior to 1700 reference is found to a " sideboard table," which was like this, no doubt, and I find them mentioned here as well. In the early days of this country, and in England too, the inn was the most important house in the village, and the innkeepers, many of them, were more than comfortably off, and for the convenience of their patrons had many things not to be found in middle-class homes. Some of the famous old inns, which have been carefully restored, have still enough of their old-time comfort clinging to them to justify this conclusion, and if you should visit, for example, the Wayside Inn at South Sudbury, Massachusetts, or the Red Lion at Stockbridge, in the same State, you would find choice pieces of old furniture in mahogany, and the delightful old china for which so many of us are eagerly

7

striving. But these inns belong to the eighteenth century.

Before me lies the inventory of the estate of William Trask, who kept the famous Black Horse Tavern, in Salem, Massachusetts, and whose will was filed March 28, 1691. The whole estate was valued at £413, — a round sum for those times, and one rather wonders where he stowed away those travellers who wished to remain all night, for there must have been some such, even taking into consideration the poor roads and the dangers of going far from settlements at that time. A portion of the will is as follows:

	£	s.	d.
Imprimis. A dwelling house, one barn, one orchard, and ye upland and marsh adjoining .	110	00	00
Parlour. 1 standinge bedstead, and feather bed and beding	6	00	00
1 trundle bedstead, featherbed and beding	4	00	00
1 longtable and forme		12	00
1 cupboard, 8 chairs, 1 wainscot chist, 1 box, 1 warming pan	1	10	00
Weareing app'l, 1 pr. Irons and tongs, 12 glass bottles, 1 psl flax and yarn . . .	8	05	00
Goods in Kitchen.			
Brass and Pewter, 2 Iron Potts, 1 pr. Iron doggs, 2 hakes, 1 pr. tongs, 1 Grid Iron, fryeing pan and spitt	2	18	00

There was, besides, one " old " feather bed and bedding, and this was the entire furnishing. Of course, the chief room in the house was the taproom, and all the furnishings that he had in any great number were bottles; and it is specified with some particularity that they were of glass, for leather bottles were also in

8

use; and in Heyward's "Philocothonista" I find the following:

"Other bottles we have of leather, but they are most used amongst the shepherds and harvest people of the country. Small jacks we have in many ale-houses of the cities and suburbs, tipt with silver, besides the great black jacks and bombards at the court, which when the Frenchmen first saw they reported, at their return into their countrey, that the Englishmen used to drinke out of their bootes."

Fifty years later saw a great difference in the furnishings which were owned by a successful Boniface. In 1730 Abel Chapin died in the little town of Chicopee, Massachusetts, and he had grown rich in keeping an inn. The inventory of his estate contains six hundred items, among them being thirty-six linen sheets and six tablecloths.

In the private home it was long before the separate room was used for dining. If the warm and comfortable kitchen was not used, meals were served in the "great room," or the hall, which was a much more important part of the house than we make it. At first, even in manor or castle, there was but a screen put up to furnish privacy for the family, since the retainers and men-at-arms all ate in the same room and at the same time as the family. Little by little the dining-room gained favour, and even then held a bed, along with the Flanders' chests, forms and joint stools, and the long table-board.

The dining-table, which was in use at this time — that is, about 1650 — and for the next fifty years, is shown

9

in the next figure, No. 5. It is variously known as the "gate-legged" or the "hundred legged" table, and it was one like this, made of oak, which had a place in the dining-room of William Penn, though his had fewer legs.

About the middle of the eighteenth century there were improvements in the serving-tables, as can be seen in Figure 6; for this has two leaves, which can be pulled out, so that its capacity can be increased. The example shown is a very handsome one, with a carved frieze rail, and two carved rosettes at the top of each leg. The wood is mahogany.

The dining-tables kept pace with the serving ones, and Figure 7 shows one of the same period as Figure 6 and which was called an "extending-table," though what we call an extension-table was not made till about 1800.

Chippendale made some very elegant tables, for side or serving-tables, with marble tops or those of solid mahogany, and with richly carved frames, very few of which found their way over here. What there were seem to have been gradually absorbed by museums, and there is one at Memorial Hall, Philadelphia, which I have shown elsewhere, and once in a while you will find one belonging to some rich collector.

In Figure 8 is shown such a sideboard table, one of a pair, twelve feet long, of richly carved mahogany. They came from the fine old English house, Luton Hoo, in Bedfordshire.

The first man to make what we know as sideboards

10

was a cabinet-maker named Thomas Shearer, of London, England, who issued a book of designs in the year 1788. That they were immediately popular is shown by the fact that all the other cabinet-makers took to making them too, and in 1789 Hepplewhite published a book with his designs, and two years later came Sheraton with his.

Figure 9 shows a Hepplewhite sideboard, with the " spade foot " which was so characteristic of this maker. This board is solid mahogany, with a curved top, and though in England they commonly veneered them on oak, those made in this country, and there are many of them, are veneered on pine, as we did not use so costly a wood as oak for that purpose. The curve under the drawers was to accommodate the wine-cooler, and the usual ornament for the top of the sideboard was not a pair of candelabra, but a pair of knife-boxes, made of the same wood as the sideboard itself, and left open to display the wealth of knives inside, particularly if they had the fashionable handles of green ivory or silver. These knife-boxes, like the sideboards, were always costly and elegant objects. Those of an urn shape were difficult to make and they were often inlaid, which added to the cost. Inside was a frame filled with holes, which held the knives, and there were also in some of them places for spoons, which were put in with the bowls up. A pair belonging to General Washington are shown in Figure 10. And a set of knives and forks in Figure 11.

An example of a wine-cooler and also a pair of knife-boxes is given in Figure 12. Indeed, in convivial days, these wine-coolers were very important parts of dining-room furniture, and were arranged to hold six, eight, or twelve bottles; and one holding eighteen bottles belonged to General George Washington himself, and is now in the possession of some of his descendants, with a large number of the bottles which stood in little compartments, intact, and each capable of holding a gallon.

Major Church, of Rochester, New York, has an autograph letter from General Washington, addressed to Colonel Hamilton, in which he says that he is sending him a wine-cooler capable of " holding six bottles, one of four which I imported during my term of governmental administration." There were elegancies of many kinds at Mount Vernon, and the General himself looked after the furnishings of the house, as well as after the purchasing of his own, Madam Washington's, and Miss Custis' clothes. These were imported from England, and were bought by his factors in London in pursuance of minute directions given in the voluminous letters which the General wrote with his own hand and despatched by every ship. The very " minikin " pins with which the clothes of Nelly Custis were to be fastened were not too small items for his attention, and he gave special orders for her doll to be dressed in the " newest fashion."

He took advantage of every opportunity to better and increase the household articles at Mount Vernon, and it is strange to think of this truly great man bid-

12

ding at auction for pickle-pots, bolsters, pillows, and bottles, as he did when the contents of the splendid mansion of the Fairfax's, " Belvoir," on the Potomac, was sold at auction. Among the expensive pieces of furniture, nearly all of them mahogany, which he bought on this occasion, was " 1 mahogany sideboard, £12 05 00," showing that fine pieces of furniture brought good prices even then. He bought side tables as well, and his dining-room must have been a dignified and elegant apartment, even if the meals were a trifle solemn.

Hepplewhite also excelled in a style of work which was called " tambour," which consisted of small strips of wood pasted on heavy cloth. This rolled up in a hollow space, and he used it on desks, work-tables, and sideboards. See Figure 13.

Figure 14 shows a style that is not unusual, and is known as Sheraton, whether made in England or here. It comes in both solid and veneered mahogany, and with inlay or without. This example has some very pretty inlay of whitewood which spreads out into fans on the cupboard doors. In the two lower drawers are spaces for the wine bottles, and I have seen some examples like this which had the drawers lined with zinc, making them air-tight. Some of the early sideboards by Shearer and Sheraton have brass rails at the back and sides. They are very pretty, but by no means common. You will find many patterns for such in their books of designs.

In Figure 15 a piece is shown in Sheraton style, and

13

this board is interesting in all its details, besides being one of those treasures which fell into the hands of its owner at a cost so delightfully small that it seems well-nigh incredible. This picture was sent me by a collector who has had remarkable success in filling her whole house with equally choice pieces of old furniture, and while the description of this piece is carefully written on the back of the photograph, the owner has neglected to add her name, and I have lost the accompanying letter. I should place the date of this piece at about 1800, as the handles are rosettes and the feet are of the pattern popular at that time. This sideboard, besides having solid doors, which even in the photograph show their beautiful graining, has a strip of satinwood which extends the whole length of the board above the drawers. There was also a place for the wine-cooler, and the bottle drawers are air-tight.

In addition to the straight sideboard which stood against the wall there were those which were made to stand in corners, and thus take up less room. In fact the first sideboards made by Shearer had their tops the shape of a half circle, and the flat side stood against the wall. These were almost without exception veneered and inlaid, and some of the most costly and choice were beautifully painted with figures and scenes on the top, but I have never seen one like this in this country, at least one of the veritable old ones. The simple corner ones, however, are to be found here, of excellent workmanship and of fine wood. One is shown in Figure 16. This choice piece, of mahogany inlaid, has the es-

14

cutcheons of ivory, which always gave a look of elegance to the furniture to which they were applied. The date of this piece is about 1770, or in that neighborhood, and it is owned in Vermont, where some years ago there was much fine furniture to be had. Even in remote parts of the State now, patriotic and historical societies have been organized, and these are gathering the antiques and preserving them, so that the individual collector has a smaller chance to secure the objects for which he pines. The sideboard in Figure 16 is a typical piece of this style, but in Figure 17 is given one in which the individual maker has given expression to his own ideas. This, too, is of mahogany, with a slightly curved front and flat sides, and with a modified form of French foot. The age of the piece is not to be judged by the handles, which have been recently put on and are modern. It is a pity that better ones were not secured, since the piece is otherwise in excellent condition. I saw one of these sideboards the other day, which had been " cleared out " by a woman who was moving and who sold it for two dollars. There is more of the story, however, for it cost the purchaser fifty dollars to get it restored. The sideboard in Figure 17 has a prettily curved front, almost serpentine, different from the half circle which these boards usually have. It has the board at the bottom, which was so much used at the end of the eighteenth century, but I think the shelves were a later addition. Even so, it is an agreeable piece of furniture and an ornament to any room.

15

There has been a great exhibition of old furniture at the South Kensington Museum, London. There was much shown which had a deal of history connected with it. Who could help " thrilling " when he saw a chair which some monarch or great person had used familiarly, and upon which he could gaze his fill? Many of the objects were undoubtedly some of the choicest relics in England, and worthy of the highest respect, but there were others that caused you to smile, even if you did come from the home of the youngest nation, where anything is antique that survives our chop and change for fifty years. Every object had attached to it the label made out by the owner, and we are not the only ones who add years and years of age to our possessions. There were pieces of furniture marked with the name of Chippendale, and their date set down as 1720, when the great maker was but a lad at his mother's knee. You cannot always trust a collector's estimate of his own possessions, and the only safe way is to study them yourself, and then draw your own conclusions, always taking care to keep them to yourself if they do not agree with the statements of the owner. If you attempt to set him or her right you will only get yourself disliked.

With the French Revolution styles in furniture altered very much. When Napoleon came on the scene they altered still more, particularly after his victories in Egypt had called his attention to Egyptian ornament. About 1800 a style was evolved called " Empire," which was heavy and ornate, with none of the

16

graceful lines and delicate ornament of the previous century to recommend it. This style was freely copied by both the English and the Dutch, the latter adapting it to their excellent standards and turning out much handsome furniture. The English, on the other hand, made their Empire furniture very heavy and added much brass, both cast and wrought, in which was seen the influence of that style of decoration which had been so popular during the reigns of Louis XIV, Louis XV, and Louis XVI.

In Figure 18 is given an English rendering of the Empire style, and shows a very plain and solid sideboard, with a sparing use of gilt at the tops and bases of the pillars. It has leaves which will draw out on the sides, for the use of the carver, and a rising back. It is made of mahogany and is not veneered. It is a good, plain piece of furniture, but is distinctly inferior, from an ornamental point of view, to those pieces which have preceded it.

In Figure 19 is given a much more ornamental piece, with richly carved legs and pillars and handsome panelled doors. This style, which is on the Empire order, is sometimes called "Colonial," which is manifestly wrong, since that term rightly belongs only to furniture made before 1776, and this was not invented till about 1800, long after our Revolution.

A pattern of sideboard which was popular about 1810 is also given, the glass knobs being thought quite "the thing" by the housekeepers of those days. A fine dining-table with heavy carved feet went with such a sideboard, and was often of mahogany. (Figures 20 and 21.)

In addition to these tables, which were distinctly for dining-room service, there were others, which could be found in different parts of the house, and were used for various purposes. I have no doubt that those most in use were the numberless little work-tables (see Figures 23, 25, 26) at which our grandmothers sat, laboring often far into the night to complete the many garments which had to pass through their hands, when neither sewing-machines nor "ready-to-wear" clothes were to be obtained. I have heard an old lady who had a family of ten children, seven of them girls, say that she made thousands of buttonholes every year, until each girl grew big enough to be taught to make her own. But if they used the work-tables pretty steadily during the day, some evenings in the week were devoted to a game of cards, and many handsome tables were sent here from England, like those in Figure 22. Hepplewhite and Sheraton made delicate and elegant ones, still to be found in many homes. Most of these tables are ornamented with inlay, the familiar "husk pattern" running down the legs, which so often tapered to a spade-foot, or had a piece of whitewood let in a few inches from the floor. These tables generally closed over on the top, so that they could be set against the wall when not in use. Rosewood card-tables were made in this country, elegantly carved and covered with baize on the top, but the Hepplewhite and Sheraton tables have usually plain wood tops.

18

The little work-table shown in Figure 23 is interesting because there is one exactly like it at Mount Vernon, standing in the room in which General Washington died. The "Dutch foot," a name which is given to this style of turned-out foot, is by no means common on tables, though it was often to be found on chairs. This table, like the one at Mount Vernon, is of mahogany, like the so-called "pie-crust" table also given in Figure 24. The old pie-crust tables always show the marks of the carving tool along the edges of the crust, while the modern ones, and there are many of these latter, are sandpapered down so as to be perfectly smooth.

The most modern of all these tables are to be seen in the last three illustrations. The one with the wooden bag (Figure 25) is not at all pretty, but it is quaint, and I know of only two or three such. This is made on what would be called Sheraton style, and from a fine piece of mahogany.

The Empire table with brass-tipped feet (Figure 26) is a choice specimen of its type, and in fine condition, while the papier-mâché table (Figure 27), in addition to the painting in the centre, has a border of inlay, chiefly of mother-of-pearl.

II — ENGLISH POTTERY AND PORCELAIN

THAT the interest in old china is not subsiding is very evident from the inquiries of many correspondents who ask about pieces which they own. Recently I have had letters referring to an article published in 1901, the writers having had their questions in mind all that time, but "just getting round to it."

Indeed, the true collector, when once embarked on his career, is seldom content to keep in one narrow path, but strays out in many directions, and finds pleasure in them all. In support of this theory I am tempted to quote a letter from an unknown correspondent, who finds much under her own roof, and is not only interested herself, but has managed to interest others. The letter begins, "Dear Friend," and after some kind and complimentary remarks, goes on as follows:

"I have made a fine collection of quaint old things from 'up garret' and elsewhere at home. Father's ancestors were among the earliest settlers of Ipswich, Mass., and my father is now living at the age of ninety years. My mother's family had a grant of three thousand acres in Orange County, N. Y., from Queen Anne, where they were all born, lived, and died, from that time; even my mother was born there. From these Huguenots I have little else than a 'Bull's Eye' watch, but

20

from a generation later have linen coverlets, bullet-mould, powder-horn, etc., and shoe-buckles of General Washington's time. Now I sigh thinking of lovely, old things sold to the ' Junk man.' Every time I read anything you have written, I go ' a-rummaging'! The family all laugh at me, and call me ' Old Antique,' but they were interested enough, I notice, when I found an original ' led-pencil' and showed them the evolution of the Pen. First a quill, from a desk of 1755, the feather part all moth-eaten, then steel pens dedicated to Washington, Webster, Croton Water-works celebration in 1845, Free Mason, etc., down to our own Fountain pen. Such queer handles as there were among them! I send this sketch of Pewter Shaving-box and soap-box with queer cake of soap, old and dried. Not the one stolen in 1777, I hope!"

(This latter remark refers to an advertisement mentioned in the article on Pewter.)

To the majority of us china exerts a fascination which we cannot resist, and from the very nature of the field, since this country was so largely settled by emigrants from England, English china is what most naturally comes our way. Nor is there no possibility of collecting choicer wares also of English make, and in this chapter a number of specimens of porcelains, collected in this country, are given.

" How shall I know pottery from porcelain? " This question is asked me many, many times. They may be distinguished by the following very simple test: If you hold your piece up to the light and can see light through it, that is, if it is translucent, it is porcelain.

Pottery is opaque, and is not so hard and white as porcelain. The main differences in the manufacture

21

of stoneware, earthenware, and porcelain are due to the ingredients used, to the way they are mixed, and to the degree of heat to which they are subjected in firing.

Most of the old English wares found in this country are pottery or semi-china, although the term china is commonly applied to them all.

The potteries in Staffordshire, covering an area ten miles long, were the most important in England, in view of the fact that besides Hanley, Cobridge, Fenton, Longport, Shelton, Tunstall, Lane End, and Stoke-on-Trent they included Burslem and Etruria, made famous by being the seats, first at Burslem and then at Etruria, of Wedgwood's potteries.

I have spoken before of the small price at which these pottery wares were sold when they were first made, and how the price has risen little by little until it has become quite preposterous. It must be distinctly borne in mind, however, that it is the historic crockery only which is so valuable, decorated with scenes relating to our own early history or to our heroes, and, with but a few exceptions, made in rich, dark blue.

One of the earliest Staffordshire products was what was known as "saltglaze" ware, — a certain coarse pottery which was glazed by putting salt in the kiln in which the objects were being fired. This ware was formed in moulds, and in the case of plates the borders were often exceedingly pretty and intricate, like that shown in Figure 28.

Occasionally the borders were openwork, and the surface of the ware is always pitted like orange peel.

22

Fig. 18 A Sideboard with Serving-Leaves

Fig. 19 Empire Sideboard

Fig. 20 Sideboard with Curved Front

Fig. 21 Dining-Table with Carved Feet

Fig. 22 CARD-TABLES

Fig. 23 WORK-TABLE

Fig. 24 "PIE-CRUST" TABLE

Fig. 27 Papier-mâché Table

Fig. 26 Empire Table

Fig. 25 Table with Bag

Fig. 28 Salt Glaze Plate

Fig. 29 "Near Fishkill"

Fig. 30 Catskill Plate

Fig. 31 "FLEURS" AND "BLENHEIM"

Fig. 32 ADAMS' JASPER WARE

Fig. 34 "York Minster"

Fig. 33 Adams' Parian Figures

Fig. 35 VIEW OF SOUTHAMPTON

Fig. 36 "MARYLAND ARMS"

Fig. 37 "MARYLAND ARMS"

This formation is caused by the way the salt forms on the surface of the ware while in the kiln.

Many of the moulds used were those of metal cast aside by silversmiths. Complete dinner and tea sets were made, as well as small figures. Very rarely flat ware is found painted in color upon the glaze.

There is a class of pieces made a little later than the dark blue and less interesting. They are printed in various colours, and have the merit of being decorative and comparatively cheap. Figure 29 shows such a piece; it is part of a set called "Picturesque Views," made by Clews, and this particular view is called "Near Fishkill." You will find them in black, red, green, purple, brown, and a medium shade of blue. An artist named Wall, from Dublin, Ireland, made the original sketches of these scenes, and there were about twenty-five in all. You can always tell them by their border, which is of flowers and scrolls, with two birds placed at intervals among the scrolls. Besides the views of Hudson River scenery, the "Picturesque Views" contain two views of Pittsburg, with boats in the foreground, and one of "Fairmount Water Works, Philadelphia." You will find these pictures on flat ware, i.e., plates and platters, on vegetable dishes, and pitchers. Plates in good condition, ten-inch size, like the one shown, are worth, at the very highest, five dollars; smaller sizes, less. Platters, fifteen-inch size, well printed and clear, will perhaps fetch ten dollars.

There are views by other makers, like Adams or Jackson, which are harder to find and more desirable.

23

In Figure 30 is shown such a plate made by Adams, and called " Catskill Mountain House." The Adams pottery is always good, and there are over a dozen different views taken in various parts of the Eastern States. They range in price from two to two and a half dollars higher, size for size, than the Clews pieces. Jackson's pottery, of which there are over thirty views, varies much in price, the " Hancock House " plate commanding twenty dollars, while " The President's House, Washington," is worth but half that sum.

In the deep blue Staffordshire I show in Figure 31 two English views, and there are doubtless many pieces belonging to these and other series tucked away in odd places and half forgotten. The beautiful fourteen-inch platter at the top is by Adams, and shows the " Castle of Fleurs, Roxburghshire," on one of the finest estates in Scotland. The castle was built in 1718, and belongs to the Duke of Roxburghe, who recently married an American girl, Miss May Goelet, so that the interest in this piece may well increase till it becomes as popular as the views below it, which are of " Blenheim," the seat of the Duke of Marlborough, who married Miss Vanderbilt.

Both of the lower views are of Blenheim, the one on the right being by Adams, and much the rarer and finer of the two. The other one is by an unknown maker. The Adams piece has long been esteemed by collectors for the beauty of its colouring and printing, and the international complication has just given it an

24

added touch of interest. Both the Fleurs platter and the Blenheim plate belong to the same series, as will be seen by examining the border. It cannot be too often mentioned what a very important part the border takes in these old plates. By its means the maker of a piece can usually be identified, for, although the old potters "borrowed" the central views from each other with the greatest freedom, they were very scrupulous with reference to duplicating borders. Only in a few instances, where potteries and the blocks on hand passed to other owners, was there confusion. These instances are quite well known, as, for example, the similar patterns used by A. and R. Stevenson, and the famous bluebell border used by both Adams and Clews. Adams was, however, generally quite particular to sign his name, and it appears in the scroll with flowers which is on the back of the plate.

Indeed, there is hardly anything ceramic which bears the name of Adams which is not worthy of the collector's interest. There are those who confine themselves to articles made by the Adamses only, and they possess varied and beautiful objects. The Adamses came of a race of potters, and William Adams, the friend and pupil of Wedgwood, was one of the few who used the splendid jasper body invented by Wedgwood with almost the skill and taste of that master himself. The years when Adams worked, from 1787 to 1805, was the time when the classical figures of Flaxman had such a vogue. In Figure 32 is shown a group of the jasper pottery made by Adams, and the grace and elegance of the figures speak for themselves.

It is often said that Adams "copied" Wedgwood, but while it is true that he worked in the same manner and material, there are details which are all his own, and his use of colour and form was quite original with him. It is also true that of all the potters working at that time, his work, in its finish, came the nearest to the perfection of Wedgwood's, and after the death of the latter, in 1795, many pieces of Adams' jasper had his name erased from them by unscrupulous dealers and were sold as Wedgwood.

After the death of William Adams his son carried on the business, and in 1849 and 1850 made some of the earliest Parian figures put on the market. The earliest use of this material was by the firm of Copeland and Garrett, who succeeded Spode. They potted at Stoke-on-Trent and had used Parian in 1848. But the Adams figures far excelled all others, and how charming they were can be seen from the small group shown in Figure 33.

Still another field for the collector who delights to specialise is in collecting one branch of the splendid English views, like the cathedrals. In Figure 34 are shown three views of York Minster, — the upper one by Stevenson, the lower one with the steamboat a rare piece by an unknown maker, and the other one by John Geddes, also uncommon.

Views of cities like the one of Southampton (Figure 35) are always attractive and ornamental, and you do

26

not realise the beauty of colour and the immense variety of shades used by these Staffordshire potters till you have a dozen or more pieces by different potters on your walls.

The coats of arms of the different states is an interesting if limited field, and although a number of these pieces were made by T. Mayer, at Burslem, England, for the American market, in the popular dark blue, about 1829 and later, they are not easily found. Two even less common renderings of the arms of Maryland are given in the next two figures (36 and 37), and though these are highly coloured, they are Staffordshire ware, the one with the designs on the rim having the impressed mark " Ironstone," while the other has no mark.

Religious scenes are represented by The Woman of Samaria (Figure 38), by Wood, which is a handsome dark blue plate, and there are other designs by such makers as Adams and the Ridgways, who also put out religious subjects. There are patterns on cups and saucers which interest collectors, and though they are not so easy to display as flat ware, still they do not take so much room as jugs. Wesley appears not only on cups and saucers, like the one shown (Figure 39), which, although modern, being printed in 1891, is already quite rare, but in Staffordshire busts, some of them nine inches high. Such are to be picked up occasionally, and I saw one the other day at auction go for twenty dollars.

Washington china, that is, scenes and pictures of

27

Washington himself, command the attention of collectors who do not mind paying fancy prices for the old blue. Everything connected with Mount Vernon has an interest for all of us, and though we may not all buy such fine jugs as the one given in Figure 40, we would like to.

Other patterns of Staffordshire ware which are immensely popular among the collectors who do not mind giving large prices for their hobbies are the Dr. Syntax and Wilkie designs and those referring to Don Quixote. Just why the last-named series does not command the same high prices as even the Wilkie set cannot be explained. It is by Clews, is well printed as a rule, has a good border, and is not half so gross as the Wilkie set, one of which is given in Figure 41, and which is called " Playing at Draughts."

There are many reasons why the Syntax designs have such a great popularity, one of them being that love for the grotesque which is latent in almost every one of us, another being the interesting facts in connection with the production of these drawings and the accompanying verses, and third, the beauty of the printing of the pieces, which were made by the Clews in their very best style.

The drawings by Rowlandson were made about 1810, and the verses were reeled off, to accompany them, by William Comb, a most prolific writer of all kinds of matter, which nevertheless was not profitable enough to enable him to pay his debts, since he was an inmate of the King's Bench debtors' prison for twenty-three

28

years, and it was in that far from cheerful spot that he wrote the lines for the three tours of Dr. Syntax, the first one, " Tour in Search of the Picturesque," being followed by " Tour in Search of Consolation," and the third, " In Search of a Wife."

The designs were made on china between 1820 and 1830, and the prices realised for this printed pottery seem marvellous. Twenty to forty dollars for plates, one to three and four hundred dollars for platters, seem too high figures to be maintained, but so few of these pieces remain to be picked up that it is thought that the prices may go higher still. The dishes shown in Figure 42 have scenes on them from all three Tours, the one showing so plainly on the side of the tureen being " Dr. Syntax and the Gypsies "; the verse which accompanies it is as follows:

" Patrick, unwilling to be idle,
As he held Phillis by the bridle,
With half a score black eyes around him,
Darting their glances to confound him,
Thought, while his master chose to trace
The history of the Gypsy race,
It would be ungallant, nay wrong,
Thus to stand still and hold his tongue . . .
Well then, these brown ones did not wait
For him to open the debate . . .
They jabber'd forth that they were willing
To tell his fate for half a shilling.
Pat smiled consent, his sixpence paid,
And thus the witch commenced her trade."

And so it goes on. One of the designs which commands the highest price is called " Pat in the Pond,"

to which retreat he had betaken himself to rid himself of

> " Bugs or fleas, whate'er they be,
> Their stings have played Old Nick with me."

As might have been expected, when it was found
that this china brought such large prices, counterfeiters
set to work and made spurious copies of " Dr. Syntax
telling the Bees," " Dr. Syntax painting a Portrait,"
" Dr. Syntax taking a Gentleman's House for an Inn."
This has, of course, made collectors very chary of
buying any of these patterns, since it has lessened even
the price of the genuine ones.

At Liverpool there have been potteries since 1600,
and the first wares were, of course, excessively crude,
and were blue and white, in imitation of the Dutch,
who in their turn copied from the Chinese.

Very little of the " Liverpool Delft," as it is called,
can be found here, and it is chiefly in the form of tiles.
There is, however, much other Liverpool pottery, commonly known as " black-printed ware." It is very
decorative, of small cost, and good to have in a collection or for ornament merely. Printing on china was
a Liverpool invention, perfected about 1752 by a man
named John Sadler. By this process the production
of decorated china was materially lessened in cost, since,
previously, all the decoration had been done by hand.
The body of Liverpool pottery, that is, the paste
itself, is a fine cream colour, very even in tone and very
light in weight. Figure 43 shows an exceedingly
popular pattern, and I have found these plates all

30

over the country, sometimes even set up in museums with high-sounding names applied to them. Although they are nice and interesting, they are not worth more than one dollar and a quarter.

But while such a piece as this is reasonable, you may spend almost a fortune on printed wares, particularly if you get together such a collection as that shown in Figure 44. Each one of these pieces is a treasure, and many varieties of English ware are here shown.

During the last quarter of the eighteenth century there was started in the town of Castleford, near Leeds, England, a pottery from which was sent out much basaltes (black ware), Queen's ware (cream coloured), and a white pottery known as Castleford ware. These works were closed in 1820, and the white ware for which they were chiefly noted was no longer made. A quantity of this ware was sent to this country, and the pieces which seem to have survived are the teapots. They were made not only with the lifting lid, like the one in Figure 45, but with the lid fastened with metal pins. As can be seen, the ware was extremely pretty, with a wreath of graceful ornament, and this specimen is unusual in having a panel decorated in colours. Even less common were the pieces decorated with portraits of Washington and Franklin, which were in medallions, either in plain white relief or on a blue background. I heard from the owner of a pitcher with such medallions only a few days since. Sometimes the surface of this Castleford ware is pitted much like saltglaze ware, but this was caused by hav-

31

ing the inside of the mould thickly set with small points, which left corresponding depressions on the surface of the object.

The name Spode always stands for what is good and advisable to have. In 1770 Josiah Spode, then about forty years of age, began working as a potter. All the ware which he made is called "Old Spode," to distinguish it from the later product of the factory, and it is extremely valuable. His son succeeded to the factory at the death of his father, in 1797, and about 1800 commenced to manufacture stone china, and a little later to make porcelain. William Copeland became a partner in the firm in 1797, and it is his descendants who manufacture pottery and porcelain at the present time. Old Spode is marked "Spode," in printed letters, impressed. This mark is prior to 1797. From 1800 to 1827 the mark is impressed or painted on in red, blue, or purple. Occasionally "Stone China" or "Feldspar Porcelain" is added. Jasper ware, black ware, and the decorated ware, in blue, red, and gold, and made by Josiah Spode himself, are valuable. After 1827, when the younger Spode died, the firm name was entirely changed, and if Spode was used at all it was put "Late Spode." I give two examples of the second Spode, — one a plate, with decoration in medium blue, and the other a very beautiful one of "St. Peter's and the Castle of San Angelo, Rome" (Figures 46 and 47).

The town of Bristol, England, was one of the first to take advantage of the growing popularity of pottery ware, "Bristol Delft" it was called, and there are records of potters' work at that town as early as 1706. The drug or medicine jars were one of the early products, and in the specimen given (Figure 48) the earthenware body is covered by a stanniferous glaze, and the decoration is in a gray blue. It was not long before the ware was greatly improved, and they were making such pieces as the plate shown in Figure 49. Bristol porcelain and that made at Plymouth, the manufacture of which ceased at both places before 1800, has such a value and is so rarely to be found in America that we will not linger on it.

In Figure 50 is given a vase of Plymouth porcelain, which was formed in a mould, and is of that brilliant milky white which was such a marked feature of this porcelain.

More easily to be obtained, though just why one cannot say, are specimens like that shown in Figure 51. This is a twelve-inch platter of Crown-Derby porcelain, marked with the crown and "D" in vermillion, which places its time of manufacture at about 1788, what is known as the second Duesbury period. In the limited space of a single chapter it is impossible to tell, even in the most concise manner, the various changes and the different hands into which these old potteries passed. It is enough to say that any of these early specimens are choice, and it is very seldom that they come under the head of "bargains," like the little platter shown. It is painted in the familiar reds and blues, with sparing touches of green, and some gold, and it and another two inches larger were recently bought in Rochester, New York, for five dollars each.

I can hardly bear to think of these platters, for as I hesitated a moment the one shown was bought, not by a collector, but by one who liked the " pretty colour- ing." The owner herself put the price upon them, but they are worth many times this sum, and would be eagerly bought if the present owners could be induced to part with them.

Some Crown-Derby cups and saucers are also shown (Figure 52), rather less ornamental in pattern than the little platter, but still bearing the old crown mark.

In the following illustration (Figure 53) is shown a cup, saucer, and plate of Old Worcester porcelain, which must not be confused with " Royal Worcester," — a modern ware which has flooded this country for years and has many imitators, both professional and amateur.

The Worcester Old Works were started in 1751, and remained in operation till 1847, though they passed through many different hands. Blue in a cobalt or turquoise shade, and also enamel blue, made the Worcester porcelain very much in demand, and a very high-class transfer printing was made here also, the designs for which were made by two artists, Richard Holdship and Robert Hancock. Both these men had a way of signing their drawings " R. H." in a mono- gram, thereby producing endless confusion and much wrathy discussion among china collectors of the pres-

34

ent day. Figure 54 shows a teapot decorated with one of the well-known designs of Robert Hancock. I have heard it called " General and Mrs. Washington having tea at Mount Vernon," the presence of a small black boy near at hand helping out the idea. It is an English scene, however, and it was the fashion of those days to have pages, either black or white, constantly at hand to do the bidding of my lord or lady.

This teapot is one of a collection which is creeping up to two thousand, the majority of which were obtained in this country. The cup, plate, and saucer are museum specimens, and are at Boston. They are painted, not printed, the decoration on the plate being that shade of gray blue known to the Oriental as " sky seen through clouds after rain."

The history of the Worcester potteries since they were first started by Dr. Wall, in 1751, is a long and interesting one. At one time and another there have been, besides the " Old Works," Chamberlain's Works and Grainger's Works. In 1902 all the companies which were still in existence were taken over by the " Worcester Royal Porcelain Co. Limited," and it is through the courtesy of that company that I am able to show specimens of Worcester transfer printing, which was made about 1756, when this style of work was first done at that place. Its clearness and beauty is plainly to be seen from the photograph (Figure 55).

Specimens of Chamberlain's porcelain, and some mugs, and a cup of the early Worcester are also shown (Figures 56 and 57).

35

Within the last year, at Cooperstown, New York, a quantity of old porcelain has come to light. A farmer was ploughing, when suddenly the plough struck some hard substance, and a moment later there was a crash as of broken crockery. Investigation proved that he had struck a wooden chest, filled with china articles. There were eighty pieces in all, and fifty were saved in a perfect condition. As for the chest, it had crumbled to bits on exposure to the air, only the rough iron lock and hinges surviving. The history of these specimens is known. They were buried one hundred and twenty-five years ago by Percifer Carr, who was employed by Colonel Edmeston, an officer in the French and Indian Wars. The Colonel received for his services a grant of one thousand acres, and Carr had a comfortable home on this land. Indian troubles caused him to leave for a time, and he buried his china. Among the pieces are some very choice Old Worcester, with both Hancock's and Holdship's designs, very similar to the teapot shown. Other pieces are in plain blue, and in brown and pink.

The farmer who ploughed up these treasures, for they are almost as valuable as gold, has not been allowed to retain them, as he only rented the farm. The owner of the property stepped in and claimed them, and after they had reposed in a bank under the care of a sheriff for some months, the court upheld his claim. Collectors from all over the country have been interested to have them come on the market.

In Figure 58 is given one of those lovely graceful

36

creamers which go by the name of " Helmet Pitchers."
For over half a century such pitchers and other china
of similar paste and decoration have gone under the
name of " Lowestoft," and have been the delight and
pride of hundreds of collectors. It is only within the
last few months that it has been definitely decided that
no such ware was either made or decorated in England, but that it is entirely of Oriental manufacture.
At the little English town of Lowestoft have been
unearthed fragments both of moulds and bits of pottery, which go to prove that the ceramic products of
that town were no different from what was made in
other English towns at the same period.

So now all this fine bluish white pottery, with its
birds and flowers and coats of arms, comes under the
head of " armorial china," and it has not lost in value
nor in beauty, if it has taken a less high-sounding
name.

Lovely as are the porcelains of Chelsea, Derby, Bow,
Plymouth, and Worcester, as mere artistic productions,
they yield the palm to the work of one man. None
of these porcelains mentioned were the product of a
single mind; they were the result of experiments by
many.

On the other hand, the great Wedgwood invented
most of his own products, formed the first specimens
with his own capable hands, and directed and controlled
those vast works which were the growth of his own
genius. He disputes with Palissy for the position of
" greatest potter."

37

Specimens of Wedgwood's wares are to be found in this country, and within the past year I have come across a cup, saucer, and plate with brown-printed jessamine border for decoration; a tray for fruit of the early rich green glaze decorated with strawberries and leaves, and a vase twelve inches high, of the black encaustic ware, dull finish, with beautiful classic figures on it in red, and a handsome egg-and-drop border enhanced with a little white enamel. Each of these pieces is marked, and the vase is numbered as well. The cup, saucer, and plate were bought for two dollars; the fruit tray was got of a Polish Jew for a quarter, the purchaser believing it to be some modern majolica, and selecting it solely on account of its colour. The vase I saw standing on the mantel-shelf of a house where there are many choice and beautiful objects. In reply to my questions the hostess answered:

"Yes, it is a nice old vase. We've always had it as long as I can remember. It has been mended, for it was knocked on the hearth once in dusting." She did not know who made it, its value, or anything, save "they'd always had it." Yet on the base of the plinth was the name Wedgwood clearly and neatly cut, and beside it the number 34. The vase had not been broken, but the fall had loosened the plinth from the body of the vase. These two parts were joined together by an iron screw and nut, and the latter had apparently rusted out. The repairer had simply put a new brass nut on the old iron screw. It was quite impossible

Fig. 39 WESLEY CUP AND SAUCER

Fig. 38 "WOMAN OF SAMARIA"

Fig. 40 MT. VERNON JUG

Fig. 42 "Dr. Syntax" Tureen

Fig. 41 Wilkie Plate

Fig. 43 Black-print Ware

Fig. 44 CABINET OF PRINTED WARE

Fig. 45 CASTLEFORD WARE   Fig. 48 "BRISTOL DELFT"

Fig. 46 SPODE PLATE   Fig. 47 "ST. PETER'S," SPODE

Fig. 49 BRISTOL PLATE

Fig. 50 PLYMOUTH VASE

Fig. 51 CROWN-DERBY PLATTER

Fig. 52 CROWN-DERBY CUPS AND SAUCERS

Fig. 53 OLD WORCESTER CUP AND SAUCER

Fig. 54 WORCESTER TEAPOT

Fig. 55 WORCESTER TRANSFER WORK

Fig. 56 CHAMBERLAIN'S WORCESTER

Fig. 57 WORCESTER MUGS AND CUP

Fig. 58 Helmet Jugs

Fig. 59 Queen's Ware

to resist dilating on the beauty and rarity of this vase and its value.

When next I saw the owner she said:

" What you told me about our black vase has destroyed my pleasure in it! "

" Why? " I asked.

" Since I knew it was so valuable I 've been nervous for fear it will get broken, and have locked it up in the cabinet, and now we cannot enjoy it at all! "

Wedgwood's products are easily and clearly grouped. He never made any porcelain. Nor did he ever protect any of his valuable inventions, save in one case, but allowed his brother potters to benefit by his experiments and to reap the reward of his labours. His earliest wares were the tortoise-shell and agate pottery, and the highly coloured green glaze already referred to.

Then came the perfected cream-coloured or " Queen's Ware," like the teapot in Figure 59, either decorated or plain. The name " Queen's Ware " was given to this pottery in honour of Queen Charlotte, who visited the pottery works and admired it. It varies in colour from pale cream to almost a deep straw or sulphur yellow, and has an admirable clearness of tone, which makes it a very good background for decoration.

As early as 1761 Wedgwood was making teapots, and in fact whole sets for either tea or dinner, for caudle as well as for many other uses, and all in this

39

ware. It was not expensive, for a dinner set of one hundred and forty-six pieces cost at wholesale about twenty dollars. That some of these sets came over here is well known, for, artist though he was, Wedgwood was a man of business as well, and did not neglect any market, particularly such a promising one as the American Colonies offered.

I have found in early newspapers advertisements of wares that I am sure were Wedgwood's, like the following, for instance, where James Gilliland, dealer in earthenware, Delft, and glass, with a shop in Wall Street, New York, enumerates " enamelled and cabbage teapots " among other goods. This was as early as 1760. Not only was this cream-coloured ware painted, but it was printed as well, and so beautifully and carefully executed that it was almost as handsome as if painted.

Perhaps the thing in which Wedgwood took the most pride, and naturally too, was the dinner set made for Catherine II, Empress of Russia, for use at the Palace of Grenouilliere, which was a part of Tzarsko-Selo, near St. Petersburg. The commission was arranged through Mr. Baxter, who was English Consul at St. Petersburg at the time, and in June, 1774, the set was finished. The firm of Wedgwood and Bentley, as it was at that time, considered it of sufficient importance to advertise it, and this was the way they did it:

" Wedgwood and Bentley inform the Nobility and Gentry, that those who chuse to see a Table and Desert Service, now

40

set out at their new Rooms, in Greek-street, may have free
tickets for that purpose, at the ware-house in Great Newport-
street, and that none can be admitted without tickets."

All the world flocked to see the set, and many have
recorded their impressions about it. The designs used
to ornament it were English country seats and land-
scapes, and as soon as the ware was made at Etruria
it was sent to Chelsea to be painted, where Wedgwood
had gathered together the best pottery painters of the
day. There were 925 pieces, each one of which had
a different scene on it, and on the underside of each
piece was a shield, enclosing a green frog. A few
duplicates were made, and some pieces which had im-
perfections were set aside. Some of these duplicates
are in museums, and the plate shown here, Moore
Park (Figure 60), is from the collection of Mr. E. J.
Sidebotham, of England, who is the fortunate possessor of three pieces.

Of the original set nothing is known now. But it
seems impossible that so many hundred pieces should
have disappeared, even in Russia. Collectors are always hoping that it will turn up in some corner of
that great and distracted empire.

Then Wedgwood perfected black ware, or basaltes,
— a form of pottery long known, but never brought
to its highest excellence till the master potter turned
his attention to it. He used this basaltes in many ways,
— for vases, portrait medallions, teasets, and for special
use in the "Colonies," in the form of a small round
inkstand, which, according to the maker, had many

advantages over any other inkstand then on the market.

In Figure 61 is shown a portrait medallion in basaltes set in silver, which brings out admirably its velvet blackness. These medallions are splendidly finished, being cut by hand after they were taken from the mould, so as to bring out the head sharply from the background and make it perfect in every detail. Some of these exquisite heads and figures are small enough to be set in a ring or an ear-drop, while others are four by three inches. The most common size is two by one and three-quarter inches, like the one shown. When the name of the subject of the medallion was printed on the front, the name Wedgwood was scratched on the back. When the name of the subject is not given, then Wedgwood is often impressed on the front.

People often tell me that they own Wedgwood. I always ask, " Is it marked? " You may set it down as a rule that all real Wedgwood, that is, " Old Wedgwood," is marked with his name. It was trial pieces only, and such as escaped the workman's notice, that left the pottery unmarked. There are peculiarities about this marking, too, which must be noted. The name, in small capitals, is always clearly and carefully marked, whether impressed or printed in colour. " Old Wedgwood " is that pottery made before the decease of Josiah Wedgwood, in 1795. The firm was continued and is still potting, but the cunning of the master's hand has left the work. After 1795, besides the name Wedgwood, other marks were used. Three letters, like " R. S. B.," " A. T. Q.," etc., and others in combination were frequently seen, and there were arbitrary marks as well to indicate special patterns and periods.

Greatback and Hackwood, two of the best modellers in the time of Josiah Wedgwood, sometimes put their initials on the back of a piece, but Wedgwood objected to this, and suppressed such marks as much as possible. Undoubtedly the highest and finest product made by Wedgwood was, in the estimation of the public, his jasper ware. He calls it " a white porcelain bisque of exquisite beauty and delicacy, possessing the quality of receiving colour through its whole substance. This renders it peculiarly fit for cameos, portraits, and all subjects in bas-relief, as the ground may be made of any colour throughout, and the raised figures are in pure white."

Of the pieces shown in Figure 62 little need be said, since their beauty is so obvious.

Many of the figure subjects used on jasper vases were drawn by John Flaxman, who became celebrated for his drawings of classical subjects. At the time he entered Wedgwood's employment he was a poor and unknown young man, and it was due largely to the encouragement and liberal payment given by Wedgwood that Flaxman became as well known as he did in after years. Every ornament and slightest detail that came from the Wedgwood potteries prior to 1795 was finished with the greatest care. Nothing slovenly

43

or slipshod would pass muster before the conscientious proprietor. His life, busy and prosperous, is a model to be studied by anyone anxious to succeed, and shows that the heights of success are reached only by unceasing and persevering effort.

III — CHAIRS AND SOFAS

WHILE all specimens of antique furniture have an interest all their own, chairs seem to arouse it in a peculiar degree. There is a personal sentiment which they possess, a something which brings one in touch with owners long since dead, that is not shared by such objects as a bureau or a table, no matter how venerable. If one could sit for a brief moment in, say, Will Shakspere's chair, would it not seem possible that inspiration might be derived for a little sonnet? Or if one had for daily companionship the antique chair of Elder William Brewster, now at Plymouth, Massachusetts, would it not be likely that one would imbibe some of the courage which upheld that doughty pioneer?

The oldest piece of cabinet-maker's work known is Queen Hatasu's chair, of the eighteenth Egyptian Dynasty, sixteen hundred years before the Christian Era. It is made of ivory, ebony, and various metals, and is in the British Museum, London. There is another old chair in which one may take a more personal interest, and whose early history is so enveloped in legend and myth that it is impossible to tell where tradition ends and truth begins. This is the Coronation Chair of England, in which all English sovereigns since 1273 have been crowned. The wood has become very solid and hard, but still shows in various places the traces of paint. In 1298 Edward I brought from Scotland the stone upon which all the Scottish kings had been crowned for centuries, and this was inserted in the seat of the English chair. It is a piece of coarse sandstone, twenty-six inches long, seventeen broad, and ten and one-half inches thick. It shows very plainly in the photograph, which also displays to advantage the Gothic character of the chair (Figure 63).

Sir James Ware, who lived from 1594 to 1666, writing about this same stone which is set in the Coronation Chair, says:

" Nor ought we to pass by unmentioned that fatal stone, antiently called liafail, brought into Ireland by the Tuath-de-Danans, and from thence in the reign of Moriertach Mac Erc sent into Argile to his brother Fergus, but which was afterwards inclosed in a wooden chair by King Keneth to serve in the coronation solemnities of the King of Scotland, and deposited in the Monastery of Scone, from whence it was at length removed to Westminster by Edward I. Wonderful things are reported of this stone, but what credibility they deserve I leave to the judgement of others. In particular fame reports, that in times of heathenism before the birth of Christ, he only was confirmed Monarch of Ireland, under whom, being placed upon it, this stone groaned or spoke, according to the Book of Hoath."

One can imagine what grief it caused to Ireland when this sacred stone, endeared by a thousand superstitious ideas, was removed and taken to England.

If you will hunt among old documents, both in this

46

country and in England, you will find frequent mention of " joint stools." I could give many extracts from old wills which specify these stools, and I show one in Figure 64. The cradle does not properly belong in this article, but when I reflected how often a weary mother had sat on that same joint stool and rocked that cradle, I let it stay. It must have been in pretty constant operation in some of those pioneer families, where twelve children were an ordinary number, and twenty not very unusual! Such a cradle and such a stool, no doubt, found their way over in many of the earliest lots of household gear, since, though these patterns were found by 1560, they were made till a century later, and when once part of the household goods of a family, descended till they fairly gave out from excessive wear.

Stools were in common use at table till well into the seventeenth century. In an old play called " The Roaring Girl " (1617), when chairs, stools, and cushions are called for, a chair is called a back-friend, and Sir Adam, who is favoured with one, says, " I thank thee for it, back friends are sometimes good."

Holinshed, who wrote his famous " Chronicles " before 1580, has much to say about the increase of luxury both in dress and household furnishings in all classes, and mentions what may be found in even the farmers' homes. He says:

" The furniture of our houses also exceedeth, and is grown in manner even to delicacy; and herein I do not speak of the nobility and gentry only, but likewise of the lowest sort in

47

most places of our south country, that have anything at all to take to. Certes in noblemen's houses it is not rare to see abundance of arras, rich hangings of tapestry, silver vessels, and so much other plate as may furnish sundry cupboards, to the sum oftentimes of a thousand or two pounds at the least; whereby the value of this and the rest of their stuff doth grow to be almost inestimable. Likewise in the houses of knights, gentlemen, merchantmen, and some other wealthy citizens, it is not geson to behold generally their great provision of tapestry, Turkey work, pewter, brass, fine linen, and thereto costly cupboard of plate, worth five, six, or a thousand pounds, to be deemed by estimation. But as herein all these sorts do far exceed their elders and predecessors, and in neatness and curiosity the merchant all other; so in time past, the costly furniture stayed there; whereas now it is descended yet lower, even unto the inferior artificers, and many farmers, who by virtue of their old and not of their new leases have for the most part learned to garnish their cupboards with plate, their joined beds with tapestry and silk hangings, and their tables with carpets and fine napery."

Burton, in his " Anatomy of Melancholy " (1621), speaking of luxurious selfishness, says that the great man " sits at table in a soft chair at ease, but he doth not remember in the mean time that a tired waiter stands behind him."

Some of the luxurious chairs of this period are shown in the next three Figures (65, 66, and 67), and are of Italian, Flemish, and English make, and all rejoice in rich carving, the one in Figure 65 being exceptionally beautiful. This type of chair is more common in this country than one would deem possible, unless it is known how many of them were brought here. There

48

is hardly an inventory among the well-to-do who arrived here from 1650 and onwards that does not mention among the commoner chests, stools, and forms at least one chair of this style.

In the inventory of John Oort, one of the husbands of Sarah Bradley, who finally married the notorious Captain Kidd, is the mention of a dozen turkey-work chairs; and Theophilus Eaton, Governor of New Haven Colony, who died in 1657, had in his hall " two high chairs with sett work 20*s*. 4*d*. each." These chairs varied in many ways. Sometimes the seat was leather, and the back also. The back might be of carved wood, like the one shown, or leather, cane-work, or set-work, or embroidery. They were made in Spanish, as well as Flemish, English, and Italian style.

The stall seats, "dwarf stalls" they are generally called, are relics from the cathedrals. They are found here sometimes, and are now used as hall chairs. The two shown in Figures 68 and 69 are, as are all the other objects so far shown in this chapter, made of oak. They date to the seventeenth century, and are French in their origin. The posts supporting the arms as well as the legs in the chair in Figure 68 are enriched with fine carving, and the open back gives it a lightness not possessed by the previous one.

The chair shown (Figure 70) is another early specimen, and though it looks decidedly uncomfortable, it was not an uncommon type of chair about the middle of the seventeenth century. The name "wainscot" was often applied to such chairs, since the panelled

4

back was carved in the same patterns that the wainscots were. Many of them are more heavily carved than the one shown here, and, like this one, they are almost always oak.

In connection with such chairs as these it is easy to be seen how very important cushions were. The best workers in tapestries at an early date were the Flemish, and in Carte's "Life of Ormonde" he mentions that "Piers, Earl of Ormonde (died 1539), brought out of Flanders and the neighbouring provinces sundry artificers and manufacturers, whom he employed at Kilkenny in working tapestry, drapery, Turkey carpets, cushions, and seats." The Turkey carpets referred to were not floor coverings, but table covers. The only things used on floors at this early date were rushes.

In early colonial times houses were small, often not having more than four rooms, and in most of them the hall was the living-room, as well as the place where the best furniture was gathered.

The widow Frances Kilburn had in her hall when she died, in 1650, at Hartford, Connecticut, "tables, formes, chairs, stools, benches," all valued at £1. Governor John Haynes, also of Hartford, Connecticut, died in 1653, and in his hall were many articles, among them "5 leather and 4 flag bottom'd chairs, 1 table and 3 join'd stools." His parlour had "velvet chairs, turkey-wrought chairs and a green cloth carpet," this latter being a table, not a floor, covering.

There were various other styles of chairs which came

50

into use about the eighteenth century that had certain marked characteristics. A very nice one, with a rush bottom, is given in Figure 71. There are a number of noticeable points about this chair which it is well to study. In the first place it is made of turned wood, except the feet, which are carved. Compare it with the previous figures and you will see the difference. Its front legs are finished in what is known as the " Spanish foot," which always turns out and is ornamented with grooved lines. The back is of the shape so generally called " Queen Anne," but which is, properly speaking, Dutch, and the splat, or centre of the back, is without decoration, which shows its early origin. This form of back grew and was varied in many ways, as will be shown later.

Figure 72 shows chairs with exactly similar backs, but varying legs, one having the ball-and-claw and the other the Dutch foot. These chairs were made in Massachusetts about 1768, and were part of a bride's outfit. They are made of Spanish mahogany, which can always be told by its weight, making such large chairs very clumsy to carry about, but enabling them to resist the wear and tear of more than a century.

An armchair of the same period, with very richly carved legs in low relief, and with the original cover of needlework, is shown in Figure 73.

These chairs were the housekeeper's pride and joy. They were carefully preserved in the " best room," and no child was permitted to sprawl on them; and I am afraid that the goodman, even if he had digged that

51

day and delved, had to rest himself on something less choice.

He could smoke his pipe and take his ease in some chair like the one shown in Figure 74, which is extremely comfortable even to-day, that is if one fancies a straight-backed chair. No doubt it was constant sitting in such chairs as these which enabled our grandmothers to accomplish their endless household tasks. There was no inducement to lolling; your backbone was called on to fulfil its whole duty!

The comb-back chair (Figure 75) was not much of an improvement on the straight-backed one, but it had a finer appearance. The style of chair on which the comb is placed is known as the " roundabout," and is not particularly comfortable except for men. This is a fine stout example, was made between 1770 and 1775, and has long done duty in a Salem mansion.

Among the ballads by William Thackeray is one entitled " The Cane-bottom'd Chair," which is so little known that I give a portion of it here:

" In tattered old slippers that toast at the bars,
And a ragged old jacket perfumed with cigars
Away from the world and its toils and its cares,
I 've a snug little kingdom up four pair of stairs.

To mount to this realm is a toil, to be sure,
But the fire there is bright and the air rather pure ;
And the view I behold on a sunshiny day
Is grand through the chimney-pots over the way

This snug little chamber is cramm'd in all nooks
With worthless old knick-knacks and silly old books,
And foolish old odds and foolish old ends,
Crack'd bargains from brokers and keepsakes from friends.

52

Old armor, prints, pictures, pipes, china, (all crack'd),
Old rickety tables, and chairs broken-backed ;
A two-penny treasury, wondrous to see ;
What matter ? 't is pleasant to you, friend, and me.

.   .   .   .

But of all the cheap treasures that garnish my nest,
There 's one that I love and I cherish the best :
For the finest of couches that 's padded with hair
I never would change thee, my cane-bottom'd chair.

'T is a bandy-legg'd, high-shoulder'd, worm-eaten seat
With a creaking old back, and twist'd old feet ;
But since the fair morning when Fanny sat there
I bless thee and love thee, old cane-bottom'd chair ! "

While the chairs shown so far, with perhaps but three exceptions, can well be classed as " simple," there was furniture of such magnificence, made even before the Middle Ages, that one must pause a moment to consider it. Immense prices were paid by the Romans for single pieces of furniture. Cicero did not hesitate to pay a million sesterces ($45,000) for a table, and there is a record of one being carried into Spain in the fifth century by the Goths, which was surrounded by three rows of fine pearls. It must have been of great size, for the record states that it was supported on 365 feet, these feet being of " massy gold."

Coming to more modern times, there was, during the reign of King James (1603–1625), a great fancy for furniture made from solid silver, and this took the style of the period which was known as " Jacobean." Some of this choice furniture is still preserved in the castles for which it was made, and at Knole, the seat of Lord Sackville, may be found some of the most

53

elegant. It would hardly seem of use to show within the limits of a book intended for the practical collector such rich articles as these were it not that some pieces are on sale in this country, and have been exhibited by Tiffany and Co. in New York. A silver chair once in the possession of the late Prince Waldeck is shown in Figure 76.

As the French always excelled the English in the magnificence of their interior furnishings, silver furniture was by no means rare in that country. Louise de Querouaille, who was created Duchess of Portsmouth by Charles II, brought with her from France a taste for these costly bibelots. She was in favour with the English king for fifteen years, till his death in 1685, and her dressing-room, as described by John Evelyn, was truly regal. He says with reference to his visit to the palace:

"But that which engag'd my curiosity was the rich and splendid furniture of this woman's apartment, now twice or thrice pull'd down and rebuilt to satisfie her prodigal and expensive pleasures, while her Majesty's dos not exceede some gentleman's ladies in furniture and accommodation. . . . Then for Japan cabinets, screens, pendule clocks, greate vases of wrought plate, tables, stands, chimney furniture, sconces, branches, braseras, etc., all of massive silver and out of number, besides some of her Majesty's best paintings."

It is supposed that some of the silver furniture now at Windsor Castle was from this very apartment described by Evelyn. He tells of another dressing-room, this time in one of the great country houses where

54

Fig. 60 "RUSSIAN" PLATE   Fig. 61 MEDALLION

Fig. 62 OLD JASPER WARE

Fig. 63 CORONATION CHAIR

Fig. 64 OAK JOINT STOOL

Fig. 67 Flemish Chair

Fig. 66 English Oak Chair

Fig. 65 Italian Chair

Fig. 68 Oak Stall   Fig. 69 Oak Stall   Fig. 71 A Rush Bottom

Fig. 70 Wainscot Chair   Fig. 73 Walnut Chair

Fig. 72 AMERICAN CHAIRS

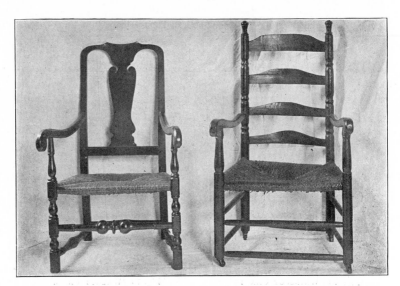

Fig. 74 RUSH-BOTTOMED CHAIRS

Fig. 75 Comb-Back Chair   Fig. 77 Rush-bottomed Chair

Fig. 76 Silver Chair   Fig. 78 Wing-Cheek Chair

Fig. 79   Spoon-Back Mahogany Chairs

Fig. 80   Mahogany Ladder-Back Chairs

court fashions were followed as nearly as possible. This extract is dated April 17, 1673, and runs as follows:

" The Countess of Arlington carried us up into her new dressing-room at Goring House, where there was a bed, two glasses, silver jars and vases, cabinets, and other so riche furniture as I had seldom seene; to this excesse of superfluity were we now arrived, and that not onely at Court, but almost universally, even to wantonesse and profusion."

That Louis XIV possessed much silver furniture is most probable, and that much of it sought the melting-pot is also likely, when his exchequer became depleted from one cause or another. As late as 1691 De Launay, who was silversmith to the king, was turning out silver furniture, and some of it found its way to England, although the Edict of Nantes in 1685 had without doubt sent over skilled Huguenot silver workers among the refugees.

It can be noticed in the example given that the ornamentation is carried to the highest extreme, and all the pieces now remaining are of the same florid style. Cherubs' heads, coats-of-arms, floral forms, and flowing designs were all used, and it is a matter for speculation to the mind of a housekeeper how all this elaboration was kept clean. In order to make the chairs and stools comfortable many splendid wrought cushions were used, and the effect must have been very rich and beautiful, if not very comfortable.

From the silver luxuriance of the chair just shown to the simple homeliness of the one in the next illus-

55

tration (Figure 77) is a far cry. In the kitchen, even when silver was in the drawing-room, were to be found chairs, straight-backed and rush-bottomed, which were much esteemed, and made comfortable and serviceable seats. When the slats of the back were set in perpendicularly they were known as "banister backs," and there were many of them made in this country, as there was always somebody in each town who could reseat them. It may interest readers to know that this chair was recently sold for fifteen dollars. I should like to say to owners of like chairs that their value is decreased by being "done over," and it is best to leave them exactly as they are, no matter how bare of paint. Their age is a patent of nobility, and to cover it up is in bad taste.

With elegance in the parlour and ease in the kitchen there came also a desire for something more comfortable in the bedrooms. This want was supplied by a style of chair known as the "wing-cheek," which must have been much in demand in those cold and draughty houses of a century and more ago. With your face to the fire and your back and sides protected by one of these well-stuffed chairs, you might get what comfort you could in those "good old times" we love to talk about with affection, and yet would hate to have return. The chair in Figure 78 is one of these easy-chairs with ball-and-claw feet and an underbrace. When the feet were less ornamental a large ruffle was put on the edge of the chair and hung nearly to the floor.

I have mentioned how the splat, or centrepiece, of

56

the back of chairs gradually took on a great degree of ornament. The two rich mahogany chairs given in Figure 79 show the early steps, when carving was beginning to be applied to this portion of the chair as well as to the legs and back. Such chairs as these found their way to many a home in this country — to the wealthy Dutch settled in and around New York, up the Hudson, and in Albany and Schenectady, as well as to the homes of the English settlers. The Dutch inventories, which were very particular, mention first in many cases the " feder bed," or the family Bible, and then the chairs. " Armed cheares " and chairs with silver lace, easy-chairs, Russia-leather chairs, and chairs with bull-hide seats figure many times, and show that, while " ye barbarous enemy " may have prowled out-of-doors, there were necessities and luxuries, too, within doors.

By 1750 England led the world in the beauty and worth which she put in her furniture, though in the previous century France had produced furniture of such elegance and beauty that it will never be excelled. Most of it was too fragile and costly for everyday use, and royalty only could afford to own it. The French patterns and designs were copied freely in England, as well as in other countries, till a great man, Thomas Chippendale, arose and, after feeling his way through copied work, founded a style of his own, which we look upon now as the epitome of what is best and most serviceable in fine furniture.

His earliest heavy chairs had the " bandy " or cabriole

57

leg, as it was called, which has been shown in the chairs in several illustrations. He then began to use the straight leg, and put much variety into the backs, carving and piercing them, and having them "ladder backs" (Figure 80), or splats with ornamentation (Figure 81). These are only simple forms of this great man's work, but they show his style admirably. It was Chippendale who first used mahogany to any great extent, and one cause which led to this was that he was primarily a woodcarver, and this close-grained wood gave beautiful effects.

The old method of treatment of wood, which was known as " oil and elbow-grease," had by Chippendale's time become obsolete at least to the trade, and " French Polish," the composition of which was kept a close secret for years, was in use among cabinet-makers. It is rather wonderful to note how far the cabinet-makers of the eighteenth century advanced when it is taken into consideration that they had no encouragement from royalty. The three Georges neither cared nor knew anything about art or design, and Chippendale, a merchant always, took what he found and catered largely to the tastes of his times.

He rather prided himself upon appealing to the tastes of all classes, and among the patrons and subscribers for his book is William Frank, bricklayer, as well as the Duke of Northumberland.

He never used inlay in any form, and if this fact is borne in mind there will be fewer mistakes in assigning to him furniture ornamented in this way. To

58

make up for his restrictions in this line he carved the backs of his most costly chairs with a wealth of ornament, introducing "ribbon-work," as it was called, in the most elaborate patterns and fanciful designs.

As soon as such pieces became the fashion, of course others copied them, and there are hundreds of pieces in this country as well as in England which are called Chippendale, but which never saw the hand of that master or England. The fact that none of the furniture was signed in any way is a sad bar to giving it an authentic history. Pieces which have long been in English families, and where, as in some cases, the bills of sale are still preserved, bring perfectly fabulous sums. During the past few months at the auction sales at Christie's, the best known auction house in London, some pieces of Chippendale's furniture sold for the following prices:

A pair of Chippendale armchairs, ball-and-claw feet, £47 ($235.00).

Set of six Chippendale horn-backed chairs, £93 ($465.00).

A Chippendale four-legged stool, £10 6s. ($51.50).

A large Chippendale easy-chair, £14 ($70.00).

I have given these prices to show the estimation in which furniture by this maker is held in England.

Chippendale began to be well known by 1752, and worked steadily along, but rivals arose in this field, the most worthy of them all being Sheraton. Before his day came the two Adam brothers, Robert and James, who, originally architects, soon began to design furniture for the houses they built, which furniture was made under their direction. Their work was all on classic lines, and so careful and painstaking were they that they even designed the covers for the chairs and sofas, or any other small detail that they considered necessary to carry out the perfection of their scheme. They are not very well known over in America, yet, as there is more or less furniture designed by them, and it is pretty in shape and of a style that appeals to feminine taste, it has been extensively copied and put on the market. Furniture houses that claim to deal only in the antique have great stocks of this class of goods, and I have found it within the last year in half-a-dozen cities, and in every case had its antiquity guaranteed. This was in the face of the fact that I could see the glue still fresh upon it, and symptoms of warping and cracking in every direction. The style of Adam furniture to which I particularly refer are the lovely satinwood sets, the originals of which were made about the last quarter of the eighteenth century, and which are painted with medallions and exquisite groups of figures, by such artists as Angelica Kauffmann and Pergolese, and still further beautified by the most delicate classical ornaments on legs, arms, and rails.

In Figure 82 is given an Adam chair, showing a shape often used, but in this example the beautifully carved woodwork is gilded.

After the Adam brothers came Hepplewhite, whose fame largely rests upon his chairs, settees, and window seats. These latter have arms at the ends daintily carved, and the seats are upholstered. This cabinet-maker had one peculiarity by which his work may be generally recognised; he had a decided preference for a shield-shaped back to his chairs. The necessity for structural excellence never interfered with his plans for having his furniture pleasing to the eye. A good example of his style is shown in Figure 83, and it has its original covering in the striped material which was so often chosen by Hepplewhite for his coverings. He seldom carried the backs of his chairs down to the chair seat, and so, although the chairs are graceful and elegant, they are not strong, the break coming in the two posts that support the shield. When you observe the style and fine appearance of these chairs you are willing to pardon some defects.

Within the last few months many interesting details with reference to the Hepplewhites have been brought to light through the researches of an English woman, — Miss Constance Simon. The " A. Hepplewhite " who wrote the " Guide," or at least was responsible for it, turns out to be Alice Hepplewhite, the widow of George Hepplewhite, who died in 1786. It is supposed that before his death George Hepplewhite prepared many of the designs for the book, which was sufficiently popular to reach a third edition.

Hepplewhite used frequently for the design of his chair backs three feathers, as a compliment to royalty. Wheat ears was another favourite pattern, but they are not particularly pretty or graceful.

For many years there had been a fancy for things

61

in "Chinese taste"; mandarins with umbrellas and pigtails were carved here, there, and everywhere. They sat or stood on mirror frames, on door and window casings, they grinned at you from china cabinets and mantel shelves. What was called "fretwork" was also immensely popular, and hundreds of designs were made for chair backs, railings, to set glass in, and for any other purpose to which it could be applied.

Fashions in dress have more to do with shapes in furniture than one would deem possible. Immense hoopskirts could not be comfortably placed in an armchair, so chairs without arms became the mode. Chairs with large seats must have large legs to support them, and large legs must have underbraces, so there we have a reason for many of the styles of the late eighteenth century.

By the time Hepplewhite had come on the scene clothes had shrunk in proportions, and the taste was more for what was elegant and light in decoration. The fashion for satinwood furniture continued, and even mantelpieces were made of it to carry out the scheme of the room. Beside the shield-shaped back which we associate with Hepplewhite — although his book gives designs for eighteen chairs with banister backs — the legs of his furniture had peculiarities also. The chair shown in Figure 84 shows what is known as the "spade-foot," — a curious device for giving an appearance of solidity to an unduly slender leg. It is the little block-like foot in which the leg terminates. He had also the fancy for using dozens of brass-headed nails to tack down furniture covering, or to fasten on fringe, or to put on in a pattern for ornament.

He specifies in his own book of designs for furniture that the proper dimensions for chairs are: " Width in front, 20 inches; depth of seat, 17 inches; height of seat frame, 17 inches; total height, 37 inches." Haircloth, plain, striped, and checkered, was fashionable now, but the best taste demanded that the curtains should match the furniture covering. Hepplewhite laid down many arbitrary rules for what was " proper," and though some of them are absurd, his furniture was deservedly popular. Not only was much imported to America, but our cabinet-makers copied it, and there are numerous chairs which we may safely call " Hepplewhite style," if not Hepplewhite.

The next maker to claim attention is Sheraton, whose work is always admirable. He combined elegance with strength, and much of his fine furniture, or at least that made from his designs, is in use to-day, and has been ever since it was made, over a hundred years ago. I know of one set of Sheraton chairs brought to this country by the ancestors of their present owner about 1780. In these chairs, when they stood in a famous old manor-house near Albany, have sat Washington, Lafayette, Alexander Hamilton, and many of the Dutch patroons, those ". Lords of the Manor " of which we read in old records. The table that goes with them still holds its own, but the original set of forty-eight chairs has been broken by the division of inheritance, and though both side and armchairs are left with the table, their number is much reduced. These chairs have never needed repair, except to have the leather cover renewed.

In Figure 85 are given one arm and one side chair of what was a very favourite pattern with Sheraton. One will find it diversified in many ways, inlaid with coloured woods, or with slender bands of brass, or with carving, as in the figure, but always agreeable.

Other familiar patterns are shown in Figure 86, and they are, as are all the designs of this maker, admirable. He combined strength with an appearance of lightness, and although some of his ornament is rather florid, it is generally pleasing to look on.

In the lovely and historic old church of St. Michaels, at Charleston, South Carolina, is a large pew called the " Governor's Pew," and instead of having the regular seats, it is furnished with a set of Sheraton chairs. General Washington sat in one of these chairs, Sunday afternoon, May 8, 1791. Lafayette used it later, and since that time many other celebrities have sat there as well.

Another style to which Sheraton was much addicted was painted furniture, in which the background was black and the pattern applied in gold. The seats of such chairs were rush-bottoms.

Quite recently I was shown an arm and a side chair of exquisite curly maple, the wood left its natural colour, and a design painted on it in a charming style. The lady who had bought them considered she had perfect treasures, as indeed she had, and they were worth many times more than the sixteen dollars she paid for them. It was some time after she bought them before they came home, and she talked a great deal about them. Finally they arrived, and she set them out before her husband and said in triumph, "Well, what do you think of my chairs?" He looked at them for some moments and then replied, "I think they look like thirty cents!" Which goes to prove that when you select a hobby it is well to have the other members of the family share your enthusiasm.

A pair of what were known as Windsor chairs is shown in Figure 87. They are sturdy old things, and they were very popular during the last quarter of the nineteenth century. You will find them advertised for sale in all the old newspapers of the country, a typical notice being the following:

"Windsor chairs made and sold by William Gautier. High-backed, Low-backed, Sack-backed, and settees, also dining and low chairs."

The Windsor rockers are not so common as the side chairs, and of these latter those are most esteemed which have a little carving on the arms — "five fingers," it is called — but it is very crude work.

In the next Figure (88) is shown a Windsor chair and a Pembroke table, which are of more than usual interest. They belonged to George Washington, and were in use at Mount Vernon. In the year 1774 there was a sale of the furniture at "Belvoir," the Virginia seat of the Fairfax family, where they had lived with

5

almost feudal magnificence. George Fairfax and his wife went to England to attend to the estate in that country, and never returned to Virginia, so the next year they instructed that their dwelling and its contents be sold.

George Washington, Colonel Washington he was at that time, seems to have given more attention to acquiring household possessions than did Madam. There are constant records of his purchases, and he was a large buyer at the "vendue" which took place at Belvoir. He bought mahogany, brass, and copper ware, a toasting-fork, pillows and feather-beds, pewter plates and pickle-pots, china ware, Persian carpets and curtains. From Colonel Fairfax' own room he chose a shaving-table and a desk, and also a mahogany Pembroke table, for which he paid £1 12s.

Could it have been this same table? There is no record of Windsor chairs in this sale, which seems to include every other article of household furniture.

Although Windsor chairs made their appearance over here about 1725 or a few years later, and were made at Philadelphia, it was not until about twenty years later that they became common. The usual colours in which they were painted were black or dark green, and in these colours we are most familiar with them.

Beside the regular makers of furniture many " handy men " who could use tools eked out a narrow income by making chairs for sale, or made them for use at home. I have such a one, of maple, without any paint on it, and now grown a beautiful brown. It has not a nail in it, the parts being fastened together with wooden pegs. It is somewhat on the Windsor pattern, but has two flat ornaments let in the back. One day, in looking over it carefully, I found on the under side, scratched in, " Made by Jarret, 1795." It came from the far South, and I like to think that Jarret made it for a spinning-chair for Mrs. Jarret!

Besides such humble chairs as the one just described may be found others which belonged to those whose names have become household words. In the group of three in Figure 89 is one which belonged to Nathaniel Hawthorne. It is the large leather one at the right, and it does not look particularly comfortable. It is of a nondescript style, with legs at the front of turned wood, and a heavy object to lift.

Of about the same degree of comfort is the next chair, shown in Figure 90, which also belonged to one of our distinguished men. This chair is of mahogany, with a sparing use of good carving, and belonged to Daniel Webster. It is of the familiar pattern which was in vogue from 1820–1850. Both of these chairs are preserved in Salem, Massachusetts.

An even more distinguished relic than either of these chairs already mentioned is one which has been recently sold at auction at Sotheby's in London. This is a chair which belonged to Napoleon, and in which the great emperor passed his last days at St. Helena. The chair is a simple affair (Figure 91), not much to look at, somewhat on the Sheraton pattern, with a cane seat and light frame. It is said that it was on this

67

throne that the emperor sat when he dictated his memoirs to Las Cases.

It seems as if the chair had been made for the emperor, to fit agreeably his short and somewhat rotund figure. The dimensions are somewhat unusual for a chair of this style, the cane seat being nineteen by sixteen inches broad, while the legs are but seventeen inches high. This relic is apparently well authenticated, for underneath the seat is this inscription:

" This chair was used by Napoleon Bonaparte, and purchased at the sale of his effects at Longwood, by Andrew Darling, St. Helena, 1821."

After buying the chair, Mr. Darling had a brass plate put upon it, which seems rather conclusive evidence that the chair was the one actually used by Napoleon at St. Helena. The belongings of this great man are sadly dispersed, and it is a pity that they cannot be placed in some National Museum. It makes one almost shiver to see his camp bedstead at a place like Madame Tussaud's.

Following along in somewhat similar lines to the chairs were the forms, settles, and settees, which eventually developed into the sofa.

The rude board settle, examples of which can even yet be found in some conservative old kitchens, was followed by something not much more comfortable, it is true, but a trifle more ornate. They were often rudely carved in Gothic style, or they had wainscot trimmings, and cushions were used to render their uncompromising angles less sharp.

68

One of these settees is given in Figure 92 and has a simple bandy leg, a panelled back, and is made of oak. Like the old oak wainscoting, it is quite free from polish or finish of any kind, the wood being almost black from age and use. Forms frequently did not have any backs to them, and must have been not very conducive to lingering at table, even when the seats were cushioned. All during the seventeenth century quantities of settees were made of varying patterns and woods, some caned like the chair seats, and with openwork wooden backs, and some with rush seats, or stuffed and covered. I do not find many of these in this country, and can hardly account for their disappearance, since they were here with the chairs which matched them. In many old inventories there is mention of settees or couches, though in the latter case it is generally specified that they are covered.

In the inventory of Theophilus Eaton (1657), Governor of the New Haven Colony, may be found the following list of cushions which he had in his "Hall," which was really one of the most important rooms in his house. I have mentioned this inventory before, since it shows what a man high in office considered ample plenishing for his family. The furniture was:

"A drawing Table and a round Table
A Cubberd & 2 longe formes
A Cubberd cloth & Cushions
4 Setwork Cushions
6 greene Cushions & a greate Chaire with Needleworke."

69

There were many other chairs and stools, and all of them were covered with set or needlework, and there were the ten cushions in addition.

A very choice example of a settee in Adam brothers style is shown in Figure 93; it has still the remains of its old covering, and the exquisite carving is in good condition. This style of settee was in vogue long before the Adam brothers' day; they only took what they found and improved upon the decoration. This represents three chairs set together, and we find these settees with two, three, or four chair backs, and rarely with five. The carving in the oval at the back is in what was called " honeysuckle " pattern, and was used by all the makers in the late eighteenth century. It was a favourite with Hepplewhite, who used it in inlay as well as in carving.

A two chair-back settee is shown in the next figure, and while it is much in the Chippendale style, I should place it a little earlier than that maker, since it has the " Dutch foot," which was so much used during the first half of the eighteenth century. Hogarth, the great painter of London life, who fearlessly held the mirror up to nature when he showed its follies and sins in such sets of drawings as the " Rake's Progress," used such settees in his pictures as this one in Figure 94. Chairs on this style are often called " Hogarth chairs," which is much more appropriate than to call them Chippendale. This settee is of walnut, and the splat shows more ornamentation than is common in this pattern and in this wood.

70

Fig. 81   Chippendale Mahogany Chairs

Fig. 82   Adam Chair

Fig. 83   Shield-Back Chair

Fig. 84 Hepplewhite Chair   Fig. 85 Sheraton Chair

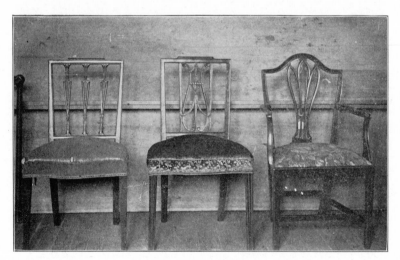

Fig. 86 Sheraton Chair

Fig. 87   MAPLE WINDSOR CHAIRS

Fig. 88   WASHINGTON'S CHAIR AND TABLE

Fig. 89 NATHANIEL HAWTHORNE'S CHAIR

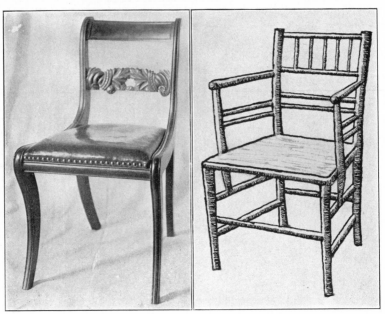

Fig. 90 DANIEL WEBSTER'S CHAIR   Fig. 91 NAPOLEON'S CHAIR

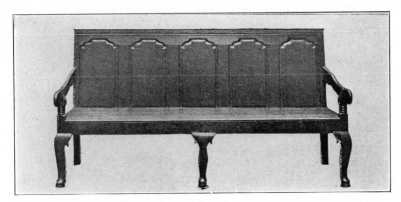

Fig. 92   OAK SETTEE

Fig. 93   ADAM BROTHERS' SETTEE

Fig. 94   HOGARTH "SETTEE"

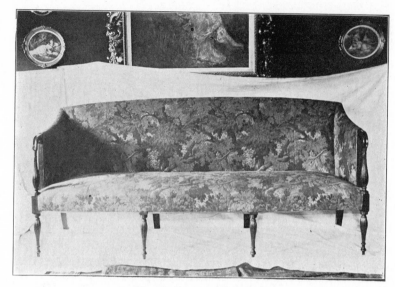

Fig. 95 TAPESTRY SETTEE

Fig. 96 SETTEE, MAHOGANY FRAME

Fig. 97   ITALIAN SOFA

Fig. 98   EMPIRE SOFA

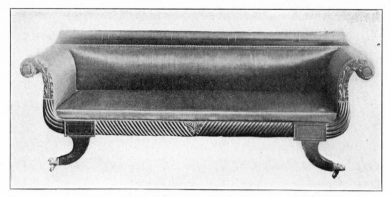

Fig. 99   CARVED EMPIRE SOFA

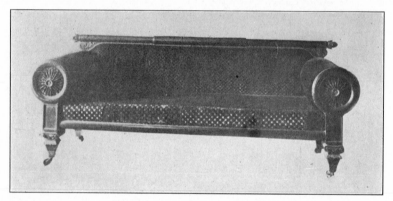

Fig. 100   SOFA VENEERED AND CARVED

Fig. 101   CARVED EMPIRE SOFA

The next two Figures (95 and 96) might have been made by either Hepplewhite or Sheraton, and it is safest to say that they belong to the last quarter of the eighteenth century than to assign them to any individual maker.

They both show decidedly the French influence and are charming pieces of furniture, the delicate fluting on legs and arms being about their only decoration. Their appearance is still further improved by the appropriate covering, which, though modern, is strictly in keeping with the style of the pieces.

An unusual and beautiful sofa, for which it is hard to assign an exact date, is next shown (Figure 97). This sofa, of splendid Italian workmanship, is part of a gift by Mr. and Mrs. Bloomfield Moore, and may be found in Memorial Hall, Philadelphia. It is of oak, the carving on the arms and back being in bold relief. I do not think that there are many sofas in this country of this pattern, yet I know of another very much like this, which has been in a house in Salem, Massachusetts, for many generations. But then Salem, with her fleet of ships touching at every port, had at her command about everything that the world afforded. Although oak was a common wood and one easily worked, it was not so much used in the eighteenth century as it had been previously. Experts on furniture are used to place an approximate date on pieces by noting the wood of which it is made, and first came the oak period, then walnut, then mahogany. Walnut was not an easily worked wood, and the great carvers,

71

like Grinling Gibbons, used something softer, Gibbons himself preferring limewood. This resembles satinwood in colour, but it has not the beautiful gloss and sheen which is one of the great attractions of satinwood.

Chippendale chose a close-set pine for many of his carvings when gilt was to be used, and some less hard wood than either mahogany or oak was adopted by the Adam brothers for the furniture they designed.

The rest of the sofas given cover a period of perhaps forty years. They are all of mahogany and may be called variations on the Empire style. The earliest one is given in Figure 98, and is curious from the fact that the ends are of solid and slatted wood, while the upholstery is confined to the back and seat. It is of a choice dark mahogany, with carved panels at the tops of the legs. This same style of frame is followed in the sofa in Figure 99, except that more carving was used. This sofa still retains its ancient horsehair covering. These hard uncomfortable articles of furniture were all too common in the first years of the nineteenth century. They were kept in the best room,—that damp, dark, musty room, which was opened and aired only on Sundays and holidays. I said that these were common in the opening years of the nineteenth century, and indeed in some parts of the country they have held their own for a hundred years and more. Within the last five years I have sat in more than one room with a haircloth sofa, slippery and chill, and tried to keep warm near an air-tight stove, which keeps your back at the freezing-point while your face is broiling. New England, as conservative as the country for which she was named, preserves her antiques and the customs which go with them more than any other section of the country. Uncomfortable as some of these be, it is pleasant to meet with those who will not sell their birthright for a mess of pottage, and to whom the venerable sofa is a throne of their ancestors.

The pieces shown in Figures 100 and 101 are partly veneered, and both have carving. The two others, in Figures 102 and 103, are solid, also with rich carving. The round cushions which often accompany these sofas are called " squabs," and in two of the sofas you may see that they are stationary; while in Figure 101 the places are left for them, but they are wanting. Mahogany was originally brought from Jamaica, and though first known in 1595, its use was so slow and gradual that not till 1700 was it used with even the least degree of freedom. By the middle of the century it was very popular, and in the hands of Chippendale acquired an immense vogue. In 1753 more than five hundred thousand feet were sent to London from that island, according to Mr. Frederick Robinson, in his book on " English Furniture," and we know that it was on sale here in the form of planks and logs. This wood is divided in the trade into Spanish mahogany and Honduras mahogany, or baywood. It is the Spanish wood which is the solid, heavy, and splendidly coloured kind which we all so ardently admire, susceptible of a high polish, and often showing a

73

beautiful waving curl in the grain, which enhances the value of the wood to such an extent that it is used only in the form of veneers.

According to Mr. Robinson:

" The finest curl and figuring of the grain of woods is found in nearly all cases at that part of the tree where the division of the branches from the trunk commences. The best curl is found at the branching of two arms only, away from the trunk, this being less confused than that caused by the divergence of several arms. A saw-cut made vertically across the tops of the two branching limbs down into the main trunk would exhibit that parting of the ways of the grain which is so valuable for the making of veneers."

The difference of weight between the finest Spanish mahogany and the inferior kinds is very great, a Chippendale-pattern chair in the fine wood being all a woman will care to lift. Tulip and satinwoods were the favourites for the old cabinet-makers to employ in inlaying, and the latter wood comes from a tree which may be found in India, Ceylon, and the West Indies. Tulipwood has the disadvantage of coming only in small pieces, and, besides, is often of such a reddish tone that it has not sufficient contrast to make it showy enough for veneer on mahogany. Lancewood is a modern substitute for satinwood, and the shafts of old vehicles, like the " One Hoss Shay," are eagerly sought for cutting into strips.

With satin, tulip, lance, and " harewood," which is sycamore stained, ebony was in great demand. The strips of this latter wood are often only one thirty-

74

second of an inch in thickness, and serve to mark the strip of light wood with better effect than if omitted.

Besides being used as an inlay, whole articles of ebony were very much in demand, and were often splendidly carved. The Dutch excelled in the use of this wood, and ebony boxes and cabinets were not uncommon, though quite costly. Horace Walpole, a collector of rare and valuable objects of whatever nature, seems to have had a fancy for this rare wood. In his letters is the following paragraph, dated May 30, 1763.

" I believe I am the first man that ever went sixty miles to an auction. As I came for ebony, I have been up to my chin in ebony; there is literally nothing in the house but ebony; all the other goods (if there were any, and I trust my Lady Conyers did not sleep upon ebony matrasses) are taken away. There are two tables and eighteen chairs, all made by the Hallet of two hundred years ago. These I intend to have. There are more plebian chairs of the same materials, but I have left commission for only this true black blood."

He speaks with the ring of the true enthusiast, and though he may have been the first man to travel sixty miles to an auction, he is not the last, for men, and women too, cross an ocean now to get a rare and desired bargain.

IV — ANTIQUE GLASSWARE

THE making of glass is an art so old and is so dignified by its antiquity that to learn about its earliest history would take us back at least fifteen hundred years before the Christian Era.

There is a glass bead still preserved, covered with Egyptian hieroglyphics which have been deciphered, showing that it belonged to Queen Hatasou, wife of Thothmes II, who reigned at Thebes 1500 B. C. The Egyptian workmen not only made beads, but attained great proficiency in the art of glass-making, and could produce bottles, cups, amulets, and images. Less pleasant things were coffins of glass in which rich and powerful persons were sometimes interred.

About the Christian Era the price of a drinking glass was half an *as*, the value of an as being about one cent, which shows that enough glass was made to allow of its being sold at a small price. Cicero (about 80 B. C.) mentions glass, linen, and paper as common articles of Egyptian merchandise.

From that day to the present the manufacture of glass has been of immense commercial importance, and besides contributing to the comfort and healthfulness

76

of our dwellings, has played a large part in giving us luxuries.

The clever Venetians early led the world in the manufacture of glass of exquisite beauty, and they still preserve their pre-eminence in this field of art. The whole history of Venetian glass-making, the laws which govern it, the almost royal privileges which belong to the makers, and the gathering together in the thirteenth century, upon the island of Murano, all this class of workers is too long a subject to be dealt with here. It is most interestingly told in Mr. Crawford's novel, "Marietta, A Maid of Venice."

Turn where you will in old records and inventories toward the end of the Middle Ages and you will generally find some mention made of Venetian glasses. These workers sent looking-glasses to England by the end of the thirteenth century, and their ornamental cups and beakers, holding within the glass itself particles of gold, were eagerly sought by those wealthy enough to buy them.

In that most interesting old book, Holinshed's "Chronicle," of which the most valuable part, "The Descriptions of Britaine and England," were written by William Harrison, we find this account of the use of glass in the year 1577, and for the immediately preceding years.

After speaking of the different foods which may be found at a nobleman's table, "whose cooks," he adds, "are for the most part musical-headed Frenchmen and strangers," he describes the rich plate on which they are served, and then goes on:

" As for drink, it is usually filled in pots, goblets, jugs, bowls of silver, in noblemen's houses; also in fine Venice glasses of all forms; and for want of these elsewhere, in pots of sundry colours and moulds, whereof many are garnished with silver, or at the leastwise with pewter, all which notwithstanding are seldom set on the table, but each one as necessity urgeth, calleth for a cup of such drink as him listeth to have, so that, when he has tasted of it, he delivered the cup again to some one of the standers by, who, making it clean by pouring out the drink which remaineth, restoreth it to the cupboard from whence he fetched the same. By this device much idle tippling is furthermore cut off. . . . It is a world to see in these our days, wherein gold and silver most aboundeth, how our gentility, as loathing those metals (because of the plenty) do now generally choose rather the Venice glasses, both for our wine and beer, than any of those metals or stone wherein before time we have been accustomed to drink; and such is the estimation of this stuff that many become rich with only their new trade unto Murana (a town near to Venice, situate on the Adriatic Sea), from whence the very best are daily to be had, and such as for beauty do well near match the crystal or the ancient *murrhina vasa* whereof now no man hath knowledge. And as this is seen in the gentility, so in the wealthy communality the like desire of glass is not neglected, whereby the gain gotten by their purchase is yet much more increased to the benefit of the merchant. The poorest also will have glass if they may; but sith the Venetian is somewhat dear for them, they content themselves with such as are made at home of fern and burned stone; but in fine all go one way — that is, to shards at last, so that our great expense in glasses (besides that they breed much strife toward such as have charge of them) are worst of all bestowed in mine opinion, because their pieces do turn to no profit."

78

The use of glass for windows was one of the greatest improvements of mediæval times, and in Whitaker's " Loidis et Elmete " he says:

" The earliest stained glass which we read of, at least in the north of England, was in the possession of the Monks of Rivaulx, about 1140. At this precise period the narrow lights began to expand, and as the use of it grew more and more general, the surfaces of windows became by degrees more diversified and wider."

Hamerton, in " Paris in its Old and Present Times," describes the Louvre as it was in 1368. He says that the rooms were low, panelled with wood, with narrow barred windows, on the glass of which were painted the arms of the person to whom the room belonged.

In the " Comptes du vieux Louvre " it says: " The King's cabinet or study was lighted by one large window with painted glass, and four smaller ones, and it was hung with black *drap de Caen.*" This was also in 1368.

In England the manufacture of glass was either unknown or neglected during the Middle Ages, and it was not till Queen Elizabeth invited Cornelius de Lannoy to settle in London that works in glass were first produced. Glass objects were much esteemed, of whatever form, and James Howell, in his " Familiar Letters," writes to his uncle from London in 1625 as follows:

" The curious sea-chest of glasses you are pleased to bestow on me, I shall be very chary to keep as a monument of your love."

79

The gossipy Pepys writes in his diary for 1661 that a Captain Lambert who had recently returned from Portugal says " that there are no glass windows, nor will they have any." His easy way of speaking of glass windows shows that they were in common use in England at that time, and in fact Harrison, already quoted, says:

" Of old time, our country houses, instead of glass did use much lattice, and that made either of wicker or fine rifts of oak in checkerwise. But as now lattices of horn are quite laid down in every place, other lattices are grown less used, because it is come to be so plentiful, and within a little so good cheap, if not better than the other."

This was nearly a hundred years earlier than when Pepys wrote.

An interesting case of glasses, while of a later period than those of which Howell wrote, is shown in Figure 104. It was made to hold not only various kinds of wine, but glasses for drinking and a tray to set them on as well. Of the old Venetian glasses from which they drank vernage, catepument, raspis, muscadell, romnie, bastard lire, osy caprie, clary, and malmesey, as well as some liquors of greater " strength and valour," few remain. Few also of the bottles or decanters have escaped the midden, but in Figure 105 are a pair of decanters such as the Venetians made three hundred years ago, and which no doubt were seen on the tables of all who could afford such luxuries. In fact bottles of one form or another, either with or without a wicker-work covering, have been in use uninterruptedly from the earliest times.

After bottles, goblets and drinking-glasses claimed attention, and a whole world of care has been given to their form and decoration. The glass found in this country, and which was in use among the colonists, came usually from England, whence most of our luxuries were imported, and was often of the style known as "cut glass," — that is, flint glass polished and ground till it receives a sparkle and brilliancy that render it extremely beautiful. During the eighteenth century much of this rich glass was sent to this country, and being quite strong, it has in many cases survived hard usage.

Less often we find drinking-mugs and glasses of German manufacture, which are generally classed, not always correctly, under the head of "Bohemian." It is true that the region forming the boundaries of Bohemia on the one side, and Saxony, Bavaria, and Silesia on the other, saw the rise and growth of the glass industry in Germany. The forests on the mountain sides, and the abundant supply of clean quartz sand which is so indispensable in glass-making, were all found here, and though there is not much literature concerning the development of the industry, two authorities remain which do much to clear up its history.

Whether the art of painting on glass came to Germany through Venice, which had long had intercourse with the East, or whether the painted glass windows had inspired some clever German to try the like on drinking-vessels, will never be known. It is probable, though, that the knowledge came from Venice. Georg Agricola, who was born at Glauchau, in March, 1490, went to Venice and studied the working of glass kilns both there and at Murano. In 1556 he published at Basle a work called "De re Metallica," which was of great benefit to the growing industry. The second authority is Johann Matthesius, who published a book on glass-making in 1562, in which he mentions that the drinking of liquor from glass was not much practised beyond his own district of Bohemia and Silesia, although we know that glass drinking-vessels had long been imported from Venice.

Two specimens of the glass work of Bohemia are given in the next Figure (106), the stein showing the splendid ruby engraved glass with which we are even yet familiar, and the tall pitcher decorated with enamelled paintings. This style of work is commonly called "Fichtel Glass," since it first originated at the kilns in the Fichtel Mountains, in the northeast of Bavaria. They still retain this name, no matter where their place of manufacture. The decoration on the jug is an ermine cloak, in front of which is a shield surmounted with a crown, — a favourite form of decoration in the eighteenth century.

While the Germans ran to a great extent to the use of colour in their glass, the English glass is distinguished by cutting and engraving, the crystal of the glass being left its natural tint. Just which art was the earlier in

82

use it is hard to say, and both styles of decoration were brought to a great degree of perfection.

Pepys mentions in February, 1668, that he went to " the Glasshouse, and there shewed my cozens the making of glass, and had several things made with great content; and among others, I had one or two singing-glasses made, which make an echo to the voice, the first that I ever saw; but so thin, that the very breath broke one or two of them." He speaks a year or two later of having his name engraved on some decanters, which gave him " great content " also.

Figures 107 and 108 show engraved decanters of great beauty, and 109 and 110, engraved beakers, one of them with cover. Such shaped glasses were in use from the seventeenth century, and the one with the tulip in its basket is undoubtedly of Dutch origin. They used one more " g " in spelling grog in the eighteenth century than we do now, and it must have been a steady head which has carried home safely the contents of more than one glass of such a size as this. Two pretty pieces, also engraved, are shown in the next Figure (111), and belong to the Water's Collection, at Salem, Massachusetts.

There is a certain elegance about cut glass which engraved glass never has, a brilliancy and a sparkle which always makes it pleasing. Figures 112 and 113 show some good old pieces, still bearing their weight of years sturdily.

Conceive what elegance a tall sugar-bowl like the one in Figure 114 added to a table on which the other furniture was porcelain, or some fine English ware, or even pewter polished to the brightness of silver. Such pieces as this are treasured relics in many old families, and some years ago could be picked up for very small sums. I bought a pair, of which this is one, in New York City, for three dollars. They are very hard to find now. In the next Figure (115) is found quite a singular piece; it is even taller than the one in Figure 114, and is a beautiful dark green. Even rarer still are such objects as the cut-glass vase, of the old "hob-nail" pattern, shown in Figure 116, which I saw one day in an "antique shop" and took a snapshot at. Going there a few days later to get a better picture of it, I found that it had been picked up by some lover of fine glass and taken out West.

In Figure 117 is shown a collection of English glass. The two covered dishes were used for sweetmeats, and the wine-glass at the end is tiny enough to be what was known as the "minister's glass," which was always two or three sizes smaller than those of his congregation. This glass is also interesting, since it is among the earliest I am able to show coming under the head of "bell-shaped," which form was copied directly from the Venetian pattern, and it dates to early in the eighteenth century. The glass in Figure 118 is known as the "drawn-bowl" shape.

They are called "drawn" glasses because they seem to have been drawn from a single piece of glass, both bowl and stem having been formed by drawing out with a single spiral movement. They come in many

84

sizes, and on tall or short stems, and are nearly as early as the "waisted" ones, some fine examples of which are shown in the next Figure (119).

The drawn-bowl glasses never are "knopped" in the centre, like the first and third glasses in Figure 119, but they are frequently decorated with a twisted ribbon of white glass, or a twisted tear of air, while those for tavern use frequently had a bead of air introduced at the top of the stem. These choice varieties of glass were made for wealthy patrons, who used them to drink wine from. Even in America many were in use, and in the Figure 120 can be noted many examples which did duty at Mount Vernon, when President and Madam Washington had guests to dinner. In fact all the elegant articles shown in this picture belonged to them, and it is well to note the fine glass candelabra on the top shelf, which must have been very ornamental when lighted up with candles.

The very choicest of all the glasses were engraved, most often with floral forms, sometimes with wreaths of grapes and leaves. A point to be noted in the row of glasses in Figure 118 is the extreme solidity of the stems and bases, which are very different from the slender stems of the modern wine-glasses. These old glasses were made so that they could not upset easily, — a very necessary qualification in days when temperance was far less considered than it is at the present time, and when squire, and parson too, were frequently taken from under the table, so potent had been the contents of these seemly glasses. I should

85

call all these glasses spirit glasses, since the beer and wine-glasses all held more copious draughts. Some of the liquors and cordials which were drunk from these small glasses were imported. Among such were Clove or Caraway Waters, Oil of Venus, Oil of Hazel-nuts, Parfait Amour, Essence of Tea or Coffee, Free Masons' Cordial, and many others.

Patriots who chose only home-brewed "cordial waters" might, in 1766, go to Richard Deane, who, at his distillery on Long Island, could supply them with Aniseed, Orange, and Clove Waters, All Fours, or the Cordial of Cordials, Golden Cordial, Cordial of Health, Royal Water, Royal Usquebaugh, Red Ratifie, Cinnamon, Cardamun, and Angelica Waters, Ros Solis, Stoughton's Elixir, Whiskey, Brandy, Rectified Spirits of Wine, as well as Aqua Mirabilis or Wonderful Water, and Aqua Coelestis, or Heavenly Water! It must have been after the perusal of this list that Benjamin Franklin wrote his "Drinker's Dictionary," consisting of many strange and curious words which signify intoxication. But though he deprecated getting "tann'd, jagg'd, glaz'd, or crack'd," he wrote the following pretty recipe for punch:

> Boy, bring a bowl of china here,
> Fill it with water cool and clear ;
> Decanter with Jamaica ripe,
> And spoon of silver, clean and bright,
> Sugar twice-fin'd in pieces cut,
> Knife, sieve and glass in order put,
> Bring forth the fragrant fruit, and then
> We 're happy till the clock strikes ten.

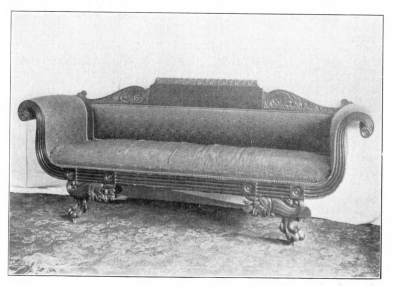

Fig. 102 CARVED EMPIRE SOFA

Fig. 103 CARVED SOFA WITH "SQUABS"

Fig. 104 LIQUOR CASE AND GLASSES

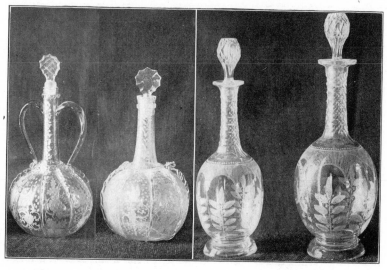

Fig. 105 VENETIAN GLASS   Fig. 108 ENGRAVED GLASS

Fig. 106 GERMAN GLASS

Fig. 107 ENGLISH GLASS

Fig. 109 ENGRAVED BEAKERS

Fig. 110 BEAKERS OR FLIP GLASSES

Fig. 111 PITCHER   Fig. 112 DECANTERS

Fig. 113 CUT GLASS DECANTERS AND GLASSES

Fig. 114 Cut Glass Sugar-Bowl   Fig. 115 Green Glass Sugar-Bowl

Fig. 116 Cut Glass Vase

Fig. 117 ENGLISH GLASS

Fig. 118 ENGLISH GLASS, FLINT, AND OPAL

For the drinking of punch in England, and the more popular flip in this country, came a glass of generous size, which was capable of holding nearly a quart. Cider mugs were often made of pottery, though no doubt it was often partaken of from flip glasses, particularly if it was "royal mulled" or "damasked." Molasses, spruce, and persimmon beer were some of the temperance drinks of the day, while tiff, Sampson, and hotch potch are but a few of the mixed condiments. Israel Acrelius, in his "History of New Sweden," 1758, mentions half a hundred beverages now no longer recognised by name or taste.

A large flip glass is shown in Figure 121, beautifully engraved, and beside it on the table lie the other necessaries for a "convivial evening," as our great-grandfathers would have said. The iron implement lying in front of the bowl is a loggerhead, which was heated red-hot and then plunged into the flip, causing it to mantle high, and imparting to it the burnt taste which was so much esteemed. The way our ancestors lived, the things they ate, how they were clothed, what they read, and how they amused themselves, are subjects of unfailing interest. But when we come to what they drank, we stand aghast! It was no doubt the fact that they had to work unceasingly and largely out of doors which was their salvation.

There was much glass of a finer quality which found its way over here, like the two tall goblets shown in Figure 122. They are of English glass, not decorated with engraving, but with a pretty floral pattern in

87

gold, and also with gold rims. One of these glasses is filled with cotton to show the pattern. These goblets are about a hundred years old, and are from a set of five, which are still in good condition, out of the original dozen. The gold is not impressed in the glass as in the modern gold-decorated glass, but is on the surface, and much more likely to wear off. The two goblets shown in Figure 123 are also quite unusual, and of about equal age. They are made of ground glass, after the fashion of the lamp-shade in Figure 118. On the base are cut very deeply several rays, and the glasses are enormously heavy, so that they are inconvenient to use when filled with water. These are also of English origin.

Three glasses, very beautiful in both execution and design, are given in Figure 124, the one on the left being particularly noticeable, since on one side it has the American eagle and shield, and on the other a coat-of-arms with the three princes' feathers. It seems incredible that glasses of such beauty as these, and those for wine which have been given, should have been wantonly destroyed; yet Madame de Sévigné writes in 1675 that it was customary after drinking the King's health to break the glass, and "roystering blades," both in this country and Europe, during the last ten years of the eighteenth century, had a fashion of biting out a piece of the wine-glass and grinding it with the teeth, and swallowing it, the pleasure to the company being to see how a newcomer stood it. Mortimer, the artist, did it, so Southey says, and never recovered from it.

88

Wedgwood, the great potter, set the fashion of making shallow bowls or cups, mounted on stems, which he called " tazzi." Sometimes these had handles. Tazzi were also made in glass, and Figure 125 is one in Bohemian glass, very prettily decorated with a raised all-over pattern and lines of gilt.

That the glass from Italy, Bohemia, and England was to be found in America very early in our history is shown by both inventories and advertisements. Colonel William Smith, of St. George's Manor, Suffolk County, in 1705, was worth £2,589 40s. He died a few years later, and in his inventory is mentioned, " 1 case Venice glasses, £3. Flint glasses, £3.14.0." Captain Giles Shelly, New York, 1718, had an enormous amount of household gear, and as many as " 45 beer glasses."

Governor Montgomery, at Fort George, New York, had among other fine things a complete set of cut-glass cruets, as well as water and champagne glasses. In the " Boston News Letter " for August 24, 1719, there were advertised:

" Fine glass Lamps and Lanthorns well gilt and painted both convex and plain. Both suitable for Halls, Staircases, or other Passageways, at the Glass Shop in Queen's Street."

Thomas Lepper, in 1754, had on sale " all sorts of bottles, from one quart to three gallons, and upward, as well as a variety of other glassware." There were " cream-jugs, syllabub, and sweetmeat glasses, cruet stands, flowered wine and water glasses, glass salvers,

89

small enamelled, shank wine-glasses, flowered, scalloped,
and plain decanters, jugs and mugs, salver and pyramids, glasses for silver, salts and sweatmeats, poles with
spires and glasses, smelling bottles, sconces, tulip and
flower glasses of the newest patterns, finger bowls and
tumblers of all sorts," advertised for sale in New York
before 1760.

You could buy in New York in 1773, "Very rich Cut
Glass Candlesticks, Cut glass Sugar Boxes and Cream
Potts, wine, wine-and-water glasses, and Beer glasses
with cut shanks, Jelly and Syllabub Glasses, Glass
Salvers, also Cyder Glasses, Orange and Top Glasses,
Glass Cans, Glass Cream Buckets and Crewits, Royal
Arch Mason Glasses, Glass Pyramids with Jelly Glasses,
Globe and Barrel Lamps, etc."

A most unusual article, at least in this country, is
shown in Figure 126 standing on a beautiful Sheraton
candlestand. This is a glass globe filled with water,
which was used to concentrate the light of the candles,
and throw it upon a particular spot.

A less choice arrangement of this order, glass bottles
of very thin glass filled with water, was used in both
England and Holland during the eighteenth century,
and doubtless earlier, by the lacemakers to throw a
shaft of light on their work. Sometimes a single candle
on a stand was surrounded by bottles, and the workers
drawn in a circle, on chairs and stools of varying
heights, had only this to make the most delicate and
eye-destroying of all fabrics.

In our own country the first glass factory was started

90

in 1607 near the ill-fated Jamestown, in Virginia, and, like the Egyptians of old, we made beads. We used them for barter with the Indians. It is said that occasionally beads are found near Jamestown, striped green and white like gooseberries, and it is thought they may have been made here.

After the various settlements were a little more secure, the necessity for glass bottles stimulated the colonists to pay bounties to men of this calling who would come and settle here. Salem, Massachusetts, a most progressive town in its early days, had a brick kiln in operation in 1629, and a glass-house in 1639. Window glass was brought over here easily as ballast, but round or hollow glass was more perishable; and to encourage home production, many enactments were passed in Massachusetts, Virginia, Pennsylvania, and New York. None of these early ventures were particularly successful, but by the eighteenth century many bottle factories were started, most of which have passed out of the hands of the original owners.

The factory at Glassboro, New Jersey, was started in 1775, and the one at Kensington, Pennsylvania, a few years earlier. These two establishments are still in operation to-day, and are the oldest ones in America which still exist. The first glass bottles were coarse and of a dark green glass, although blue and brown colouring was produced by using oxide of cobalt and manganese. The making of even the roughest bottle takes more skilled labour than one would think at first glance, and when it comes to a fine object, graceful

91

in shape and elegantly ornamented, the work becomes an art.

About 1810, and until the last quarter of the century, glass bottles were made here in various shapes and with different devices. Among the earliest were those bearing portraits of Washington and Lafayette, those with eagle and shield, and some with a car drawn by a horse, and also one showing an early locomotive; but, of course, these were later still. About 1840 were made the log-cabin devices, of which there were several on bottles, in pitchers, like the one I show in Figure 127, and in small square panels, which were mounted for breastpins, one at least of these being treasured in California, since a drawing of it was sent to me only the other day. The log cabin was so favourite a device that it was seized upon for use as a whiskey bottle, and is marked on the back, " G. Booz's Old Cabinet Whiskey." Still later than this the same shape was used for " Holtzermann's Stomach Bitters." This was a patent medicine, and such a bottle is shown in another figure.

A fine group of old glassware is given in Figure 128, the most attractive pieces being the row of cup plates with historic scenes and portraits, which form the front row. Beginning at the right, the first cup plate shows the log cabin, the design being very plain, even in so small a space. This design was made about 1840, and it is not yet known whether these pieces were made in this country or, like the historic china, in England. Next comes "Henry Clay," date 1844; then the " Benjamin Franklin Steamboat"; then "Fort Meigs"; next "Eagle and Shield," followed by one of the rarest, showing the Bunker Hill Monument and having these inscriptions: "Bunker Hill Battle, Fought June 17, 1775." "From the Fair to the Brave." "Corner Stone laid by Lafayette, June 17, 1825, Finished by the Ladies, 1841."

The last plate on the row is another portrait of Henry Clay, and there is also a portrait of President Harrison, although it is not given here.

That there are many of these cup plates tucked away out of sight I am quite sure. I am also sure that they will be rummaged out directly, and that my correspondents will want to know their value. Of course, they do not begin to be so valuable as the old blue china cup plates, which bring exorbitant sums, but one with a portrait or scene on it, in good condition, is worth one dollar. I have known of seven being bought for twenty-five cents for the lot.

The era of patent medicines set in about 1850, and distinctive forms for bottles were eagerly sought. There was no limit to the ingenuity displayed in the choice of shapes, and a collection of these bottles is certainly quite ornamental, if not particularly interesting.

In Figure 129 the fish is marked under the eye, "Dr. Fish Bitters. W. H. Ware. Patented 1866." The Indian in rich brown glass is marked on the side, "Brown's Celebrated Indian Herb Bitters. Patented 1867." The cannon does not tell what it contained, but is merely labelled, "A. M. Bininger and Co., 19 Broad

93

street, New York." The graceful jug is nothing but a whiskey bottle, and is marked, " Wharton's Whiskey. 1850. Chestnut Grove." This probably came from the City of Brotherly Love.

" Van Dunck's Geneva, Trade-Mark," is found on the bottom of the toby in Figure 130, and the nice old squatty bottle of rich green glass betrays its Dutch origin, since it is a Schnapps bottle, but is probably not so old as the one shown in the next Figure (131), which has an earlier type of neck. The man's figure in mottled ware (Figure 132) is marked " Monk, 1849." This bottle is not glass, but one of those rare specimens of Bennington ware, which came from the Vermont pottery which was started in 1847, and whose brief career lasted about ten years. Beside it is the most modern piece of all, which was brought out in the Cleveland campaign.

I wish to refer to two very unusual glass portraits, called " Jefferson " and " Madison," which are mounted in strong gilt frames, and which are marked " Desprez, Rue de Recolets, No. 2, à Paris." I am able only to give drawings of these, but it would be interesting to know if any more such portraits are to be found here (Figure 133).

In Figures 118 and 134 are given several articles of opal glass, candlesticks, cups, and some small plates and lamps. About 1820 this glass was quite fashionable, and was used also for rosettes to loop back curtains, and upon which mirrors were stood. There is a cheap quality of glass made to-day which is milk white in colour, and which should never be confused with this charming old opal glass, which has playing over its surface the fleeting shades of blue and rose, which make it resemble the gem for which it is named.

Some exceptionally fine girandoles are shown in the following Figure (135), with beautiful glass prisms, and in Figure 136 some candlesticks with extra holders for the candles, and coloured glass bases.

Before closing this brief chapter on glass, mention must be made of one of its most familiar uses, — that of mirrors. The early ones came from Venice, and great must have been the delight of the fair sex when such objects replaced those made of polished metal, which up to that time had been the only ones in use. The Duke of Buckingham is given the credit for establishing in 1673 the first factory for the manufacture of looking-glasses in England, the term " mirror " often referring to a convex glass, which might or might not have sconces for candles on each side of the frame. The early Venetian glasses in richly carved frames were very beautiful, and few enough, if any, found their way over here. Indeed, looking-glasses were taxed as unnecessary luxuries by the Pilgrim Fathers, when they sought to raise money for the expense of the Indian wars.

In England they became popular at once, and both men and women wore them, a small bit serving to loop up a gallant's hat, and one of similar size was mounted on my lady's fan or hung at her side. In Massinger's play of " The City Madam," he says, " Enter Lady

Frugal, Anne Mary, and Milliscent, in several postures, with looking-glasses at their girdles."

In " Cynthia's Revels," the same author says:

> "Where is your page ?   Call for your casting bottle,
> And place your mirror in your hat as I told you."

The branch of glass-making which had the greatest success in France during the seventeenth century was the manufacture of mirrors. In 1665 eighteen workmen from Venice were established at a factory in the Faubourg St. Antoine, at Paris, and very soon after another factory was started at Tour-la-Ville, near Cherbourg. Both of these prospered, and were finally united. The plates of glass which are in the famous Salle des Glaces at the palace of Versailles were made at Tour-la-Ville. The process of casting plates of glass was revived in 1688 (for the art had been practically lost since Roman times), and it became possible to make larger sheets of glass than when the plates were produced by blowing.

But though the manufacture was extensive, the prices of mirrors were high. Only those who were possessed of means were enabled to have such luxuries.

There is a little anecdote told by St. Simon which proves that looking-glasses were not cheap in France as comparatively late as 1699. The Countess of Fiesque, a friend of Mademoiselle de Montpensier, purchased an extremely fine mirror.

" Well, Countess," said one of her friends, " where did you get that? "

96

" I had," replied she, " a troublesome estate, which produced only corn. I have sold it, and bought this mirror with what it brought me. Have I not done well? "

This glass, costly as it was, was exceeded by at least one other, which, in 1791, was valued at thirty thousand dollars in gold. This famous mirror, surrounded by a frame of jewels and gold, belonged to Queen Marie de Medici, and hangs in the Louvre at Paris, showing still to the world that the extravagance and luxury of the present day was far outdone by the lavish magnificence of the Renaissance.

These early mirrors had a bevelled glass, the bevelled edge being about an inch wide and following the shape of the frame. An interesting one in a simple frame is given in Figure 137, and shows not only the bevelled edge, but also the small sizes in which the pieces of glass were made. Very often in the upper sections some ornament was used, either in the quicksilver, or of painting. Rarely you find one in a Japanned frame, in which case the glass will be very small, and there is another early style, which has a frame of bits of looking-glass with strips of gilded wood.

Handsome glasses like that shown in Figure 138 were commonly called pier glasses, and were hung over a table. They were carved and gilt, or carved from the natural wood and not gilded, or the two were combined, as in our example, which shows a bird, which, if it had a longer bill, might well belong to the style which Chippendale used on his glasses. All the furniture makers made mirror frames, many of them of great beauty, and some of them so overloaded with ornament that to the present idea they seem absolutely grotesque. It takes a Chippendale to put on such a frame, waterfalls and Chinese pagodas, Mandarins and umbrellas, and then to crown the whole with such a bird as never was seen, and have the thing look charming!

There were some men from the middle of the eighteenth century who published their designs for these articles of ornament, and of these probably the most famous were Ince and Mayhew. Hepplewhite made some fine designs, many of which had frames enriched with inlay, and in the days when the so-called Empire styles prevailed the glasses followed the fashion of the other articles.

Very much desired by those who wanted something uncommon was a kind of glass which was known as " Bilboa." One is given in Figure 139.

The greater number of such glasses as these are to be found in Massachusetts, and have marble columns, generally pale yellow, at the sides. The frames themselves vary very much, some being of gilt and marble, some combining these two with natural wood; and there are others with fine Italian metal work at the top, showing vases and scrolls. The one shown here is a solid affair of gilt and mahogany, and looks as if it had never seen Bilboa, from which port it is stated these mirrors were brought home by the Massachusetts sailors. No matter where they came from, they are beautiful

98

objects, and the one which is given here belongs to Mrs. Nathan Osgood, of Salem, Massachusetts.

In the next Figure (140) will be found a Hepplewhite pattern, all gilt, and supported upon two Battersea enamel knobs. It is in fine condition, and forms a beautiful adjunct to any room, though particularly appropriate in a fine old house, where it has hung many years. It might be well to say a word of warning to enthusiasts who, regardless of their surroundings, are devoted to antiques. A certain propriety, which is often neglected, should be observed with reference to the placing of such things. Of course, if your old mahogany and china are heirlooms, there is nothing to say. Put them where you please and enjoy them. But if you live in a modern frame house, with low ceilings and modern arrangements, you need to be very careful how you install antiques which were made for other conditions. Also be careful how you mix ancient and modern objects together; the result is sometimes mirth-provoking, and one is obliged to face the owner with a solemn face, when one would like very much to laugh at the incongruities which are grouped there, and which their eager possessor expects you to praise with unction.

The three-light mantel mirror we are all familiar with, and with the small bedroom mirror with its painting on glass at the top. Somewhat on this fashion, but yet what we might well call "Empire," is the mahogany one given in Figure 141. It has choicely carved side-pillars, and a water-gilt mount at the top.

99

It is what is called a two-light mirror, and dates from about 1800. Still later is the cheval glass (Figure 142), which is of veneered mahogany, with turned posts and top rail. The glass was considered a generous size when it was made, and measures two feet by three. Glasses like this in standards which varied but a little could be obtained till what was known as "the black walnut age" set in, during the fifties. They did not have much to commend them, and look as clumsy now as do their cousins, the great sofas with similar legs and heavy veneered arms. Many people think that because a thing is old it needs no further recommendation, and never look for grace of line, beauty of construction, or choiceness of material.

I am frequently asked if there is any way of detecting the counterfeit hollow glasses with which the markets are so heavily stocked. There is no infallible way, but before purchasing a glass it is advisable to flick it sharply with the finger. If it is an old one, it will respond with a sharp, metallic ring, which is entirely absent from the modern reproductions. The bases of the glasses are much larger in the old than in the spurious ones, and the modern glass is always brightened or "buffed" by machinery, which can be easily detected. In the middle of the base there is a rough, sharp place, as if the extra glass had been broken off, which is another mark of the antique pieces which is wanting in the modern, and frequently the foot is "folded," — that is, has an extra piece added in the form of a rim, which gave it extra strength and firm-

100

ness. Glasses with this folded foot are extremely rare and consequently desirable. It is seldom found on specimens later than the seventeenth century.

In reference to the old German beer-glasses, the plain ones are the most common. They should have the appearance of having been blown from one piece of glass.

The grog-glasses, or "Rummers," as they are sometimes called, are always of ample proportions, and many of the old ones have a peculiarity which would easily escape notice. This is that the upper half of the glass is thicker than the lower half, magnifying the amount of liquor put in it, and at the same time reducing its quantity.

Many of the nice old glasses dating from the last of the eighteenth century are decorated with grapes and vine leaves. Others are fluted, and some have a lattice work, all of which ornamentation is engraved. In these it will be noted that the foot is much flatter than the earlier ones, and not quite so large. The collector of glasses has an exciting career before him, for there is great difficulty in deciding on what is genuine and what is not. The most rare and desirable glasses are the old square-based goblets, sometimes engraved with the owner's name, and sometimes with stars or other devices.

V — CHESTS AND CUPBOARDS

DURING the Middle Ages and through several succeeding centuries, the chest ranked next to the bed as the most important piece of household furniture. Of course, this statement does not apply to the courts, where more or less luxury was always to be found, but to the people composing the middle rank in life, — the bone and sinew of every country.

Beginning in Italy, where elegance and beauty flourished long before they reached the ruder peoples of northern Europe, we find the chest was a necessity in every household, particularly the stout one of iron to hold the treasure of the family. There were no banks, and each man stored his ducats as safely as might be, some of them, like Shylock, finding them fly with a wayward daughter.

From the sixth century the Jewish merchants were noted for their wealth. They were the money-lenders of the world, and to them is due credit for establishing the system of bills of exchange. About 1183 orders to pay money to a particular person were in use among the merchants of Lombardy and the South of France. General letters of credit were common in the Levant by 1200, while bills of exchange regularly

102

Fig. 119 Wine-Glasses

Fig. 120 Washington's Glassware

Fig. 121 FLIP GLASS AND LOGGERHEAD

Fig. 122
ENGLISH GOLD DECORATED GLASS

Fig. 123
GROUND TUMBLERS WITH CUT BASES

Fig. 124 THREE ENGRAVED GOBLETS

Fig. 125 BOHEMIAN GLASS TAZZA

Fig. 126 CRYSTAL GLOBE   Fig. 127 LOG-CABIN PITCHER

Fig. 128 GROUP OF GLASSWARE, AMERICAN

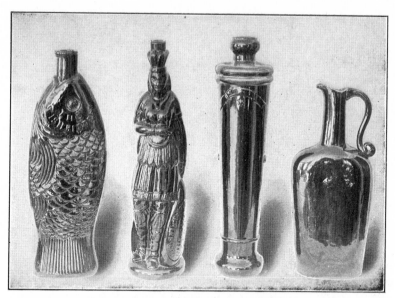

Fig. 129 Patent Medicine Bottles

Fig. 130 Patent Medicine Bottles

Fig. 131 OLD SCHNAPS BOTTLE

Fig. 132 PATENT MEDICINE BOTTLES

Fig. 133   GLASS PORTRAITS

Fig. 134   OPAL AND FLINT GLASS

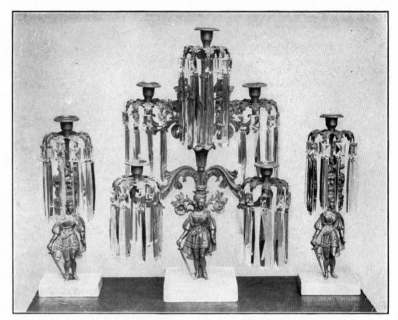

Fig. 135 GIRANDOLES

Fig. 136 CANDLESTICKS AND LAMP

negotiable were mentioned as early as 1364; and by
1400 they were drawn in sets and worded exactly as
they are now.

The earliest bank of deposit instituted for the accommodation of private merchants was at Barcelona
in 1401; so it can be readily seen what an important
article a chest was. In Figures 143 and 144 are given
some of these iron treasure-chests with their ponderous
locks and great handles, showing what heavy weights
they were expected to sustain. They have both seen
service, and belong to the sixteenth and seventeenth
centuries, bringing up in this very new country after
a world of voyaging.

General Washington's household chest, which may
now be seen at the National Museum at Washington,
is nearly identical with the chest shown in Figure 143
on the left, the one on the right being more like one
of the coffers used in churches.

A very interesting work by Mr. Frederick Roe,
called "Ancient Coffers and Cupboards," goes into the
matter of the old chests exhaustively, and he divides
them into four classes, passing over those which are
entirely of iron, and beginning with those which for
their strength and ornament depend largely on ironwork. The second class contains those which have
painting as well as ironwork for decoration, while the
third class are those which have fronts composed of
upright slabs of wood, carved with ecclesiastical forms,
like the smaller chest in Figure 144, which has a pattern of pillars and arches. Then, fourth, more secular

103

chests, having on them knights and ladies, animals, etc., these subjects being incised or burnt in.

Throughout the fourteenth century there was a continued improvement all over Europe of what we denominate luxury and elegance, though Italy still presented the fairest picture of domestic life. The use of chimneys and glass in house-building are the two most important improvements in this century, and if the houses were so crude, it may be guessed how simple were their fittings. Indeed, everything tending towards luxury crept among the people slowly, and in the very matter of chimneys they were few and far between, the masons connected with the abbeys being the only ones who could build them, so that in the farmhouses they were not introduced till about the middle of the seventeenth century. King, writing in 1656 in " Vale Royal," says:

" In building and furniture of their houses, till of late years they used the old manner of the Saxons; for they had their fire in the midst of the house, against a hob of clay, and their oxen under the same roof; but within these forty years they have builded chimneys."

It does not exactly appear what was kept in the church coffers, already mentioned, unless it was the treasures, — i. e., votive offerings and plate, and in most churches at this early period there was little enough of these. In Kennett's " Parochial Antiquities " he says:

" Ela, Countess of Warwick, who died very aged, in the year 1300, was so great a friend to Oxford University, that she

104

caused a common chest to be made, and did put into it two hundred and twenty marks; out of which such as were poor scholars might upon security at any time borrow something gratis for their wants; in consideration whereof, the University were obliged to celebrate certain masses every year in Saint Mary's Church. Which chest was in being in Edward IVth's time, and called by the name of Warwick chest."

Very few of these ancient church coffers are still in existence, and even those are housed in museums. Domestic chests have fared better, though few can be obtained prior to the Elizabethan period.

In 1572 Skipton Castle, the ancestral home of the Earls of Cumberland, and one of the most splendid mansions of the North of England, had but seven or eight beds, and in none of the chambers were there either chairs, carpets, or looking-glasses. The inventory of the entire contents of this castle is given in Strutt's "View of Manners," and shows not how much they had, but how much they had not.

But to go back a little. In 1450, and from that date until 1478, Dame Margaret Paston wrote a series of letters from the town of Norwich, England, where she was living, to her husband in London, which give many interesting details as to the dress, manners, and furniture of that time. She writes him in 1454 that she is about to send up to London his " trussing coffer," or clothes-chest, and says further, that " his meny rob his chamber and rifle his hutches "; " hutch " coming from " huche," a French coffer or chest standing upon legs.

A hutch, or coffer on legs, is shown in the next

Figure (145), though of a later period than that of which Madam Paston writes. A panelled oak cupboard goes with it, still retaining the original ironwork hinges. In these hinges may be seen a pattern known as the S-curve, which was used in furniture decoration at an early period. It appeared in flat carving, at the tops and sides of chairs (see Figure 146), and was even used in architecture, the tops of the towers of Hardwick Hall, England, built in 1590, showing it in perfection. On the two side panels of the hutch is a rosette, which frequently forms the central ornament in a design called the " guilloche," which is a pattern formed of a continuous line of circles, each enclosing a carved rosette. Frequently the larger circles have smaller ones alternating with them, or they may be compressed so that there is no room for the central ornament. Common though this form of ornament is on English furniture, the fact remains that it is of Italian origin, — that is, the use of it during the Renaissance period, for the Italians took it from the Byzantine ornaments and used it to great effect on the beautiful carved cassoni of the times. A good free rendering of the guilloche is found in the panel top of Figure 146; a wainscot chair, and the S-curve already mentioned can be seen at the sides.

Besides trussing coffers or chests, which took the place of trunks, and which were generally of stout oak planks iron-bound, there were others of more or less ornate character. The most important of these, at least in the eyes of the gentler sex, were those known as "marriage chests," generally bought while the daughters of the house were still children, and filled by degrees with linen and woollen cloth, woven under the careful eye of the mother.

In Figure 147 is one of these chests of Italian origin, which belonged to some noble and wealthy family. It is not hard to conjure up the store of fine linens, lace trimmed; the pieces of rich silk damask and cloth of gold; the Venice points and the lengths of velvet which were laid away year after year to swell the marriage portion of the daughter. Sometimes suitors who betrayed a tendency to lag could be made to show a more coming-on spirit by a view of the chests and their contents; which were the lady's dower.

Like almost everything else of Italian origin, the carved chests were extremely beautiful, whether of the Gothic period or of the more sumptuous Renaissance and later. The chest shown in Figure 147 is of carved oak. They were made of other woods as well, painted and gilded, inlaid sometimes with ivory, ebony, tortoiseshell, lapis lazuli, or anything which the mind of the maker conceived would add to its beauty. On some of these old *cassoni* were painted figures and scenes by the famous artists of the times, sometimes portraying events in the life of the owner, but oftener, if for a bride, groups of flowers and cupidons, making these chests to-day as valuable as if wrought in gold.

Our old carved chest is sixty-six inches long by twenty-four in height, and has preserved its beauty almost unimpaired. No better example of the period

107

which preceded the elaborate carving could be given than by the glimpse we get of the old Gothic chest on which it stands, the panels showing designs similar to those found in the stone-work of the church-windows of the same period.

The Venetian or Florentine bride not only had her rich clothes and linens, but her jewels were dealt out with a lavish hand. In the inventory of the trousseau of a fifteenth century bride of noble but not royal blood, the rich stuffs are calculated by the pound weight and the " great pearls " by the gross. In such a little chest or coffer as that shown in Figure 148 would these be kept, together with her girdles of gold and silver, her enamelled and jewelled garlands and buttons. There are still traces of gold and colours on this chest which could tell so much if it would, and there is a ponderous lock so that thieves should not break through and steal. There is a little of everything carved upon it, comic and tragic masks, cupids, scimitars, dragons, and garlands, yet done with so much skill that the result is infinitely pleasing, as is almost everything of the florid period known as Renaissance.

But while these chests are interesting in every way, and are to be bought in this country, since it is known that we are becoming the collectors of the world, it is with homelier and less ornate articles of this class that our interest chiefly centres. When the Pilgrim Fathers and Mothers packed their scanty belongings and stowed them away in the hold of the Mayflower, their goods were mostly contained in chests. stout ones no doubt,

108

and, I think we can say, entirely guiltless of carving. These chests for use in travelling were called " ship chests" or "standards," and were simple, box-like affairs with locks and no legs, and often with handles.

There were, even in those early days, some chests brought over which stood upon legs. The legs were formed by continuing the " stiles," as those boards which hold the sides, back, and front are called. You can see them very plainly in Figure 149. The boards at top and bottom of the panels, in the top one of which is the keyhole, are called " rails." These are often carved, the stiles generally being left plain, or ornamented only with a slight moulding.

There are many chests like Figure 149 scattered over the country. This one is a " pick-up " near Rochester, New York, within a couple of years. It is of oak, — old English oak at that, — dark, solid, and heavy, so that the boards which make the bottom seem almost like iron. It is a joined chest. The nails which you see on the stiles were put there recently to prevent the chest from positively dropping apart from age. The date of this piece is between 1675–1700.

Another pattern of carving which was often used early in the seventeenth century was the design called " linen fold." It can be seen on the chest in Figure 150. This pattern was in use as early as 1480, and Mr. Robinson, in his work on " English Furniture," asserts that it was brought from France. It was at first very angular in treatment, but it became more and more flowing, and had, in the later years of its use, gouged work in addition. The pattern, although in vogue till the middle of the seventeenth century, was seen at its best only during a period of about eighty or a hundred years after its introduction. This chest has also a panelled top, as well as panelled sides, the panels being set in with a moulding instead of a bevelled edge, showing that this chest belongs to the first half of the seventeenth century. It is a fact that no two of these old hand-made chests resemble each other. They have slight differences as to dimensions, and marked ones as to decoration. It is all the more pleasing to be obliged to study closely before we can date our specimen, and it is usually safer to assign it to a century than to a more precise date.

While oak and pine were the woods ordinarily used for chests, olive-wood was rarely chosen, and sometimes cedar and cypress. The English-made chest was commonly of oak throughout, like this one, but when we came to build them — and we started cabinet-making as early as 1622 — we used pine for the parts that did not show, like back, sides, bottom, and often lid.

In Flanders many fronts of chests were elaborately carved and then sent to England to be fitted with the other parts. When the burghers were comfortably settled here and growing rich in the fur trade, they sent home for chests in which to store their goods, and many a rich " Kas " came in their low-lying, broad-hulked vessels.

The fronts of these Flanders chests were often carved in high relief with figures, heads, animals, or even

110

lettering woven into a pattern, and were very hand-some. They are by no means so rare in this country as might be supposed; and in many cases the carved fronts have been removed from the chests and used for other purposes, as, for instance, setting in a mantel front, or in a panel, where they show to better advantage than in a chest.

Besides those that were carved there were others on which the ornamentation was of mouldings broadly splayed and bold in design, to which were added the turned drops of stained pear-wood, or of ebony, which were such favourites with the Dutch. Figure 151 shows a fine example of such a chest, and in addition to the two splayed panels, has a round arch for ornament in the centre.

Could anything be finer than the Dutch Kas shown in Figure 152? The date of this chest is approximately the same as that shown in Figure 149, but it is a very elegant article of its kind. There is a long drawer at the bottom; both sets of cupboards open, and there are shelves within. It must have taken the good vrouw and her daughter many years to grow the flax, hatchel, bleach, and spin the thread, and then weave it into linen cloth that must be bleached again many times before it came to the required whiteness which every good Dutch housewife considered necessary in her "Hollands."

The ball feet seen on this Kas were a Dutch design, copied both by the English and by us. Many plain chests are found in America with these ball feet like the one in Figure 153. This piece shows the first step in the evolution of the chest, for a drawer is added. Dr. Lyon says, in his book on "Colonial Furniture," that the first mention made of a one-drawer chest is in the inventory of the goods of the Rev. Nathaniel Rogers, of Ipswich, Massachusetts, dated August, 1655. The value was given as sixteen shillings.

Sometimes this single drawer was divided, and in the earliest specimens the runners on which the drawer moved were on the sides of the chest, — not on the bottom, as came later. The sides of the drawer had a deep groove in them, and a stout runner was on the side of the chest.

With the appearance of drawers, mouldings, such as were popular for wainscots on walls, were more freely used, and such chests were called "wainscot-chests." There were other methods of ornamentation which gradually came in fashion as the chests mounted upward by the addition of drawers. Among these were what are called "nail-head" bosses, and for these, as well as for a fretwork which was seldom more than an eighth or a quarter of an inch in thickness and was applied to the drawers, we are indebted to the Dutch. Such bosses can be seen on the chest of drawers given in Figure 154, where they are used in connection with both round and pear-shaped ornaments. These nail-heads are in this case distinctly for use, since they are but the tops of wooden pegs which answer the purpose of locking the drawers by turning a bolt. Few are so useful as these, however.

112

In Figure 155 is another style of chest, also of oak, but with splayed panels inlaid with bone and mother-of-pearl. Although this piece is dated 1541, it is probable that it was made somewhat later, since this style of ornament was made till as late as 1650. The handles point to the latter date also, and the chest does not need the added century to make it both interesting and beautiful. There is always a tendency to call such pieces as this Italian, but there is nothing about it which could not have been done in England, and it is known that inlaid furniture was made there at about this period.

The proportions of the early chests without drawers were about sixty inches long by twenty-four high. As the chests rose in height they decreased in length, so that they should not become too bulky.

The chests were almost always fitted with tills, either one or two, so that small articles could be conveniently stowed away.

The old inventories filed with wills are mines of information regarding the belongings of our ancestors. I have read scores of them, and there is always a pathetic side to these musty old yellow papers, the owners usually had so few possessions. Leather breeches " half wore out," appears many times; " old quilts "; feather-beds, " not new," is another item, and in the earlier documents things are sometimes described as " damnified."

Colonel Epes's inventory, dated October 1, 1678, Henrico County, Virginia, contains numerous items which show him to have been a man of wealth and importance. Among them are these chests: "one old middle-sized chest, with lock and key; one small old chest, with lock and key; two other old chests without keys, and one without hinges."

Sarah Oort, a rich and many-times-married widow, had at the time of her third marriage many elegant goods. Among them were three "chests of drawers," as chests *with* drawers began to be called. This was at New Amsterdam in 1691.

"One fine chest of drawers, of maple" (1703), is an item in another inventory, probably made of native wood by one of our own cabinet-makers.

By 1724 walnut, cherry, maple, poplar, hickory, pine, and ash were all being used, and in the larger centres comfort was by no means lacking. The pioneer, however, still clung to his "Kist," since he could use it both by day and night, and hide within it his few valuables.

In a number of inventories in the early years of the nineteenth century I find mention of chests, showing how long they continued to be used. Lieutenant Ozias Cone, of Canandaigua, New York, had two in 1805. He valued them at a dollar each.

Dr. Samuel Dungan, of the same place, whose inventory was filed May 14, 1818, had many possessions; among them was "one large pine chest," valued at twenty-five cents. He also specifies "a lot of bones, five dollars"! Could this have been the family skeleton?

Of course, our cabinet-makers made just such furni-

114

ture as they had been accustomed to make "in the old country." It was only in occasional instances that one branched out for himself.

Figure 156 shows such an example, for though it is apparently a small bureau, it is in reality a two-drawer chest. What appears to be two small upper drawers and the long one below them are but mouldings fastened on the front of the chest, which takes up the whole upper half of the piece.

This is a very old piece; the handles are of an early variety of the willow pattern, and fastened in with wires. It is the only piece of the kind I have ever seen, and is interesting in every way.

There are other chests, made by one man and his assistants, it is most probable, which occupy a place quite by themselves; and it is well to describe these chests before we pass on to the final steps in the growth of the chest.

In Figure 157 is given what is known to collectors as the "Connecticut chest," from the fact that so many of this pattern have been found in that State, — about fifty in all. It is a two-drawer chest of elaborate design, the turned ornaments being stained black, and the patterns on the panels carved in low relief, the two end ones showing conventionalised tulips and the centre a sunflower.

Many of these chests are built on the American plan, with pine tops, bottoms, and backs; but this chest, which is in Memorial Hall, Deerfield, Massachusetts, has a top of oak like the front and sides. It is forty inches high, forty-eight inches long, and twenty-two inches in breadth. The same style of decoration has been found on chests with but one drawer, which probably emanated from the same workshop. The date assigned to this chest is from 1675–1690, the shape of the mouldings and turned ornaments dating from about that period.

The owner of this chest is Dr. A. M. Kenney, of Boston, Massachusetts. His father has written to me concerning it, and starts a new theory regarding it. He says:

" This chest was brought to Greenfield, Mass., by my great grandmother, and had belonged to her mother and probably another generation preceding. I am in receipt of a letter from a lady in Cleveland, Ohio, who owns one like it, who desires to know where they were made, saying also that tradition makes it to have been made in Scotland, and brought to America about 1700. My father in 1843 was a warrant officer in the U. S. Navy, and while stationed in Rio de Janeiro, Brazil, visited a disused convent in that city, in each cell of which was an oak chest, nearly if not quite like this one."

No doubt the American maker copied a chest which he had brought from England, or perhaps made his own plans from memory of what he had made in the old country, so that there was a strong resemblance between those of domestic and those of foreign make.

There is still another style of chest belonging to a special locality, quite different from the one already shown. In Figure 158 you may see the " Hadley chest," so called because they are found in and near

116

the town of Hadley. While made of oak, these chests are still further ornamented by being gaily painted or stained. As they were known as "dower chests," no doubt an effort was made to have them unusually handsome on the bride's account. Like the Connecticut chests, the Hadley ones are always of exactly the same pattern, the middle panel being carved with the initials of the owner. The "S. H." seen in Figure 158 stood for Sarah Hawks, who was married in 1726.

The low relief carving extends over the whole chest, the carved part being stained red, and the natural colour of the oak forming a background. The front only is carved, the sides being panelled. Looking on this old chest, which is also at Deerfield, one can imagine how proud the bride must have been who owned one. How she must have toiled to fill one ever so scantily with linen and woollen cloth, and some bits of " 500-muslin," — which was the desire of every woman, — to be made in caps and kerchiefs!

Not far away from this chest is the door of one of the early Deerfield homes, driven full of huge spikes to repel the attacks of "ye barbarous enemy," who, even so, managed to cleave the door with their murderous tomahawks.

The owner of this chest has mouldered into dust years and years ago, yet you may lay your hand on her " dower chest " and conjure up before your mind her satisfaction in it, her hopes and fears as she filled it and carried it with her into her new home.

After the three-drawer chests, of which this is such

117

an interesting example, the next step in the upward flight of the chest was a marked one. They began now to be mounted on legs of turned wood, — six in number, four in front and two behind, connected by curved stretchers. The one shown in Figure 159 is an early specimen, made probably about 1700–1710, of walnut veneered with walnut and having the early drop-handles. Two very good indications of the age of a piece of furniture are the handles and mouldings, while the feet, as a general rule, point more to its nationality.

The drop-handles on this chest are solid, but the drops also come hollowed out at the back and indicate an earlier period. These are fastened into the drawer by a piece of wire which is twisted together on the inside. The plate through which the handle passes may be round, or diamond-shaped, or in curves, and while sometimes cut, it is more often stamped out. This is an early style of handle.

The first mouldings used to surround the drawers are quite plain; they became double after a little while, and sometimes, when used to form the top or cornice, quite heavy. The very earliest specimens of these chests on frames had but one drawer, instead of three, at the bottom, and the lower edge was in a single curve instead of a triple one.

Little by little numerous changes were wrought in these chests on frames, and the straight turned leg disappeared. Then presently two legs were dropped, and then the curved stretchers.

The places of the two missing legs in many standing

118

Fig. 138 Broken-arch Mirror

Fig. 139 Bilboa Mirror

Fig. 137 Bevel-edge Mirror

Fig. 142 CHEVAL GLASS

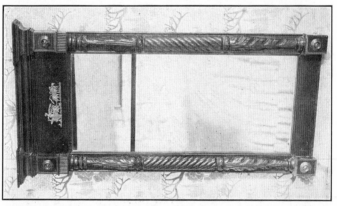

Fig. 141 EMPIRE MIRROR

Fig. 140 HEPPLEWHITE MIRROR

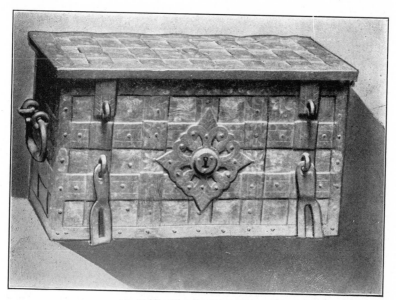

Fig. 143 WROUGHT-IRON CHEST

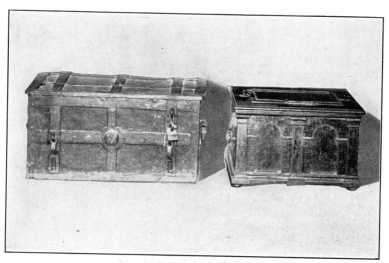

Fig. 144 TREASURE CHESTS

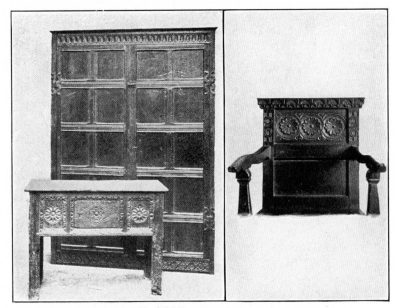

Fig. 145 STANDING COFFER   Fig. 146 "GUILLOCHE"

Fig. 147 CARVED ITALIAN CHEST

Fig. 148 Venetian Coffer

Fig. 149 Chest of English Oak

Fig. 150 "Linen-Fold" Pattern

Fig. 151 Chest with Moulding Panels

Fig. 152 DUTCH KAS

Fig. 153 CHEST WITH ONE DRAWER

Fig. 154 OAK CHEST WITH DRAWERS

chests, as they are sometimes called, is to be seen supplied by a drop ornament of a more or less ornamental character. Occasionally the place is finished off square with a little moulding.

The cabriole, or bandy-leg, became popular, and was finished either with the plain Dutch foot or with the ball and claw.

An example of the early bandy-legged high-boy of Flemish make is given in Figure 160. Although it has not very graceful proportions, it is rendered most ornamental by its beautiful floral marquetry, showing tulips, carnations, and passion-flowers in different coloured woods in a mahogany ground. By 1700 the importations of foreign woods had given an impetus to what was called "smooth-faced" furniture, — that is, what was inlaid, veneered, or enriched with marquetry, — in distinction to furniture where the decoration protruded from the surface, as in carved or panelled work.

What veneering is we all know, — the covering of an inferior wood with thin strips of a choicer kind, so that the whole base is concealed. Inlay is an enriching with wood of another colour, or with metals, stones, bone, ivory, mother-of-pearl, tortoise-shell, or anything that could be utilised by the skilful worker.

The line of demarkation between marquetry and inlay is not very sharply drawn, but marquetry is apt to cover entirely the baser wood, the decorative arrangement being used in what is called "reserves." In few pieces is the marquetry so large and the ground so small as in our example in Figure 160. As

119

may be noted, the ground forms just a frame for the marquetry on the drawers, while the usual rule was to have, say, two reserves on a drawer, each of them oval or round in shape, and allowing a large portion of the ground wood to show. Where you find a tulip entering into the decoration of a piece of furniture, you may generally ascribe it to the Dutch, particularly if the ornamentation is conceived in a free and flowing pattern.

As will be seen from the examples, nearly all these later pieces which we call " high-boys " were really chest-on-chest of drawers, or chest on tables. Sometimes these two pieces of furniture became separated, and the lower part, if in table form, was called a dressing-table, and used for that purpose. Such a derelict is shown in Figure 161, and must have been a part of a very stately piece of furniture. The ages of these chests and high-boys can be roughly guessed by the drawers.

First came those which had heavy splayed mouldings, with applied ornaments of turned drops and beadings. The framework around the drawers was beaded or moulded. Second were the oak or walnut pieces, veneered or not, with plain drawers and double beaded frame. Third came the moulded drawers with plain frames; and last were the drawers which were moulded but not projecting, the edge of the drawer lapping over the frame so that the opening did not show.

At first the tops of the high-boys were flat, finished with a small, plain moulding. By degrees this mould-

120

ing grew heavier, and was sometimes wide enough to carry a long drawer; then it rose into a curve, and the "broken arch" top was put on choice pieces made of mahogany or cherry. At the ends of the cornice and in the middle were placed ornaments of either brass or turned wood, urns, flames, or points, according to the taste of the maker; and now the simple "trussing-coffer" of the fourteenth century reached its highest expression in the "chest-on-chest" of the eighteenth century.

Figure 162 gives a very beautiful example of a mahogany chest-on-chest, which is a highly prized ornament of a Vermont home. It has its original brasses and top ornaments, the handle brasses being beautifully engraved. This chest-on-chest has a line of inlay about the drawers, and the shell carved in the lower drawer is done in a piece of solid wood and is very handsome.

Our cabinet-makers seldom indulged in very much inlaid work; a line of whitewood, holly, or satinwood usually contented them; or in some cases a double line of whitewood and ebony was sparingly used. They did use carving more freely, and these old pieces have a look of solidity and a certain irregularity which is often found in handwork when the maker did not give any too great attention to accuracy of measurement. There is an old oak cupboard of the seventeenth century in the rooms of the Antiquarian Society at Concord, which is infinitely pleasing in form. This has been copied within recent years by first-class cabinet-makers, who used the greatest care in their work, and the reproduc-

121

tions, while following in shape and colour the hardy old original, have lost the very thing which gives it half its charm.

The cupboard at Concord is very similar to the one in Figure 163, and is really that piece of furniture of which we often read and seldom see, called a "court cupboard." The old-time mentions of it always refer to it as being set out with the store of plate, beakers, tankards, etc., which its owner possessed. In Harrison's "Description of England," which has been quoted before, the mention is made of the farmer having pewter "on his cupboard." In many inventories references are made to cupboards of various styles, — such as wainscot, livery, court, joined, press, and what is variously known as a butter cupboard, or a trencher-bread cupboard. Such a one is given in Figure 164, which is in shape a court cupboard, but has the holes bored in one of the divisions so that the air may enter and keep the food within pure and sweet. Trencher bread was a very important article in the household in Elizabethan times and was generally called "manchet." It was made of wheat, and Harrison, in his "Description of England," says:

"Of bread of wheat we have sundry sorts daily brought to the table, whereof the first and most excellent is the manchet, which we commonly call white bread, in Latin, *primarius panis;* and our good workmen deliver commonly such proportion that of the flour of one bushel with another they make forty cast of manchet, of which every loaf weigheth eight ounces into the oven, and six ounces out."

122

It was to keep the trencher bread dry that the cup-board was pierced. This cupboard is a fine one, — of oak, with some good carving upon it, and the original hinges. Upon the shelf in front of the upper doors was room for a row of plate or pewter, and even on the top beakers and jugs which were not in common use could be displayed.

The livery cupboard was really a set of shelves with-out doors. Mr. Litchfield, in his "History of Furni-ture," quotes from a record in the British Museum for some joiners' work which was done at Hengrave about 1518, in which "livery cupboards" are specified. "Ye cobards they be made ye facyon of livery y is wthout doors."

Two other very splendid cupboards are given in Figures 165 and 166, the former covered with a beautiful fretwork. This piece dates to about 1630 and has still the ornate hinges and clumsy handles with which it started. It is of oak, and the handles and hinges are of iron, as they should be. The last cupboard or cabinet (it can be called by either name) is handsome of its kind, but be-longs to the seventeenth century. It is of oak, and belongs to the Water's collection of Salem, Massachusetts.

The built-in cupboards are often charming, but are generally the work of the carpenter rather than the cabinet-maker. They were made either with doors or without, and the choicest which can be found in this country are those which have a great shell forming

123

a concave top. In many of the old houses cupboards such as these still can be found, often incorporated with the wainscot, and I have seen particularly choice ones in Deerfield, Massachusetts, as well as in Concord, and at Salem in the same State.

VI — BRASS AND COPPER UTENSILS

ALTHOUGH we read in the Bible about "a sounding brass and a tinkling cymbal," it was not the yellow metal which we know as brass that was meant, but something which more nearly resembled bronze.

Brass is an alloy of copper and zinc. "English brass," as it is called, contains about seventy per cent. copper and thirty per cent. zinc. While brass is of comparatively modern origin, copper, on the other hand, has been in use from the most remote times, and when alloyed with tin in the form of bronze, was the first metallic compound used by mankind. Indeed, so general was its use at one distant period, when arms, implements, and ornaments were made of it, that we call that time the "Bronze Age." In museums and historical collections the world over are found metal objects belonging to this time, and wonderfully beautiful many of them are.

It was the Romans who spread the art of working these metals over Europe, and the first traces of yellow brass which we find in England is in the form of monumental brasses, which took the place over tombs of carved effigies and figures made of stone. These brasses are made of sheets of the metal and set into the

125

pavement. Although they began to be used as early
as 1230, the most famous one I know of is in the church
at Stratford-on-Avon, where it was placed in 1616 over
the grave of William Shakespeare. This is what it
says:

> " Good frend for jesus' sake forbeare
> to digg the dust encloased heare ;
> Bleste be ye man yt spares thes stones
> and curst be he yt moves my bones."

Shakespeare himself says in the " Taming of the
Shrew," when Gremio is describing all his wealth:

> "First, as you know, my house within the city
> Is richly furnished with plate and gold ;
> Basins and ewers to lave her dainty hands;
> My hangings all of Tyrian tapestry ;
> In ivory coffers have I stuff'd my crowns ;
> In cypress chests my arras counterpoints,
> Costly apparel, tents and canopies,
> Fine linen, Turkey cushions boss'd with pearl,
> Valance of Venice gold in needlework,
> Pewter and brass and all things that belong
> To house or housekeeping."

Truly the young man seems to have been well fitted
out.

The most important domestic uses to which brass was
put was in utensils, if I may so use the word, for heating and lighting.

In the most interesting history of " Isabeau de
Bavière," by Vallet de Viriville, he gives extracts from
the records of her household expenses which are still
preserved in the French Archives. This Queen was
the wife of Charles VI, called " the Well-Beloved,"

126

and she lived from 1371 to 1435. She had more idea of comfort than many of her predecessors, and in her rooms were chairs covered with red Cordova leather, and baths of oak. She used "suspended carriages" and had one chariot on purpose for thunderstorms, "*pour le tonnere,*" but just how it was arranged the records do not state. Queen Isabeau had also to warm her rooms *calorifères*, like little iron chariots filled with red-hot ashes which could be wheeled about, and also hollow balls of gold and silver full of hot cinders to hold in the hand, which comforts were hitherto unknown.

From this time on, articles for holding hot coals have been in use for heating, and still are largely employed in Spain and Japan and China, where the metals used are brass and bronze.

The usual name given to these inadequate heaters is brasier. One form is shown in Figure 167.

Another kind is given in Figure 168, and these were carried about from room to room. There are peculiarities about this heater which make it unusual. It is of English manufacture: the bottom part is of copper with figures of brass, and the top is of brass with figures of copper. It stands on brass feet and has a brass handle. Although the lower part is not in one piece, it is entirely hand made, and the bottom of it is curiously bent up on the sides. That this was not an ordinary article is plainly to be seen by its decoration, and, though it has found its way over here, I am sure it served its turn in some old manor or castle, which,

127

though high-sounding places of residence, were none too comfortable.

Still another brasier is shown in Figure 169. This is made of brass, very solid and heavy, as may be seen, with two handles to carry it about conveniently. It is of Spanish workmanship, but the shape was approximately the same in all countries.

The old English records of about Queen Elizabeth's time show how highly considered all metal objects were, and display some curious facts as well. John Fuller, of Rednall, Norfolk, England, had his will probated in 1598. He gives to his wife Ann "all the household stuff she brought me, such as brasse, pewter, fowles, etc., at her death to go to Thomas Fuller the younger." This was only one of several cases where I have found that there were two children in one family given the same name. The confusion in the Fuller family must have been something dreadful, since there was "oulde William" and "young William," "Thomas the elder," and "Thomas the younger." The father says in his will, "to young William my sonne, the lesser brass bason and the platter on the cupboard," and to "the children of oulde William my sonne, the cupboard and the long table in the hall. To Thomas the elder a milch cow and to daughter Batriss a great bason and a pewter dish."

Amid the belongings of those who first sought the shores of this country when the Mayflower took her troublous way hither from Delfshaven, there were copper kettles, no doubt, carefully packed within the iron

128

pot, which was the *most* necessary article of household gear which they brought with them.

The records seem to point that they were better off for such utensils than one poor village in County Craven, England, in Cromwellian times. The story goes that the village had been so completely gutted by the soldiers of the Commonwealth that not a single kettle remained, and that an old helmet travelled from house to house and was used to boil the broth and pottage in. But to return to our own early settlements.

I find in the inventory of the Widow Coytemore, dated 1647, when she married Governor Winthrop, "one copp. furnace." This was, I am inclined to believe, a small, box-like affair on legs, into which live coals were put to keep the kettle warm on the hearth. There is such a one at the Antiquarian Rooms at Concord, Massachusetts.

John Stevens, of Guilford, Connecticut, died in 1670, but he was one of the old settlers of the place, since the town records state that in 1645 he was fined for neglecting to do his share of the fencing. To his son, Thomas, he bequeaths " the mare I usually ride on and my biggest brass kettle, my best sute and my cloak and my bed and one payre of sheets and all my other bedding." Such a kettle as the one he mentions is shown in Figure 170. These great kettles bear on their sides not only the scars of time but the marks of the mallet as well. Brass utensils have been made in this country for a century or more, but the first one is not a matter of record, as is the first iron pot, the story of

9

which, though not quite within the province of this article, I shall tell here.

In 1630 Thomas Hudson came to this country and settled in Lynn, Massachusetts. He took up land on the Saugus River, near the ford, and found in the nearby marsh bog-iron ore. This find led to the establishment of the first iron works in this country, and in 1642 the first casting, an iron pot, was made. This pot remained in the possession of the descendants of Thomas Hudson till 1892, and in that year it was presented to the city of Lynn, where it may now be seen.

Another iron works was set up at Braintree, Massachusetts, in 1646, and here "pots, mortars, stoves and skillets" were made, but the works did not continue long in operation, as the good people of Braintree were afraid that the necessity for charcoal would consume too much wood, and so did not allow the works to remain operative long. Besides they had religious differences with Dr. Child, the owner, and made it very unhappy for him.

"Open kettles," as they were called to distinguish them from tea-kettles, were made here at an early date, and were hammered out of sheet brass and copper which was brought here chiefly from Wales. We know that Captain Myles Standish had three brass kettles, four iron pots, a skillet, and a warming-pan. It is also set down in Colonial records by Governor Bradford that the second contingent that arrived at Plymouth, in the ship Fortune, besides being a "rollicking lot," had no bedding, "nor any pot or pan to dress meat in."

130

Perhaps Captain Standish loaned them some of his seven.

Large brass kettles were put to other uses besides cooking. Michaud's " Early Western Travels " has this to say about a brass furnace:

"About two miles from West Liberty Town I passed by Probes' Furnace, a foundry established by a Frenchman from Alsace, who manufactures all kinds of vessels in copper and brass, the largest containing about 200 pints, which are sent to Kentucky and Tennessee, where they use them in the preparation of salt by evaporation. The smaller ones are for domestic uses."

This was in the southwestern part of Pennsylvania in 1802.

A little later on in his narrative he says:

" At Springfield or near it is Mays-lick where there is a salt-mine. For evaporation they make use of brazen pots, containing 200 pints, and similar in form to those used in France for making lye. They put ten or twelve of them in a row in a pit 4 ft. deep, and at the ends throw in billets of wood and kindle a fire. These sort of kilns consume great quantities of wood."

I have never found any of these kettles marked or stamped in any way. They are not difficult to find, and, brightly polished, are always ornamental.

Among the lists of goods belonging to the pioneers who came to this country are often to be found objects of " Prince's metal," as it was called. This was a composition of brass, arsenicum, and copper. " Latten ware," was used also, and this was largely composed of brass as well.

By 1700 the records show a great variety of household articles, and make interesting reading. Cornelius Jacobs in this year had several pairs of brass andirons, and two pairs of iron "dogs," though just what the distinction was it is hard to tell.

Captain Giles Shelly, of New York, had in 1718 a fine lot of household goods, including seventy chairs, which would seem an ample allowance to most of us, even in these days of machine-made furniture. He had as well a pair of brass candlesticks with snuffers, a brass hearth with hooks for shovel and tongs, a brass lantern, two warming-pans, a chafing-dish of brass and two of silver. In fact it was a great surprise to find how general was the use of chafing-dishes. Although brass ones are frequently mentioned, I have never seen one, but copper ones are not unusual, and there is a fine one, made by Paul Revere, at the Rooms of the Antiquarian Society at Concord, Massachusetts, which was presented to the Society by his grandson.

In 1720 Judith, the daughter of Judge Samuel Sewall, was to be married, and as the bridegroom was well-to-do, the Judge proposed that his daughter's outfit should be of unusual elegance for that time. They sent to England for it, and I shall give a list of the metal objects only which were included in it:

" One bell-metal Skillet of two quarts, one little one ditto.
One good large warming-pan, bottom and cover fit for an iron handle.
4 pair of strong Iron Dogs with brass heads, about 5 or 6 shillings a pair.

132

A Brass Hearth for a chamber with Dogs, Shovel, Tongs and Fender of the newest Fashion (the Fire is to ly upon Iron).

A strong Brass Mortar that will hold about a Quart with a Pestle.

2 pair of large Brass sliding Candlesticks about 4 shillings a pair.

2 pair of large Brass candlesticks, not sliding, of the Newest Fashion, about 5 or 6 shillings a pair.

4 Brass snuffers with trays.

6 small strong Brass Chafing-dishes about 4 shillings apiece.

1 Brass basting ladle; 1 larger Brass Ladle.

1 Pair chamber Bellows with Brass Noses.

1 small hair Broom suitable to the Bellows.

1 Duzen of large hard metal Pewter Plates new Fashion, weighing about 14 pounds.

1 Duzen hard-metal Pewter Porringers."

Perhaps in Judith Sewall's outfit, to go with her brass hearth and " Fender of the newest Fashion," was included a handsome stand like the one shown in Figure 171. This is of brass, and has places for two candles at the top. The lattice-work shovel was for scooping up the live coals and letting the ashes drop through. Of course she did not have such a splendid coat of arms for decoration, but some ornament was usually put in this place. There is a stand similar to this, but of brass and steel, at Van Courtland Manor, New York. It belonged to Colonel John Chester, of Wethersfield, Connecticut, who was born in 1748. The candle-holder in this latter case was movable.

Governor Montgomery's effects were sold at Fort George, New York, early in the eighteenth century, and among the unusual things specified were the following: "A large fixt copper boyling pot. A large iron fireplace, an iron bar and doors for a copper."

133

A very charming fireplace, dating from about the middle of the last half of the eighteenth century, is to be seen in Figure 172. The brass mountings are patriotic, since, besides our familiar eagle, there are medallions of Washington and Franklin. This fireplace is fitted with a crane, and has a delicate pair of firedogs also. One may grieve to see such a generous old fireplace walled up, but if it must be, it is fortunate that so agreeable an object has been found to take its place.

Sea coal was advertised for sale in 1744, and about this time Philadelphia fireplaces came into use. This was shortly before Franklin had invented his grate. Steel hearths and stove grates came into use by 1751, and iron stoves with brass feet were advertised for sale. Copper was sometimes used for making grates, and copper furnaces were plenty, — that is, little affairs standing on legs and holding a few coals to keep a kettle warm on the hearth.

Among the pieces of brass shown in Figure 173 is a smoothing iron with a drawer that pulls out to receive hot coals, and the thing that looks like a clumsy spoon is a spoon mould, also of brass. Into this mould was poured the spooning pewter, and then allowed to form in shape. The Colonial village which owned one of these moulds considered itself rich, and it was passed around among families as they needed it. The spoon at the back with the long handle was for basting, the handle being necessary to prevent the hands getting burned. The little candlesticks were for

134

Fig. 155   CHEST INLAID WITH BONE

Fig. 156   TWO-DRAWER CHEST   Fig. 157   "CONNECTICUT CHEST"

Fig. 159 Chest on Legs

Fig. 158 "Hadley Chest"

Fig. 160   CHEST-ON-CHEST   Fig. 162   CHEST-ON-CHEST

Fig. 161   TABLE OF CHEST OR HIGH-BOY

Fig. 164 CUPBOARD WITH PIERCED DOOR

Fig. 163 COURT CUPBOARD

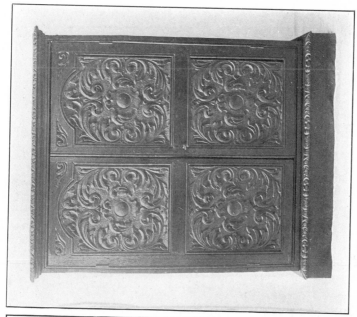

Fig. 166   Cupboard or Cabinet

Fig. 165   Carved Cupboard

Fig. 167 BRASIER   Fig. 168 BRASIER

Fig. 169 SPANISH BRASERO AND BOWLS

Fig. 170 BRASS KETTLES

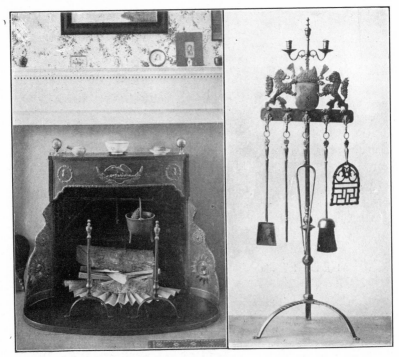

Fig. 172 Fireplace   Fig. 171 Fire Set

Fig. 173 Brass Smoothing Iron, etc.

tallow dips, and the tall one stood in the best room. The noggin was for a nightcap of peach brandy, schnapps, or that beverage which is put down in so many old account books as "W. I. Rum."

There lies before me as I write the diary of a New England judge, a man of high standing and dignity in the community in which he lived. The diary covers that eventful period in our history which was included between 1754 and 1788, and presents a wonderful picture of the life in a New England town. The noggin brought to my mind what hard drinkers our ancestors were, and I turned at random to this diary to see what the judge had to say on the subject. The page where I have opened is dated August, 1772, and I find the following entry for the first day of the month:

"I went to MacGregores and got the bushell of salt that I paid him for last fish time in shad, and a bottle of snuff, and a pair of brass sleeve buttons for which I paid him 44/ Hampr old Tenor."

On the 3d he and his son went out to mow, and after mowing "the path to the meadow, I borrowed a flask full of Rum from Wm. Caldwells wife."

On the 4th (next day), "I went and got two Quarts of Rum at Hugh Campbell's on credit." On the 13th, "I sent David to Means to get ½ Gallon of Rum and ½ pound of tea," and on the 24th he got two quarts more of "Rum on credit from Campbells." Such little utensils as are shown in Figure 174 were used in the preparation of the drinks which were often compounded of the rum, which our good judge always spelled with a capital letter. This drink was used universally in all homes from that of the parson down. It was cheap. In another place the judge says he pays a pistareen for two quarts; this was about twenty cents. The liquor was pure, and their lives were so filled with hard work out of doors that they seem somehow to have lived through their excessive drinking.

Tea was more expensive than intoxicating liquors, — about four shillings a pound, though the value of money varied so, " old tenor," " lawful tenor," pistareens, and Spanish silver, all being in use. Such a little kettle as is shown in Figure 174 had many uses. I do not doubt that the housewife boiled her tea in it, and that it heated water for many a glass of toddy. Every family had a warming-pan, and most necessary they were in the cold, damp houses which were seldom warm from autumn to spring. They were commonly of brass, but this one is of copper, as is also the ladle. The large kettle is of the ordinary type and is of wrought copper, as were most of them. It is exactly like a kettle which belongs to a collector who has a number of beautiful and valuable objects, — old china, glass, pewter, and brass. I asked her once what thing among all her treasures she liked the best, and she said, without a moment's hesitation: " That battered little old kettle, for it took me nearly two years to get it, and in all that time it was scarcely out of my mind."

She had seen it in a tumble-down old cottage where lived an old man with his daughter. They were neither

136

of them ornaments to society, and were scarcely ever at home at the same time, since their love for the flowing bowl caused them to spend much time in retirement — at the town's expense. Her first offer was the modest one of fifty cents, as the kettle was in very bad condition, — battered and rusty. This sum proved no object to them, and during the time she was in pursuit of it she rose little by little till she finally paid five dollars for it, — a preposterous price, truly, but she had become so wedded to the idea of owning it that she could not give it up.

In Figure 175 is given a group of utensils of various kinds of copper, with a kettle of different shape. It was such a kettle as this which met a curious fate at the time of the famous Boston "Tea Party." It belonged to the family of Benjamin Fish, of Portsmouth, Rhode Island. Now, although a Friend, Mr. Fish was a loyal American besides, and showed his devotion to the Federal cause by jamming and battering, and then throwing away the copper kettle because his daughters persisted in brewing tea in it. The women, however, kept an eye on it, and when the Revolution was over they brought it out, and Artemus, one of the sons, hammered it into shape again, and it once more took its old place on the family hearthstone. They all became much attached to it, and when one of the daughters, Peace by name, went to live at Rensselaerville, New York, she took the old kettle with her.

One can hardly realise what a change in many ways the banishment of tea from the usual dietary caused.

Even the Southern States were up in arms with New England, and June 1, 1774, was appointed a day of fasting in Virginia. Tea was sealed up and destroyed. Money and provisions were obtained by canvassing the counties, and were dispatched to Boston. But there were some royalist hearts which beat in Virginia, and one owner of such an one, she who had been the lovely Kate Spotswood, but who had married Bernard Moore, has had her name come down to us as continuing to sip her tea in the privacy of her closet after it was banished from every table.

Indeed, "tea" was no longer a popular meal; its place was taken by "coffee." Philip Fithian, a tutor in a Virginia family, left a very full diary of what was done among the families with which he came in contact at this time. He enters in his diary from "Nomini Hall" the following:

"Something very merry happened in our palace this Evening. Mrs. Carter made a dish of Tea! At Coffee she sent me a dish — and I and the Colonel both ignorant. He smelt, sipt, look'd! At last with great gravity he asks, 'What's this?' 'Do you ask Sir?' 'Poh!' and out he throws it, splash, a sacrifice to Vulcan."

Colonel Carter was always a patriot, you see!

Three other kettles, two of them of unusual shape, are given in Figure 176. I am very sure that, if we could find their histories engraved on their sides, they would prove interesting reading. They belong in Ipswich, Massachusetts, a town settled as early as 1633 by John Winthrop and his twelve companions.

Though these hardy spirits suffered from Indian raids and all the hardships incident to a pioneer settlement, the town grew, and soon numbered among its residents Deputy-Governor Symonds and his wife. Madam Symonds was a very fine lady, and sent to London for all her clothes, wore red Spanish-leather shoes, and kept herself cool with a fan of feathers mounted on tortoise-shell sticks, even when she was turned sixty years of age, and included in her orders such trifles as needles and pins, spices and figs. The tall vessel looks more like a coffee-pot than a tea-kettle, but no doubt served its turn in many ways.

Among the articles mentioned in Judith Sewall's wedding outfit is " A strong Brass Mortar that will hold about a Quart with a Pestle." Two such mortars are shown in Figure 177. They are handsome and must have been an ornament to the kitchen dresser when brightly polished and set on the shelf. The swinging-kettle of brass is not so modern as we are apt to think, and a fine specimen is shown in Figure 178, with handles on the base to carry it about. There is a lamp of some kind with places for three wicks, and this kettle is much later than the old coffee urns, which were made to have a piece of hot iron placed in the centre to keep the coffee warm.

The Dutch settlers who brought so many comforts and luxuries to this country did not forget to have their fine brasses come from the old country in many a ship. Among such utensils were many milk cans like the one shown in Figure 179. This one has seen

139

service, but it is handsome yet, and made of a wonderfully fine quality of brass. The little stand on three legs was often placed among the ashes to warm something, — a mug or cup, — and it, too, is " far in years," as they say in New England, and more or less damaged.

Figures 180 and 181 show other copper vessels, the great two-handled pot in Figure 180 being made from a single sheet of copper. To what use the vase-like piece was put it is hard to conceive, unless it was for ornament only.

Of the pieces in Figure 181 the covered dish and the battered pot were used for cooking. The two-handled cup is a sada, or Jewish utensil, their ritual forbidding them to grasp the cup from which they drink with an unwashed hand. The flight of Russian Jews to this country has brought here much beautiful old copper and brass, in quaint and curious forms. While nearly every country has been despoiled by the collector for the enrichment of his shelves, Russia was one of the last to be invaded. In the Russian kitchen are to be found stores of beautiful shapes in brilliantly polished metal, for the marriage portion of most daughters is a stock of kitchen utensils, and these are of such admirable workmanship that they last a lifetime. Indeed, in the poorer families they descend from one generation to another; and it is heirlooms like these that the collector wants for his own.

It was not to be expected that when the demand arose it should not be supplied, and to-day, in the streets of

140

New York which are in the great Russian quarter, you
may find copper and brass utensils to satisfy the most
grasping collector. You may hear, too, the tap-tap of
the worker, who in back shops and cellars is making
these objects, and battering and denting them to suit
the taste of the most rabid gatherer of "antiques."
Of course these articles are hand-made, being fashioned
from great sheets of copper and brass, which are first
heated in rude furnaces to make them malleable, and
then hammered into the same shapes which the Russian
peasants have used for years. There are merchants who
have the old articles, and many of them are honest
enough to tell you which they are. One progressive
Russian, who has become imbued with the American
spirit of hustling, for several years has made an annual
visit to his native country and bought up many of these
articles and brought them over here. There is a fierce
spirit of rivalry among these merchants of the Ghetto,
and they will cry down one another's wares with the
greatest vigour. The true collector with "the gift of
tongues" will be able to make many a bargain, and,
after all, the bargaining is almost as dear to his heart
as possession.

Some beautiful Russian pieces are shown in Figure
182. The middle one is much like the Turkish shape
for coffee-pots, and the genuineness of these articles
is assured, since they were obtained from the Russian
peasants on landing. The samovar, a peculiarly Russian utensil, had also come in for its share of popular
favour, and two very fine antique ones are shown in

141

Figures 183 and 184. They belong in one of the most noted collections in New York City.

Figure 185 has, besides the brass samovar which stands on an antique tray of beaten brass, an incense burner, used on festival days for sprinkling the guests when seated at table with incense. The strange old vase with Arabic characters upon it is made from a single piece of brass, and the candlestick betrays its nationality so plainly that it is hardly necessary to say it is Chinese. These pieces make quite a polyglot company.

The only sugar-bowl which I ever found in brass is given in Figure 186, and with it, but not like it, is what might be called by courtesy a creamer. The pitcher is much the more venerable of the two, for the bowl has handles of cast brass. Both pieces are either of English or American manufacture.

In Figure 187 are some other Russian brasses, — a coffee-pot and two bowls, the bowl which stands flat on the table being of extremely crude workmanship and very old. The other is in two pieces, and they are riveted together. Figure 188 shows the metal work of three nations. The kettle to the right is a handsome piece of brass repoussé work, with a fine coat of arms for decoration. Once upon a time it had a piece of wood upon the iron bar which holds the two ends of the handle together, but this was burned off long ago, and even the iron is much corroded. This came from England. The brass tea-kettle in the centre is home-made, and furnished to cold and tired travellers hot water in plenty for their toddy. The brass pitcher with upturned lip is Dutch, and seems as if it might have borne company with the old brass shaving-bowls of a century or more ago.

Travellers from Holland bring home much brass these days, — dust-pans, snuff-boxes, and various small kettles, and once in a while one of the huge old milk-cans which are such a picturesque feature of the country. These, while pleasing, are generally quite modern, and will not keep company with the pots and pans shown here, all of which belong to the old *régime*.

Having all too briefly considered the brass and copper utensils used for heating and cooking, it is next in order to consider their use in holding a light. Before we can properly speak of the way our ancestors lighted their homes and buildings, we must glance at the scanty means which they had at command for getting that light started. There were, of course, no friction matches, their invention taking place about 1827. The earliest friction matches which were used in this country were imported from France, and there is a story concerning their early manufacture in America which goes to prove how seldom the inventor profits by his invention. In 1836, nearly ten years from their first use, friction matches imported from France were clumsy phosphoric ones. They were made by dipping the match-stick first into sulphur and then into a paste composed of chloride of potash, red lead, and loaf sugar. Each box of matches was accompanied by a bottle of sulphuric acid, into which every match had to be dipped in order to light it.

143

The attention of a young man living in Springfield, Massachusetts, L. C. Allen by name, was attracted to this subject, and he set to work to invent a match which could be lighted by drawing it across a rough surface. He succeeded, and was urged to take out a patent. This he neglected to do, and when at last he took steps in the matter he found that a patent had already been obtained by a pedlar from Chicopee, Massachusetts, who had picked up in some way the results of Mr. Allen's labours. The end of the matter was that Phillips, the pedlar, gave Allen leave to make matches under his patent, in consideration of Allen's waiving his claim and not instigating any litigation. So the inventor of friction matches became a manufacturer of matches under another man's patent.

Before the use of matches all lights had to be produced by hot coals which were kept glowing by being covered with ashes, or by flint and steel. The practice of carrying coals from one house to another when a light was needed became so common that the danger of fire to the settlements was much increased. Stringent laws were framed in many towns, ordering that " fire shall always be kept covered when carried from house to house." Among the early laws of New Amsterdam were those regulating the moving of hot coals, and several Dutch vrouws were brought to court for breaking them. The danger of fire was a constant menace, and every house was provided with fire-buckets, which were hung in some handy spot.

As late as 1742 an inventory of the belongings of
144

Peter Faneuil, Esq., of Boston, was filed. He was a wealthy man, with a large house and rich furnishings, yet in the " great centre hall " hung " one large entry lantern, twelve baggs and bucketts and some books." Apparently the bags were to carry out the goods if it were necessary.

The method of using flint and steel is unknown to most people of this generation, but it was a process which is said to have caused more strong language from our ancestors than anything else with which they had to deal. The flint was a bit of stone, as the name implies, which was roughly shaped, oblong, square, or round, about two inches in diameter with a sharp edge, which was smartly struck against the steel. This latter object was hung over the the fingers of the left hand and the handle of it firmly grasped; the flint was held between the finger and thumb of the right hand, and the steel struck quickly with the flint from above downward. This caused the sparks to fall upon the tinder in the box, the tiny spark was blown into a flame, a match covered at the end with sulphur was soon burning, and was quickly applied to either fire or candle. At the very best this process took from one to three minutes, and if the materials were damp, if the striker's hands were chilled, or if in the dark the steel was not successfully struck, it might take as long as thirty minutes to perform the operation. Many were the bleeding knuckles which were the portion of the unskilful. No wonder that the friction match was hailed as one of the greatest marvels of the age. Before friction matches were made something far more wonderful could be seen in New York City. That was the house at No. 7 Cherry Street, which was lighted throughout by a marvellous and dangerous material known as Gas. This was in 1824, and the house belonged to Mr. Samuel Leggett, President of the New York Gas Light Company, who took this method of showing how little danger there was in the new illuminant. The method of lighting it was by the sulphur match, which was lighted in its turn by the tinder-box, if no hot coals were at hand.

Figure 189 shows two styles of tinder-boxes. The round one on the left is closed, and the little tube on top held the candle. When the cover was removed the candle-holder came too, and within were the flint and steel, and a round bit of tin with a handle called a " damper," and used to put out the sparks in the scorched linen when no longer needed. The other box, somewhat like a wheelbarrow in shape, has within it yet the old sulphur matches and the flint. The steel forms the wheel. In all cases it was necessary to keep the boxes carefully covered, so that the contents should not get damp, for this added to the difficulty of getting a spark started. We can see why " early to bed " became a household word!

Wood, in his " New England Prospects," says:

" Out of the Pines is gotten Candlewood that is so much spoke of which may serve as a shift among poore folks, but I cannot commend it for Singular good because it is something sluttish dropping a kind of pitchy substance where it stands."

146

Higginson, writing about this same early period, says:

"Our pine-trees that are the most plentiful of all wood, doth allow us plenty of candles which are very useful in a house. And they are such candles as the Indians commonly use, having no other, and they are nothing else but the wood of the pine-tree cloven in two little slices, something thin, which is so full of the moisture of turpentine and pitch that they burn as clear as a torch."

We do not seem to have made much use in this country of the "light of antiquity," as the rush-light may well be called, and I have never come across a rush-light holder, nor seen one exposed for sale in this country. Rush-lights were easy to make, and in Walter Harris's translation of "Ware's Antiquities of Ireland" there is the following:

"They made use of lights made of the pith of rushes, which they stripped bare of the skin, and left only a small ridge at the back to keep the tender pith from falling asunder. When these were thoroughly dried they dipped them slightly in grease or other unctuous matter, and then had no further trouble in the preparation. This sort of light is to this day made use of among the meaner sort of Irish, and people of condition (before the use of the tallow candle which was introduced into Ireland from England) twisted a great number of these rush lights together, sometimes to the bulk of a man's arm. Nay, we have instances in the Irish annals that even within these 200 years they made them the size of a man's middle."

Rush-lights were in use among the cottage folk of England long after the first settlers came to these shores, but it was not long before oil was to be had

147

here, which was better than candlewood or rush-lights, and less precious than candles made of grease, even though the tallow came from deer suet or bear grease. One of the earliest and poorest styles of light-givers was called a betty lamp. It was little more than a metal tray with upturned edges, so that the grease would not drop out. The light was provided by a bit of twisted rag which burned in the pointed nose. It had to be constantly attended to in order to give the faintest light. Lamps similar in principle had been in use centuries before the Christian era and were made of pottery, with a spout for a wick and a hole in the top into which the oil was poured. The form our ancestors used was something like the one in Figure 190, except this one could carry four wicks, one at each corner. The tall lamp at the right is also a crude form for a round wick and oil, and known as a " baker's lamp."

When the early colonists looked about for other material than grease to use for lighting purposes they found it near at hand in the sea, where there were abundant fish. Higginson, writing in 1630, says that though there is " no tallow to make candles of, yet by the abundance of fish thereof it (the colony) can afford oil for lamps." In another quaint old record, called Josselyn's "New England Rarities," which was written between 1663 and 1671, there is another reference to oil:

" It was not long since a Sperma Ceti Whale or two were cast upon the shore not far from Boston in the Massachusetts Bay, which being cut into small pieces and boyled in Cauldrons,

148

yielded plenty of Oyl, the Oyl put up in hogsheads, and stow'd into cellars for some time, candies at the bottom, it may be one quarter; then the Oyl is drawn off, and the candied stuff put into convenient vessels is sold for Sperma Ceti, and is right Sperma Ceti."

In 1686 Governor Andros of New York asked for a commission for a voyage for " Sperma Coeti Whales," and in 1671 Nantucket, then known as Sherburne, began whaling operations, growing to be known as the greatest whaling town in the world. Oil for burning was soon in demand in all parts of the colonies. But candlesticks of brass, copper, pewter, and later of silver and Sheffield plate, were not crowded out by oil. They were considered more elegant than oil lamps and held the choicest wax candles which the housewife could make. If possible she used bayberry-wax, which was highly esteemed from New Orleans to Canada. Of so great importance was this vegetable wax that at Brookhaven the law forbade the gathering of the berries before September 15, under penalty of a fine of fifteen shillings. In Louisiana the bushes were planted on the borders of the bayous which formed the waterways and in some cases marked the boundaries of the plantations. In 1705 Robert Beverley described it as follows:

" A pale, brittle wax of a curious green color, which by refining becomes almost transparent. Of this they make candles which are never greasy to the touch, never melt with lying in the hottest weather; neither does the snuff of them ever offend the smell like a tallow candle, but instead of being disagreeable if

149

an accident puts a candle out it yields a pleasant fragrancy to all that are in the room, insomuch that nice people often put them out on purpose to have the incense of the expiring snuff."

In Figure 191 a row of stout candlesticks of good Colonial types is shown. A "sliding candlestick," a pattern much used among the thrifty, is given in Figure 192. As the candle burned away it could be moved up, so that there was no waste. There is also another early pattern of a stick with a grease tray, which caught the drippings as they fell from the burning candle. This was very necessary in the case of tallow dips, or any candles not made of wax. The big candlestick in the centre is a Russian church stick. Other candlesticks of Russian and often Jewish origin are shown in Figure 193, and all were used for religious purposes. The Jews were noted long ago for their proficiency in metal work. In Bible days at Tyre and Sidon "they traded in vessels of brass in thy markets."

The Chinese also worked in brass and other metals centuries ago, and embodied many of their strange artistic ideas in domestic articles. One of their temple sticks is also shown; it is the one with the two birds on it.

The two candlesticks with glass shades are of English make, one of Sheffield plate and one of mahogany (see Figure 194). The smaller one was for bedroom use, and the shade prevented draughts from extinguishing the candle when it was carried about. These are reproduced to-day in brass as well as plated ware, and are quite as useful in country houses as they

Fig. 174 WARMING-PAN AND KETTLES

Fig. 175 COPPER KETTLES

Fig. 176 COPPER TEAKETTLES

Fig. 177 BRASS MORTARS

Fig. 178 BRASS SWINGING-KETTLE

Fig. 179   DUTCH MILK CAN AND UTENSILS

Fig. 180   COPPER VESSELS

Fig. 181   COPPER COOKING VESSELS

Fig. 182   RUSSIAN COPPER KETTLES

Fig. 183   SAMOVAR   Fig. 184   SAMOVAR

Fig. 185   RUSSIAN SAMOVAR, ETC.

Fig. 186   PITCHER AND SUGAR-BOWL, BRASS

Fig. 187 Russian Brasses

Fig. 188 Brass Kettle and Pitcher

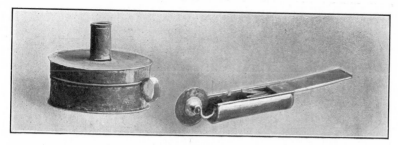

Fig. 189 Tinder Boxes

Fig. 190 Early Lamps

Fig. 191 Brass Candlesticks

Fig. 192 Sliding Stick   Fig. 194 English Sticks

Fig. 193 Russian Candlesticks

were in the days when they were the latest thing out. The tall mahogany candlestick is one of a pair which are in as fine condition as they were the day they were made. For many a long year they graced the mantel-shelf of a fine old house, being one of the chief orna-ments of the best room, and lighted only when company was expected. On such occasions conversation or cards were the amusements, and such sticks never left their dignified retreat on the shelf. On the card-tables, many of which were provided with round, flat places for the candlesticks to stand, would be found tall candlesticks like those seen in Figure 195, which belonged to Gen-eral and Mrs. Washington and were in use at Mount Vernon. This pair are silver, but there were few per-sons who could afford that metal, and, provided the stick was tall enough, it did not matter of what material it was made. I find in old records and inventories many references to candlesticks, and it is easy to see that they were important objects of domestic economy. As early as 1489 I find mention of a " bell candlestick," the word " bell " referring to the shape of the base, which was somewhat in the form of a bell and very solid and heavy. In the next century the candlestick was still of enough importance to be an object of bequest, and a Mr. Thatcher of Pirton, England, gave by will " to my grandson one fallowe cowe and best bed and one greate Brasse Candlesticke." To his youngest grandson he gave " one fallowe heifer with bed and payer of sheets of the thirde sorte and one Brasse Candlesticke."

The process of making the candles to go in these

sticks was long and trying, but casting them in moulds was easier than dipping them. The moulds were made either of tin or pewter and would hold from two to eight candles at a time. Not every family owned a set of moulds, but in those pleasant days of village life a mould was passed about from one family to another at need, just as they passed the spoon mould when new pewter spoons had to be run.

Anyone who has travelled abroad, particularly on the Continent, knows how important a part candles play among the charges on the bill even yet. Some thrifty souls take with them from place to place the candle ends for which they are charged, and are enabled to get up quite an illumination at the end of a week of travelling by lighting all the bits. I think that the penurious feeling which exists in the breast of nearly every Frenchman with regard to candles has come down for over a century or more and become ingrained in his nature.

In the days of the greatest glory of France, during the reigns of Louis XIV and Louis XV and even in the lifetime of the unhappy Marie Antoinette, candles were one of the most valuable court perquisites. During the reign of Louis XV the ladies attached to the Queen's bedchamber were paid but one hundred and fifty livres a year, — that is, about thirty dollars, which seems a beggarly sum. This they were allowed to increase by selling the candles which had been once lighted. These ends of candles would not seem to be a large item, yet it brought them an income of five

152

thousand livres—over one thousand dollars. The profit on candles was so great that it was shared among many of the courtiers. For instance, those candles which were not burned up when the play was over went to the members of the guard, while those which remained after the king's meals were finished went to other retainers of the royal family.

There was, and is, a certain elegance to wax candles; they give such a mellow and becoming light. Consider how handsome the dining-table at Mount Vernon must have looked when guests were bidden and the board was graced by the handsome candlesticks which may be seen on the upper shelf in Figure 195. All the arrangements of lighting at Mount Vernon were handsome, and the hall lantern, as well as some lamps of silver, can still be admired. They are in the National Museum at Washington.

Almost as necessary as the candlesticks themselves were the snuffers and tray to go with them, and it was a much sought privilege of the children of the house to be allowed to use them. Just how early they came into use it is difficult to say, but in the old play of "The Miser," 1733, one of the characters, Charles Bubbleboy, is made to say: "I have brought you a pair of the new invented snuffers, madam, be pleased to look at them; they are my own invention; the nicest lady in the world may make use of them." A pair of nice, plain, old brass snuffers and tray is shown in the next figure (196), and they probably are well along in their second century, though their present

153

owner cannot tell. They are owned in Salem, Massachusetts, and are some of those things which the owner "always remembers." Those made of other metals than brass were sometimes quite ornamental, but the brass ones are generally plain.

Brass sconces were also sent here from London and Paris, and a choice pair, rather florid in design, are shown in Figure 197. I have seen Dutch warming-pans made into sconces, the very handsomely ornamented lids being used, and arms for the candles set on to them. The owners had no idea what was the original purpose of the slightly convex circle which formed the most important part of their sconces.

The first invention to benefit the simple lamps which had been in use so long, as I have said, was in 1783, when Leger of Paris invented the flat wick and a burner to go with it. In the next year Ami Argand, also a Frenchman, invented a burner to which he gave his name, and which is still the parent of innumerable modifications. With all these means for illuminating at hand, it was certain that some choice lamps should find their way over here. And they did. I show two of these lamps with handsome globes (see Figure 198). Many such lamps have been resurrected within the last few years, but something is wrong with them. We either do not know how to manage them, or we expect too much, for they give a poor light unless refitted with modern burners. A friend of mine who is rather antique mad secured some time ago a lamp like one of these, but, alas! it had no shade. Being a lucky

154

collector, he laid it aside for the moment, and shortly after, being on a visit to a neighbouring city, during his rummages in second-hand shops he found a shade. He bought it on the chance that it would fit, and carried it home carefully in his hand. His luck stayed by him, and it did fit the lamp as if made for it. He fussed with wicks and burners till at last he got a light, but a feeble one. He never tried it more than once or twice, and he is now content to let the lamp stand on a nice old table and look well. I asked his wife how it happened that she was so complacent with his collecting so much miscellaneous stuff. Her reply was a wise one, and I have often thought of it: " He has no vices," she said; "he does not use liquor or tobacco in any form, so, as I think he ought to have a fad in some direction, I encourage his collecting." It is a strange thing, but judging from the hundreds of letters I receive, men compose the great body of collectors. They outnumber women two to one, and, as a rule, are quite as vague in describing some treasure which they want judged, as is the gentler sex! A fine lamp shown in Figure 199 once belonged to Governor Pierce, whose son was President Franklin Pierce.

In Figure 200 are seen lamps of a more usual form than those just shown. They belong to about the same period and were for use on the mantels, the crystal drops making them very brilliant. The reservoir to hold the oil was in the centre of the lamp, and as these were made before the use of petroleum as an illuminating fluid they must have burned paraffin oils. An-

155

other pair similar to some used at Mount Vernon are shown in Figure 201.

There was not an abundance of petroleum to be had until after 1855, although it had been known from most ancient times. In 1847 and during the next few years experiments were made in Manchester, England, with regard to using this oil for illuminating fluid. It was not till 1875 that one of the most productive oil fields ever known was developed in this country, making the oil abundant and cheap. Petroleum was first noted in this country, in the State of Ohio, in 1814. It was frequently found when digging wells for brine, and in 1829 a brine-well in Cumberland County, Kentucky, yielded such an enormous quantity of petroleum that it was regarded as a wonderful natural phenomenon. There were so many thousands of barrels of it going to waste that at last some ingenious Yankee bottled some up and sold it as a "cure-all" under the title of American Oil.

Public buildings were as badly off for lighting facilities as private, and churches were dependent on candles and oil lamps. Some rich parishes, like that of St. Michaels in Charleston, South Carolina, imported from England chandeliers of brass, which were hung by a chain from the ceiling, so that they could be raised or lowered. Some of these chandeliers held as many as forty-five candles, and it required constant snuffing to keep them in order. This same old chandelier in Charleston still hangs in St. Michaels, but within recent years it has been fitted for gas. Under its light have worshipped both Washington and Lafayette, and it has seen pass beneath it victims of war and pestilence and has withstood fire and earthquake. Amid many other interesting relics which the church contains, the old chandelier still bravely holds its own.

So far all the lights shown did duty within doors. When one stepped abroad, so dark were the streets and so badly paved that, after cocking one's bonnet and throwing on a roquelo, a stout staff was a necessity.

In Scott's Somers' Tracts, 1685, under the head of "England's Wants," is the following with reference to the lights:

"There is wanting a law wherein, although not all England is concerned, yet a great part thereof is, that, in the capital city of England, not only all the streets and lanes should be kept clean, that all sorts of persons might walk as commodiously in winter as in summer, which is of late years brought to pass in that great and populous city of Paris, in France; but also, as is done in that city all the winter nights, in the middle of the streets there should be hanged out so many candles or lamps, as that all sorts of persons in this great trading city might walk about their business as conveniently and safely by night as by day."

We did not suffer from highwaymen in our country as they did in England, such gentry being seldom met with here. To be sure, the "watch" had a lantern, — you can see one in Figure 202, — and you were lucky if you were going his way. Even New York in 1789 was a dirty city. Pigs were the only scavengers, and as they did not do their duty very thoroughly

157

an appeal for relief was made to the High Constable of the city. It was printed in the "Daily Advertiser" of December 19, 1789, and begins as follows:

"Awake, thou sleeper, let us have clean streets in this our peaceful seat of the happiest empire in the universe."

Street lamps had been introduced in 1762, but they were few and far between, apt to go out, and often unlighted. In December, 1778, the firemen of the city formally complained that they had been greatly hampered at a recent fire because most of the lamps had gone out. Things improved slowly, for in 1789 a citizen prayed for relief because, as not a lamp was burning, he had walked into a pump in Nassau Street, near the mayor's house. In the country districts the lantern was a positive necessity if one had to be abroad at night. Nor is it yet a thing of the past, as I very well know, since I have found my way about several New England villages lately by its kindly aid.

The old lanterns were similar to the one pictured in Figure 203, and sometimes I find such as these hanging comfortably on a wooden peg in barns where the ox-bow is still in use.

VII — OLD-FASHIONED BEDSTEADS

EVEN in the earliest times some attempts were made to have the resting-place soft and warm. The warrior, coming home from war or chase, threw his wearied frame on a simple couch laid upon the floor and covered himself with furs. Little by little the frame of the bed was raised from the floor, coverings grew more elaborate, greater ease was required, and gradually the elaborate structure we require to-day was evolved. As late as the fourteenth century beds were objects of luxury in England. Many a castle had but one, in which the lord and his lady rested, the remainder of the household sleeping on settles, chests, tables, or on the floor.

After Italy, France soonest had elegant and luxurious household belongings, and the palaces of royalty, as well as those of the great nobles, were rich in precious and costly things. Charles V and Jeanne de Bourbon were great collectors, and although the queen sold a set of plate of which she was very proud to pay the troops of Du Guesclin in 1369, she soon began to collect again, and the king had a list made of their valuables which still is extant in the French archives. From it we learn that they had statuettes of ivory and gold, sets of gold plates, basins and candlesticks of the same

159

metal, drinking-cups, knives, and spoons, even if there were only three forks. There were sets of hangings for windows and beds, one being entirely of cloth of gold, another of green with stripes of gold, while a tent to put over the queen's bath was of white satin embroidered with roses and fleur-de-lis. The beds in use at this time were enormous. If only six feet square they were called *couchettes* or little beds, and they had to be eight feet and a half to twelve feet by eleven before they were called couches or beds. These beds were mounted on wide steps or dais, and hung with exquisite materials. The bedding mentioned in this same list seems to have been kept in chests in the bedrooms. A quantity of white silk sheets are spoken of as being in a coffer in the king's room, and in a gilded chest were towels, tablecloths, and sheets of *toile de Reims*, also richly embroidered pillows, one of which had on it a knight, a lady, two fountains, and two lions. There were *couvertoers*, or warm coverings for winter, and *couvertures* or sheets of fine material to be thrown over the beds by day. One of these is mentioned as being of ermine, fastened to an old sheet of *marramas*, from which the king had caused a breadth to be cut to make a chasuble.

There were bills from a Marie Lallemande for blue and white stuff for the window curtains of the royal bedroom, and for eighteen feather-beds with pillows. In the midst of all this elegance it is amusing to find duly set down: " Item, an old matrass all torn and a pillow the same which had belonged to King Jean."

160

There is also mention of two banners embroidered with fleur-de-lis and bordered with pearls which had been used to drive away the flies while the king was at table. The bedsteads which accompanied these rich belongings were of oak, carved, but there are none of them left now for us to gaze on with wonder and amazement.

The word "bed" in old deeds and records, in England as well as in this country, generally covers the bedstead and furnishings. Some of these ancient ones were very grand affairs of carved oak, with mattress of feathers, sheets of linen, rugs and blankets of fine down, and with coverlets of tapestry, damask, or "cloth woven of samite" and heavy with gold threads. Richard, Earl of Arundel, in 1392 left to Philippa, his second wife, "a blue bed marked with my arms and the arms of my late wife." In 1434 Joanne, Lady Bergavenny, devises "a bed of gold swans, with tapettar of green tapestry with branches of flowers of divers colours, and two pairs of sheets of Raynes, a pair of fustian, six pairs of other sheets, six blankets, six mattresses, six pillows with cushions and bancoves that longen to the bed aforesaid." The famous "Great Bed of Ware" mentioned by Shakspere in "Twelfth Night" is about twelve feet square. It is still preserved at Rye House, near to the Saracen's Head Inn, where it formerly was. The beds now in use in Hatfield House, the historic home of the Marquis of Salisbury, are built on the plan of the "Great Bed of Ware," and the sheets for them have to be specially woven in Germany.

11

The earliest beds which remain for the edification of the student are those which date from the Elizabethan period. These, like those of an earlier period, are of oak, and there are some in this country which have been brought here from England, and in the great public collections in the latter country there are other fine examples to be studied. In Figure 204 is a choice specimen that claims attention on more than one account. It is of the Tudor period, with a canopy, and with four arched panels carved and inlaid, and with carved and inlaid borders at the sides. The canopy is panelled as well as inlaid and carved, and the low footboard is also carved. This bed is but five feet two inches wide and seven feet high. It is in perfect condition, and once belonged to the poet Lord Byron, who gave it to his housekeeper, Mrs. Broughton. Her daughter sold it to the late Mr. Wilson of Tuxford Hall, Nottinghamshire, England, and within a few months, at the sale of his effects, it was purchased by a firm who deal in antiques. These beds, while sumptuous to the eye, were not very soft to lie upon, as they were laced across with ropes. Many beds of feathers were necessary to give them comfort, and as early as 1509 regulations were drawn up with regard to the quality of feathers to be used, and I quote the ensuing words from the Lansdown MSS.:

"Upholders forbidden to mix scalded feathers and flocks with dry pulled feathers and clear down, in beds, bolsters, and pillows; and also to use horse-hair for down, neat' hair, deer's hair, and goat's hair, which is wrought in lime-fats, in quilts,

162

mattesses, and cushions, because by the heat of man's body the savour and taste is so abominable and contagious, that many of the King's subjects thereby become destroyed. They were to be stuffed with clear wool or clear flocks alone, one manner of stuff. For their own use however, and not for sale, persons might make, or do to be made, any of the aforesaid corrupt and unlawful wares."

These regulations had been called out by the increasing use of mixed materials in the beds. In the " Paston Letters," which are so interesting, is given the furnishing of the bedroom of Sir John Fastolf, in the year 1459. He was a rich man, and presumably could have had anything he wanted, yet, as will be seen, his mattresses were not both of pure feathers.

"In primis. I fedderbedde. Item I donge of fyne blewe.
Item I bolster. Item II blankettys of fustian.
Item I payre of schetis. Item I purpeynt.
Item I hangyd bedde of arras. Item I testour. Item I selour.
Item I coveryng.
Item III curtaynes of grene worsted.
Item I bankeur of tapestre warke.
Item IIII peces hangyng of grene worsted.
Item I banker hangyng tapestre warke. Item I cobbord clothe.
Item II staundyng aundyris. Item I feddefflok.
Item I chafern (brasier) of latten.
Item I payre of tongys. Item I litell paylet. Item blankettys.
Item I payre schetys. Item coverlet.
Item VI white cosschynes. Item II lytell bellys.
Item I foldyng table. Item I long chayre. Item I grene chayre.
Item I hangyng candylstyk of laton."

Not quite one hundred years later Harrison, in his " Description of England," discourses as follows on the

163

improvement in comfort in the houses. He considers the first improvement was the use of chimneys.

" The second is the great (although not general) amendment of lodging; for, said they, our fathers, yea and we ourselves also have lain full oft upon straw pallets, on rough mats covered only with a sheet, under coverlets made of dagswain or hopharlots (I use their own terms), and a good round log under their heads instead of a pillow or bolster. If it were so that our fathers or the goodman of the house had within seven years after his marriage purchased a mattress or flock bed, and thereunto a pillow of chaff to rest his head upon, he thought himself to be as well lodged as the lord of the town, that peradventure lay seldom in a bed of down or whole feathers, so well content were they, and with such base kind of furniture; which was also not very much amended yet in some parts of Bedfordshire, and elsewhere, further off from our southern parts. Pillows, (they said) were thought meet only for women in childbed. As for servants, if they had any sheet above them, it was well, for seldom had they any under their bodies to keep them from the pricking straws that ran oft through the canvass of the pallett and rased their hardened hides."

I have given the Elizabethan era as the earliest one from which we can hope to find examples of bedroom furniture. There was a reason for this, which Mr. Robinson in his " English Furniture " points out. Not even the royal palaces were proof against the changes of fashion, and beds passed on in their downward career from royal chamber to guard-room, and thence, one cannot tell where. Besides the question of perquisites came in, and in Sandford's " Coronation of James II " is the statement " that the Lord Great Chamberlain

164

claimed to carry the King's shirt and clothes to him on the morning of the coronation, and with the help of the Chamberlain of the Household to dress his Majesty. For this service he claimed the bed, bedding, and furniture of the King's chamber, with forty yards of crimson velvet and other perquisites. The Court of Claims disallowed the furniture, but conceded the velvet and other things claimed, and compromised for the rest for £200."

Cardinal Wolsey, according to the records of Hampton Court, had two hundred and eighty beds, most of them hung with silk. It was not until the fifteenth and sixteenth centuries that much attention was paid to the woodwork of beds, since the hangings were the most important part, and concealed all else.

In John Evelyn's Diary are many notes on the manners and customs of his times. In November, 1644, he mentions having seen a bed at the villa of an Italian prince. "But what," he notes, "some look upon as exceeding all the rest is a very rich bedstead, inlaid with all sorts of precious stones and antiq heads, onyxs, acates, and cornelians, esteem'd to be worth 80 or 90,000 crowns." In the next year he speaks of another gorgeous Italian bed, all inlaid with "achats, chrystals, cornelians, lazuli, esteem'd worth 16,000 crowns." He mentions another fact which may have had something to do with the disappearance of some of these huge wooden beds which is not always taken into account. He says, "The bedsteads in Italy are of forged iron gilded, since it is impossible to keep the wooden ones

165

from the chimices." These are the same little pests with which the American housekeeper is called on to struggle occasionally, and which has rendered so popular in our day and generation these same forged beds of iron, or equally sanitary ones of brass.

The furniture of a bedroom at about the middle of the seventeenth century may be judged by the inventory of Mr. Sarjeant Newdigate, who left his goods to his son. The inventory is published by Lady Newdigate-Newdegate in her "Cavalier and Puritan." It runs as follows:

"A very large bedstead with embroidered curtains and valence of broadcloth lined with carnation-coloured sarsenet, and seven plumes of feathers in the bedtester. Also two embroidered carpets, two armed chairs, four stools embroidered suitable to the bed, a looking-glass, six flower pots, two stands and a hanging shelf, all gilt; a pair of brass andirons, a picture over the chimney and carpets round the bed."

The fashion of putting a bed and the other bedroom furniture in mourning was not at all uncommon. It had prevailed in France and Italy, as well as England, and Catherine de Medici, while not conforming to the rules of mourning considered seemly in her person, had her bed draped with black velvet embroidered with crescents and pearls, and had all the room furniture to correspond. This bed is mentioned in her inventory at her death, in 1589. In the "Verney Memoirs" there is mention of a great, black bed with hangings of the same colour at Clayton, England, about 1640, and it was lent to different members of the family whenever

166

Fig. 195　General Washington's Candlesticks

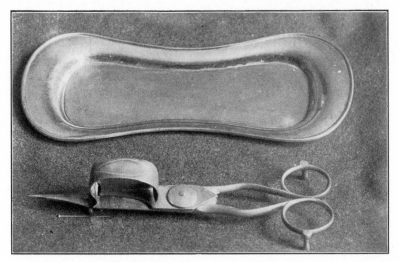

Fig. 196　Brass Snuffers and Tray

Fig. 197   Brass Sconces

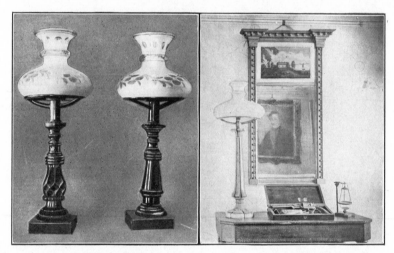

Fig. 198   Brass Lamps   Fig. 199   Governor Pierce's Lamp

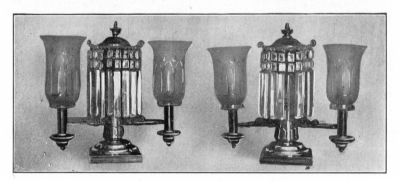

Fig. 200   Brass Lamps with Drops

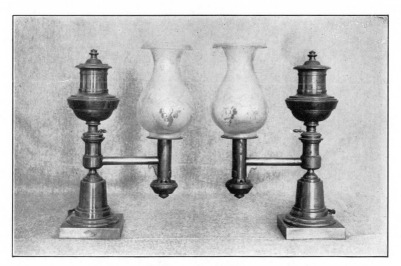

Fig. 201 BRASS LAMPS

Fig. 202 WATCHMAN'S LANTERN

Fig. 203 LANTERN

Fig. 204   Tudor Bedstead, Oak

Fig. 205   "Stump" Bedstead

Fig. 206　General Washington's Bed

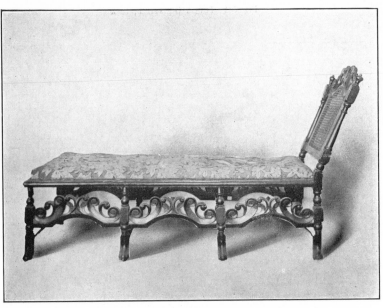

Fig. 207　Joseph Bulkley's Stretcher

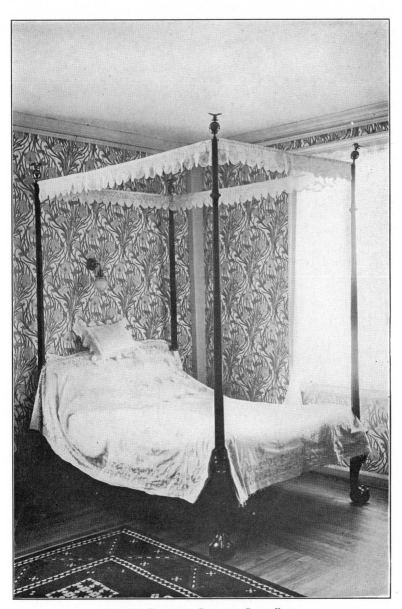

Fig. 208 BED WITH BALL-AND-CLAW FEET

Fig. 209   Dutch Bed Chair

a death occurred. One would think that the sight of such a thing might induce suicide; and perhaps it was such a monument of woe which induced the Lord Treasurer Clifford to try and hang himself from the tester of a four-poster on August 18, 1673.

Then there were the great, upholstered beds of about the time of Queen Anne. They were made after the French fashion, and completely covered with embroidered silk or velvet. Their chief claim to our notice is their extraordinary height, some of them being sixteen or eighteen feet tall, to keep pace with the great height of the chambers in which they were placed. The best place to see a collection of these enormous structures is at Hampton Court, London, where quite a number of beds belonging to royalty have been preserved.

In lower walks of life the bed continued to be an article of parlour furniture into the seventeenth century, and the will of Robert White, of Messinge, Essex, England, a long and elaborate document, has in it this item:

" Item. I give and bequeath unto my said son John White, the Ioyned standinge bedstead wch is in the parlour, with the featherbed, flockbed, bolster coueringe with other furneyture thereunto belonginge. Alsoe the presse cupbord, the cupborde table and my newest chest, all whch are in the said p'loure to be delivered him after the death of my said wife Bridgett White, or instead thereof the sum of twenty marks of like lawful money."

This will is dated June 2, 1617.

The " ioyned standinge bedstead " mentioned was not

probably as handsome a one as is shown in Figure 205, which belongs to about this period, and which is of the type known as "stump" from the fact that it has no foot-board. This bedstead is of oak, carved, with panelled head-board, and beside it is a joined table and stool. The pewter bell-candlesticks are also of this period, and the room is furnished as closely as possible as it would have been in the first quarter of the seventeenth century.

There are not many such beds as these already mentioned, and our interest centres on the beds which found their way to this country, some of which still survive, although the very earliest have gone the way of their owners. I find there were four styles of beds in use, say from 1660 to 1830, — the high four-post bed, the field bed, the low four-post bed, and the "French" bed. In addition are shown a settee bed, stretcher, or day couch, as it was called, and a Dutch bed-chair, because rare specimens of these are still occasionally to be met with.

There was also the slawbank or built-in bed, which was a feature in so many of the houses built by the early Dutch colonists who settled about New York, New Jersey, up the Hudson in Albany, Schenectady, etc. I do not include these, because they were taken out of the houses when the bed was relegated to a room of its own and no longer was part of the furniture in kitchen and best room.

The early records, inventories of property filed with wills, show us how our ancestors lived, and with what simple appliances many of them got along. The bed was generally the most costly possession, and comes first in the list.

In 1640 William Southmead's house in Gloucester, Massachusetts, was valued at £8 ($40), and his feather-bed, bedstead, and appurtenances at the same sum. Cornelis Barentsen, in 1656, sued Cristina Capoens for payment for a bed he sold her, payment to be made in fourteen days. The price was six beavers, and Cristina seemed unable to meet her obligations; but payment was ordered by the court at New Amsterdam.

In June, 1666, the administrators of the late Jan Reyerson of Albany, New York, sold some " beasts " (horses, calves, and hogs), as well as furniture, at public sale. The payment for the beasts, " also the bed, boulsters and pillows," was to be made in " whole mer-chantable beavers, or otherwise in good strung seewant, beaver's price, at 24 guilders the beaver." (A guilder was worth about forty cents of our money.)

Nicholas Van Rensselaer, of Albany, New York, who died in 1679, was a wealthy and important member of the colony. There is a list of his entire household fur-nishings. There were two beds, two looking-glasses, two chests of drawers, two tables, one of oak and one of nutwood, also a table of pine with six stools of the same, a sleeping-bank or built-in bed, twenty pictures, a desk, and many brushes and kitchen utensils. These goods were distributed through four rooms.

In the South were found more luxuries than at the North. Captain Mathews, who died in 1690 at York,

Virginia, had in his parlour both a bedstead and a truckle-bed, that is, a small, low bed which could be pushed under the large bed when not in use. It was generally occupied by the children of the family.

No matter where you turn, North or South, among English or Dutch, the "ffether," "feder," or feather-bed is always mentioned in the inventories. Sometimes they were not able to have the beds entirely of feathers, so flock beds were used, or, if not flock, the soft down from the cattails which grew so abundantly in the marshes. I have found lists where the bed was specified as part chicken feathers and part cattail.

Till quite recently in our history the feather-bed has played a part, and in New York State where many comforts found their way, these were not lacking. At Canandaigua, which was not settled till near the end of the eighteenth century, I find many records like these.

Isaac Colvin estate, settled 1796, had three beds valued at £10 each, and they consisted of bed, under-bed, bolsters, and pillows.

Israel Chapin, inventory filed 1800. Among other things were three pink blankets valued at £3, feather-bed, bolsters, and pillows, £5, 1 copper kettle, £1 16s., and brass kettles, £3.

In 1809 was filed the inventory of Daniel Curtis. His "best bedstead and poorest underbed" were valued at $1.50, while "one old featherbed" was set down at $4, and one "turkey and hens featherbed" was worth $5.

The inventory of W. H. Cuyler of the same place,

170

filed in 1813, is interesting as it gives the value of so many household articles about a century ago. Among his wearing apparel was a plaid coat, and " Cherry valleys," whatever those were, valued at $2. His sword and belt were worth $25. Six pair of flannel sheets were $30, eight linen sheets, $30. One set of bed curtains, $7, one bed, bolster, pillows, straw bed, and bedstead were put at $27. Another bed, with rope to lace it, two feather-beds, two bolsters, and four pillows were valued at $42.37. One trundle bed and rope, also bolster, $8.50. One clock, $16, and one buffalo skin, $12. In a number of the inventories given, sheets of different kinds have been mentioned, and really, a chapter might be devoted to this part of the bed alone. Silk, fine and soft, linen of the choicest Holland make were none too good for sheets and " pillow-beres," as the cases used to be called. In the MSS. of the Countess of Pembroke there is this passage for the year 1676, in which she died.

" I saw George Goodgeon paid for 249 yards of linen cloth that he bought for me at Penrith, designed for twenty pair of sheets and pillow-veres [this is her spelling] for the use of my house. And after dinner I gave away several old sheets which were divided among my servants. And this afternoon did Margaret Montgomery, from Penrith, the sempstress, come hither, so I had her into my chamber, and kissed her, and talked with her; and she came to make up the twenty pairs of sheets and pillow-veres."

Nor was it only customary to have the sheets and pillow-cases of fine materials. For centuries they were

171

richly trimmed, so that their cost was enormous. Lace, embroidery, even of gold thread, was not considered out of place, and the household accounts of royalty in France and England are full of the amounts spent for bed furniture. In the "Creevy Papers," which consist of the Diary and Correspondence of Thomas Creevy, M.P., and which extends over the years from 1768 to 1838, he makes a mention of lace-trimmed sheets as late as 1827. This is the way it reads:

"Lord Charles Somerset complains that he could not sleep either of the three nights at Wynyard, never before having slept in cambrick sheets, and that the Brussels lace with which they and the pillows were trimmed, tickled his face so that he had not a moments peace."

Wynyard was the seat of Lord and Lady Londonderry, and the latter was fond of declaring that she could not use handkerchiefs which cost less than fifty guineas the dozen.

The amount of linen which was to be found in this country at an early date is rather surprising, till we take into account that the splendid Dutch housewives who came here soon grew flax and wove linen, not only the coarser kinds, but sheer and fine, suitable for their caps and kerchiefs. Holland furnished to the world many kinds of linen fabrics which have strange and unfamiliar names, and were used for various purposes, bed curtains and coverlets, window curtains and cushions, for it was the mode for many years to have all these match. In fact, all the world, or at least those ports at which trading

172

vessels touched, contributed their quota of goods, which were not only to be found in the cities, but at the country stores as well. These stores, particularly in the Southern States, were most important institutions. They were attached to a plantation, or in some cases the plantation grew to be an attachment to the store. An inventory of the Hubbard store, in York County, Virginia, in 1667, shows what a vast stock of valuable goods could be found in one. There were, " lockrams, canvass, dowlas, Scotch cloths, blue linen, osnaburg, cotton, Holland serge, Kersey, flannel in bales, full suits for adults and youths, bodices and bonnets, laces for women, shoes, gloves, hose, cloaks, cravats, handkerchiefs, nails, hatchets, chisels, augers, locks, staples, sickles, bellows, froes, saws, axes, files, bed cords, dishes, knives, flesh-forks, porringers, sauce-pans, frying-pans, gridirons, tongs, shovels, hoes, iron posts, beds, tables, physic, wool-cards, gimlets, compasses, needles, stirrups, looking-glasses and candle-sticks, candles, funnels, twenty-five pounds of raisins, one hundred gallons of brandy, twenty gallons of wine, and ten gallons of aqua vitæ." These goods were valued at £614 sterling (equal to about $3,000 of our money).

The earliest four-post bedsteads that were brought here were, no doubt, more or less carved, and made with valance and curtains. Often two sets of curtains were used, — an outer and an inner, the latter to be drawn so that unpleasant draughts of wind could be kept out.

The materials of which these bed curtains were made might be perpetuana, kitterminster, serge, darnic, silk

173

darnic, camblet, mohair, fustian, seersucker, camac, bancour, paly, printed calico, checked and striped linen, India and Patma chintz, corded dimities, harrateen, lutestring, moreen, French and pompadour chintz, " fine laylock and fancy callicoes," and muslins. A full-dress bed with " petticoat valance " and window curtains to match, trimmed with fringes and tied back with cords, was costly and handsome.

In addition to all these goods there were scores of others brought from the East Indies, with unfamiliar names and high prices. None of these materials were by any means cheap. Harrateen, a favourite stuff, cost, as late as 1750, four dollars a yard, and a set of curtains all made was worth two hundred dollars.

Camblet was another popular material, and as early as 1678 Colonel Francis Epes, of Henrico County, Virginia, inventoried " One large new feather-bed with camblett curtains and double vallins lined with yellow silke, boulster, pillows, counterpane, rodds and hooks, tops and stands, one curtaine and some ffringe damnified — twenty-four pounds, five shillings."

But such curtains lasted years, and were passed down with the bed from one generation to another.

The well-known Peter Faneuil, of Boston, Massachusetts, died in 1742. He never married, but lived with his sister in great comfort and luxury. The list of belongings in his house and stables showed that he looked well after his own ease, and letters of which he left copies prove that his sister's appearance was a matter of moment to him also, for he ordered all her clothes from London, and was much annoyed because they sent six pairs of worsted stockings for her instead of " three prs. thread hose, one pair of Galons hose, and two pr. of thread ditto." The worsted stockings went back to London by return ship. Mr. Faneuil was dark, no doubt, for he chose yellow as the colour of his room, and beside " small arms," bottles, and a " looking-glass tipt with silver," he had a " yellow mohair bed counter-pane, feather bed, bolster, 2 false pillows, false cur-tains, 6 chairs, 1 great chair, 2 stools, window curtains, etc." Excluding the small arms, the furnishings of this room were valued at £245 (about $1,225 of our money). Many a house is furnished nowadays very prettily for about half that amount.

The four-post bed shown in Figure 206 is at Mount Vernon. Upon it General Washington rested in his last illness, and it is supposed to stand in the spot where he had it during his life.

Many of these old four-post beds are very narrow, — about four feet wide. This was the standard width in those days, and each extra inch of width was charged for. This size was the rule as late as 1795, when the second edition of the "Journeyman's Cabinet and Chair-maker's Philadelphia Book of Prices " was published. It says, " extra width or extra length shall be charged for at the rate of two pence per inch." This Washing-ton bed is of mahogany, of unusual width, over five feet, and no doubt was purchased by the General him-self, as he never missed an opportunity to add to the comfort and elegance of his home.

175

In 1774 Belvoir, the home of the Fairfax family, one of the most splendid mansions on the Potomac, was closed on account of the continued residence of the family in England, and its contents sold. General Washington (he was Colonel then) bought goods valued at £200 sterling, and among them was a "mahogany settee bed with Saxon green covers for same, 13 pounds."

This form of bed went by various names,—stretchers, day couches, or settee beds. The one I show (Figure 207) is still in perfect condition, yet it belonged to Joseph Bulkeley, and is mentioned in his inventory as a "stretcher." He died early in 1700, and brought this to this country in 1690, or thereabouts. As can be seen, this stretcher is a very handsome piece of furniture. It is of oak, of Flemish workmanship, with handsome carved underbraces and the curved Flemish foot. The seat and back were originally of cane, and the back is yet perfect, but the seat has worn out with much service. Some of these single beds (for that is what they really were) had cords laced across and a mattress laid on them, and some had canvas seats also, with cushions or mattress. They were made as late as 1800, but not many of them have survived.

It is customary for people owning old furniture to always call it mahogany, which often is erroneous. Our native cabinet-makers (and Phineas Pratt of Weymouth, Massachusetts, was at work before 1630) used cedar, ash, elm, pine, maple, cherry, poplar, walnut,

176

and nutwood (which was hickory), so they had many varieties to choose from.

The legs and posts of these old beds varied greatly. Some were so high that when the feather-beds were added a pair of steps was required to mount into one with comfort. The width differed, as has been pointed out, and the decoration of the posts also shows much variety, some being plainly turned, others having the two foot-posts carved, the head-posts being plain, as they were concealed by drapery. Head-boards were often omitted, their place being filled with curtain stuff.

Ball-and-claw feet are sometimes come across, though these were usually confined to desks, bureaus, chairs, etc. There is a bed with such legs in the rooms of the Concord Antiquarian Society. It was part of the wedding outfit of Martha Tufts, who was married in 1774. The quaint old curtains are dropping with age, and still display men ploughing, cows and other animals in dull shades of blue and green. A choice example with ball-and-claw feet is given in Figure 208. The posts are unusually slender, and ornamented with brass balls and eagles on the tops.

Such beds had no springs, which were not invented till later, but were laced across with ropes, in many cases requiring the strength of the entire family to pull them tight enough. A mattress of straw was laid over the cords, and upon this was piled the feather-beds, — as many as the household could muster.

The next Figure (209) shows a Dutch bed chair,

very rarely found, and of which few were brought over here. This one is of maple, very handsomely inlaid in a floral pattern with satinwood. The hinges on the front of the chair show, and a piece comes from beneath the seat, the back lets down, arms and legs come together for its support, and the result is a long, narrow bed. They are occasionally mentioned in inventories, but this is the only one I ever saw. It is in the museum connected with the School of Art at Cooper Institute, New York City, and is in a state of perfect preservation.

Another style of bed made chiefly by the Dutch is given in Figure 210. As can be seen, it is nearly covered with a beautiful pattern in marquetry, the darker wood being maple, which contrasts very prettily with the light, inlaid woods. This bed is six feet six inches wide, but I have seen them in single widths also. One peculiarity of these beds, as well as many of French workmanship, is that the decoration is on one side only, the intention being that one side shall go next to the wall. Often the wood of the wall side is different from the rest of the bed, and recently I saw an exquisite, carved rosewood bedstead, with the wall side of deal, stained to match the colour of the rest. It seems a strange economy, and may be classed with making the lids of chests of pine, when the bodies of them were of oak.

An unusually elegant four-post bedstead can be seen in Figure 211. It is of mahogany, richly carved, with a decorated frieze and water-gilt mounts. It is plainly

178

of French make, and belongs to the latter half of the eighteenth century. The head-board and two head-posts are plain, and it was intended that they should be covered with drapery.

Another four-post bed, very much simpler but pleasing for its very simplicity, is given in Figure 212. I am inclined to believe this to be of American make, since the posts are all finished alike, and the fluted posts were favourites with our own makers. I have seen beds of the same pattern which came from Charleston, South Carolina, during the first half of the nineteenth century, and which were made of very choice curly maple. They were foolishly cut up by their owner into hall chairs and goodness knows what other fripperies!

Another style of four-post bedsteads was called " field beds," of which an example is given in Figure 213. They were in use early in the eighteenth century, for about 1730 Governor Montgomery had a sale of his effects " at the Fort " in New York City. Among the articles enumerated were " a fine yellow Camblet bed, lined with silk and trimmed with fine lace, which came from London. A fine field bedstead and curtains."

These field bedsteads were popular for at least seventy-five years. Where they have all gone it would be hard to say. I know of but two, — the one given in Figure 213, which is in the old house in Ipswich, Massachusetts, now called the Whipple House, and one at Washington's Headquarters, at Somerville, New Jersey.

Since the above statement was first published, about

179

a year ago, I have received letters from three people who own these field beds. In two cases the old curtains are with the beds, one set being netted and one of chintz, with a design of peacocks on it. None of them are of mahogany, and the owner of one specifies hers as being of maple.

They were fashionable in England as well as here, for those great makers — Chippendale, Hepplewhite, and Sheraton — designed patterns for them, each making the curve of the " sweep," as the frame which held the netting was called, a little different.

There is no doubt that many such beds were imported, and it was from these that our native makers copied. In the " Journeyman's Cabinet and Chairmaker's Philadelphia Book of Prices," 1795, which has been before quoted, I find the cost of making " a field bedstead of poplar, the roof sloped each way, one pound. If of buttonwood, two shillings extra." " A field bed of mahogany, one pound, four shillings, sixpence." As a matter of fact, the field beds cost a little more than the four-post mahogany, these latter being listed at one pound, four shillings, sixpence. Probably the extra work on the sweeps was the cause of the extra price.

The bed shown in Figure 213 is of mahogany, with ornaments at the top of the gracefully turned posts. The ornamental brasses that covered the holes through which the screws were put to hold the bed together are all in place, two on each foot-post, one on each head-post. They are in most cases of pressed brass, in a

180

rosette pattern, and should be found on high and low four-post beds, and on field beds. In many cases, unfortunately, they are missing. This bed has a plain sweep, and is covered with the netting work, which was so much prettier than cloth drapery.

The coverlet is of the blue-and-white hand-woven material, which was a favourite with housekeepers on account of its durable character and neat appearance.

The furniture in the room is all of appropriate age, and it is interesting to note the tiny size of basin and pitcher. This handsome old house was built probably between 1640 and 1645, and the original oak beams and floor joists show in every room. It is supposed these beams were sawed by hand in a pit, as they bear no signs of axe or adze, and there was no water saw-mill in Ipswich till 1649.

The low four-post bed seen in the next Figure (214) is restored. It has had a stormy career, but has once more renewed its youth. Hundreds of these beds were made and carved in this country, of choice mahogany as well as of other woods. It is not generally known that mahogany was used here as early as 1700, and was quite freely on sale a few years later.

These posts are richly carved with the acanthus leaf, which, after all, is much like our familiar dandelion, — a plant that lends itself readily to decoration, leaf, flower, and bud all being beautiful. Each post is finished with a pineapple. These low four-posters date from about 1800 to 1835 or 1840. They may or may not have foot-boards, but always have head-boards.

181

This particular bed was found in Central New York State, in a barn, where for many years it had furnished a more than usually handsome roost for chickens. I say the bed was found, but, to be quite correct, there were but the four posts,—the sides and head- and foot-boards had long since passed out of sight, perhaps through the kitchen stove! The posts in their dilapidated condition, though fortunately there was not even a nick in the carving, were bought for three dollars. The man who got them for that price turned quite a neat penny, for after holding them for a week he sold them for fifteen dollars.

The last purchaser had the posts rubbed, scraped, and hand polished, the sides and head- and foot-boards made from patterns of similar beds, the brasses to cover the screw holes reproduced, and the result is this very handsome bed. The price, in the meantime, has mounted into the hundreds, since the cost of restoring was heavy. Many beds like this are tucked away out of sight; some, alas, have been painted. I was shown one the other day that was painted a lively green. Carefully scraping it with a bit of broken glass, the original wood came into view. It was curly maple, grown a splendid golden-brown with age. If you wish such a piece done over, you should put it in the hands of a skilled workman. Sometimes this is not possible, and I have seen pieces which looked extremely well treated as follows at home: Bits of broken glass, or a knife with a rounded blade, can be used to get off paint or varnish, care being taken to hold the glass or scraper so that it will not

182

Fig. 210 MARQUETRY BED

Fig. 211 CARVED MAHOGANY BED

Fig. 212 Mahogany Bed

Fig. 213 FIELD BED

Fig. 214 LOW-POST BED

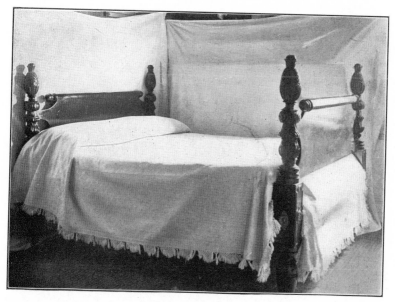

Fig. 215   Low-Post Bed

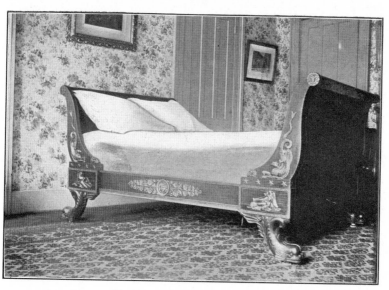

Fig. 216   French or Empire Bed

Fig. 217 PLAIN COPPER LUSTRE JUGS

Fig. 218 GROUP OF COPPER LUSTRE JUGS

Fig. 219 COPPER LUSTRE PITCHERS

Fig. 220   Silver Lustre Jug

Fig. 221   Teapots, Silver Lustre

scratch the wood. If there is carving, the varnish must be got out with alcohol and a pointed stick, which will get into the crevices. After the varnish is all off you may feel that the worst of the job is over, and then rub carefully down with fine sand or emery paper.

If your piece is veneered, you must be particularly careful not to catch your scraping tool in the joints, and it is always safe to scrape *with* the grain of the wood. When you have scraped and thoroughly dusted and wiped your treasure, go over the entire surface with a coating of boiled linseed oil, applied with a bunch of waste or a flannel rag, — never with a brush, — and whatever you do, apply no varnish; it is an abomination. After the oil has soaked in for about twenty-four hours, begin to rub with more oil on waste or flannel. Then rub and rub and rub; rest a while and rub some more.

The longer you rub the higher polish will come on your wood, but just at the present time the fancy is for rather a dull finish. I know of a pair of card-tables, beautifully inlaid and with twisted, carved legs, which have been entirely done over, a little at a time, by the small owner, who is not very strong either in her arms or back.

Another low-post bed is shown in Figure 215. This one is perfect, and has a roll-over head- and foot-board. It is of mahogany, elegantly carved, and is as choice as one would expect, since it belongs in Salem, Massachusetts. I give this bed for the benefit of those who own posts and wish them to be refitted. Either this

183

style of head- and foot-board, or the one shown in the previous figure, are appropriate.

The last style of bed shown (Figure 216) is often called " French " bed. The more correct name is really Empire, for it was this style which prevailed in the early years of the nineteenth century, when France, having passed through the throes of the Revolution, emerged as an Empire under the great Napoleon. It was his wish that styles of dress and furniture should be altered. All the exquisite furniture of the times of the three Louis' was banished, though much had been destroyed in the looting of the royal palaces. The Empire style sought its inspiration from classic models, though after it had passed through the hands of a French artist like David it could scarcely recognise itself. There was little carving, but the chief ornamentations were " ormolu mounts," — that is, beadings and decorations made of carved or pressed brass applied to the surface of the wood.

During the reign of Louis XV this style of work, under the hands of masters of their craft, had reached its greatest excellence and beauty. Under the Empire it became but overloaded ornament. After the Egyptian campaign chairs and tables, stools and commodes blossomed out with carved sphinx heads, and Egyptian ornaments, and though the furniture is poor, artistically, it is interesting as the memorial of a man who impressed his personality on everything with which he came in contact.

The bed illustrated is an excellent example of its

184

class. It was imported from France, and stood for many years in the bridal chamber or guest-room of the Van Rensselaer mansion at Albany, New York. The mounts are carved from solid brass, each smallest piece being made with the beauty of goldsmiths' work. The figures of Fame, with her trumpet, repay the closest examination. Indeed, this bed has been reproduced several times for different members of the family, each reproduction costing a thousand dollars, owing to the work in copying the brasses. The carved dolphins' heads are also fine, the usual foot being a plain bracket or round foot, rarely carved.

Empire style became very popular in England, where it was poorly carried out by the use of pressed instead of carved brass. Of course, we followed European styles, and our rendering of Empire is both handsome and solid. We did not use the brass ornament, but much wood-carving, keeping only to the general lines of this style. I have seen Empire beds made in Massachusetts which were elegant and patriotic as well. The wood was solid mahogany, and the sides of foot- and head-boards ended in very spirited carvings of eagles' heads, — our own national war eagle. These were the only ornaments, the bed relying otherwise on the rich grain of the wood for its beauty. Much of the best furniture to be found here now is of the so-called Empire style. It is either in solid or veneered wood, in which latter process our native makers were very successful.

VIII — LUSTRE WARE

THERE is scarcely a china collector who does not number among his or her possessions at least one piece of lustre, which ware forms a group of its own in English pottery.

All lustre ware may be divided into three classes — copper, silver, and gold — the first being the most common, least valuable, and least interesting. The process of making this ware was simple enough, consisting in dissolving the metals employed by chemicals and forming a solution which could either be applied by dipping or with a brush.

Who first invented, or rather applied, this method of metallic coating to English pottery is not known. Admirers of Wedgwood claim that he first used gold as early as 1776 for lustring picture frames. Other authorities give the merit of the discovery to John Hancock while employed by Spode, to whom he was apprenticed in 1769. Still others credit the firm of Gardiner & Stennys with the introduction of lustred pottery. Be this as it may, by 1770 R. Frank was making copper lustre ware at Brislington, near Bristol, England.

Wilson, in Staffordshire, was making it in 1785.

Lustre ware of all three varieties was made at the

186

Market Street Works, Longton, and was frequently marked with a " B " impressed in the body. The works were in operation at the same time that Wedgwood was working at Etruria, and the firm was originally Cyples, then became Cyples & Barlow, and then was conducted by Thomas Barlow alone.

Moore & Co. and Dixon & Co. were both at work in Sunderland by 1820, and produced much handsome ware. Lustre was also made at Leeds before 1800, in Preston Pans, at Dillwyn, where the famous Swansea gold and silver lustre was manufactured, and at many other pot works all over England.

The body of lustre ware is generally earthen, of a reddish colour and coarse texture, which sometimes detracts from the elegance of the shape of the vessel, though when copper lustre was at its best, about 1801, there was little criticism to be passed upon either its colour or the shapes it covered.

Some of the best examples of copper lustre approach more nearly to those elegant Hispano-Mauro specimens of the fifteenth century than any of the other varieties, and has a depth of colour that forcibly reminds one of the splendid old Italian ware. Since an article on lustre was published by me some years ago, I have received a number of letters from owners of pieces, written in a most earnest spirit. One declared that the so-called "silver lustre" was but a mock, and that he possessed specimens of the true silver lustre which was on glass, and another, a lady this time, gravely informs me that she owns a mug of copper lustre which came over in the

Mayflower! When I suggested that perhaps she had dated her mug a little too far back, she replied that she had been told that in 1805 the mug was considered very, very old, that family tradition was enough for her, and that declared the Mayflower as being the carrier which brought her piece to this country. If only Italian lustre was made as early, why then her mug was Italian. By the way, this mug, which is described as light as aluminum, has survived all these years without so much as a chip! She speaks with some scorn of two marked pickle dishes by Wedgwood which belonged to her husband's family, but pins all her faith to this piece of copper lustre, and nothing will shake her. Family tradition is a power that cannot be gauged till you run counter to it in dating specimens.

In the choicer porcelains and higher class wares it is possible to find characteristics by which they can be distinguished. It is not so in the more common or peasant productions. Highly coloured and more or less crude wares which we quickly assign to England may have been made in Sweden, Denmark, or Belgium, or may even be traced as far south as Italy. Many pieces of lustre are also made in Germany and look so much like the English wares that they deceive all but the most expert. One seldom takes into account that potters travelled from one country to another with the methods which they had learned, and were able to produce in Denmark examples of pottery exactly like those which they had made in Staffordshire.

It is only necessary to trace the movements of a

famous man like Billingsley, who was noted for the roses
which he painted on china, and which during fifty years
appeared on many celebrated English wares as he went
from one factory to another. As with him so with less
renowned potters, so that with unmarked pieces it is
almost impossible to assign the place of manufacture.

In an article on "Historic Pitchers," published in
1902, I showed the "Cornwallis jug," which is the most
valuable piece of copper lustre known. Such a jug in
perfect condition is worth $45, on account of its his-
torical association, since in shape, size, and quality of
ware it is in no wise superior to hundreds of other
copper lustre pitchers. I know of but a scant dozen
of these jugs — in speaking of this Cornwallis pitcher
the term "jug" seems more appropriate — and of these
two are imperfect, one having a bad crack and the other
having lost its "foot" — that is, the base on which it
stands.

I have been criticised for placing the value of these
jugs so high, but, for those of large size and perfect it
is what the dealers ask. I have inquired in several shops
where antiques are sold, and I find that this is the general
figure in the large cities. No dealer will give such a sum,
and you will do well if you can get half so much, for he
too has his profit to make. Next in rarity and beauty
come the perfectly plain copper jugs, fine and simple
in form, and beautifully lustred inside and out. Some
of these of different sizes are shown in Figure 217, and
even in the photograph you can see their wonderful
lustre. These old specimens have a deep-seated lustre,

189

if it may be so expressed, while the modern reproductions are more on the surface, and seem to have a more metallic appearance than the old.

In the Figure 218 are shown seven copper lustre pitchers, embracing all the familiar types, showing the different styles of handles and the ways these were applied, the pitchers having a thumb rest and large pointed lip being the oldest. The best pitcher in this group is the one at the end at the left side, on which are white figures on a copper ground. This pitcher is similar in style to those made by Wedgwood, Wood & Caldwell, and other well-known potters.

The pitchers in Figure 219 show only their good shape and proportion in the photograph, for the broad band of decoration which passes about the upper part of the pitcher just below the handle is a splendid and unusual shade of olive green which does not "take" well.

These pitchers are unusually handsome, the shade of lustre being very deep and rich, and the harmony of that with the green very satisfying. They are of undoubted age, and are now at the Whipple House, Ipswich, Massachusetts, where are gathered so many relics of that interesting old town. The pitchers belonged to Aaron Jewett, janitor of the Old Court House from 1820 to 1850, and were used as water pitchers by the judges of the court during that time.

I do not doubt that this temperance beverage was an unfamiliar invader of these hospitable jugs until they came to do legal duty, for the usual liquid which poured from their generous lips was cider. It was not only to pewter vessels that the terms " gallonier, pottle pot, pot and little pot " were applied, but to pitchers which held respectively one gallon, two quarts, one quart, and one pint. The idea of temperance seems to have been one of the last to enter the minds of our forefathers on either side of the water.

These larger-sized pitchers were made for cider or beer, or some of the numerous decoctions which are compounded of these ingredients and several others, and then heated with a loggerhead.

Bowls, tea-sets, pepper pots, mugs, goblets, and very rarely coffee pots are found in copper lustre, a very handsome specimen of the latter being similar to the helmet-shaped teapot in another illustration (Figure 224).

Two correspondents, one in Mexico (where, she writes me, there is much old china to be picked up) and one in Virginia, own large gallon pitchers of plain copper lustre, very similar in shape to the largest pitcher shown.

The second period of copper lustre was about 1830, when the glaze was inferior, being filled with bubbles and little holes, showing that the pieces were hastily dipped and stood on their bases, where the glaze collected in drops. Since this time copper lustre has been made in quite a number of potteries, and modern lustre can be found easily in Canada, I understand. There seems to be little in the United States, for I have sought in dozens of stores without coming across one pitcher. Whole tea-sets of a certain brilliant lustre, with a band

191

of bright blue, have been offered me as "antiques," every line and its hard, brassy colour showing in an unmistakable fashion its recent manufacture.

There is a depth of colour, a smoothness of glaze, and a "feel" to old lustre that is not easily mistaken. You will find the bottom of the object worn smooth, the polish dulled by wear in places, and the crudeness of the modern ware absent.

The two pitchers in the centre of Figure 217 are of a more modern type than those on the ends with large curved lip and familiar handle. Sometimes such jugs come with a cover also of the lustre, which fits into the neck of the pitcher, and has a square opening so that the liquid can be poured out without removing the lid. Such pieces are very rare. It is a misfortune that such a small quantity of lustre ware of any description was marked. Its age can only be guessed at.

While copper lustre never reached an advanced state in beauty and perfection, silver lustre, as it is familiarly called, deserves a front rank in English pottery. It is not so old a form of lustre as the copper, and probably dates from not earlier than 1785. The process of producing this lustre was by applying a deposit of metallic platinum to the surface of either pottery or porcelain. Platinum was first introduced into England from Spain about the year 1750, and its reductibility and the ease with which it could be deposited were early known to chemists.

John Hancock, who was born in 1757 and died in 1847, claims for himself the first use on pottery of this substance. In 1846 he wrote to the "Staffordshire Mercury" a letter concerning this subject, of which a portion is quoted. He says:

"In the notice of the death of Mr. John Booth, inserted in your last week's paper, it is stated that he was the inventor of lustre for earthenware. I beg to state that this is incorrect, as I was the original inventor of lustre, which is recorded in several works on Potting, and I first put it in practice at Mr. Spode's manufactory for Messrs. Daniel and Brown, and continued to make it long before Mr. Booth or any other person attempted to do so. . . . By inserting this you will oblige me, whose character, at the age of eighty-nine, is at stake."

In Shaw's "History of the Staffordshire Potteries," 1829, he states:

"The first maker of silver lustre properly so called, was John Gardiner, when employed by the late Mr. Wolfe of Stoke. Next were Mr. G. Sparkes of Slack Lane, Hanley, Mr. Horobin of Tunstall, and a person named Mr. John Ainsley, who introduced it at Lane End. Since 1804 it has been practised with varied success through the whole of the district."

In 1810 Peter Warburton, of the New Hall Pottery of Lane End, took out a patent for " decorating china, porcelain, earthenware, and glass with native, pure, or adulterated gold, silver, platina, or other metals fluxed or lowered with lead or any other substance, which invention or new method leaves the metals after being burned in, in their metallic state."

Among the names which may be found on pieces of silver lustre are, " Warburton," with a heart impressed; " Wilson," " Bailey and Harvey," " Spode," " Wood,"

" Minton," "J. E. Wileman," "Harley," "Ralph Salt," — this was the same man that made Staffordshire figures, —" Wood and Caldwell," the Mayer star, and the letter " R," which is supposed to stand for Ridgway. But by far the larger number are entirely unmarked.

The process of making silver lustre was a simple one. The ware, when glazed, was dipped into a bath containing platinic chloride and dilute spirits of tar. It was allowed to dry, and was then baked for eight to twelve hours in a kiln at 1,200 F., when the organic matter burned away, leaving a surface of metallic platinum, lustrous and fine. Sometimes the platinum was mixed with the materials of the glaze and applied directly, and those pieces which have the lightest and most silvery appearance were coated with oxide of platinum produced with sal ammoniac, and fired at a low heat.

Various bodies were used. Wedgwood chose a dark red clay, others a dead white porcelain, and I have seen also a yellowish body, and common gray clay. Originally the pieces, particularly tea-sets, bowls, and mugs, were lustred inside as well as out, for silver lustre was made for those who wished to own silver but could not afford it. In the course of time, when electroplating cheapened metal ware, and the lustre ware no longer deceived, the interior of vessels was coated with a white slip or porcelain glaze and the lustre was confined to the outside. This had the merit, also, of reducing the cost. The pottery body is of coloured earthenware, red or yellow, made very thick in such pieces as tea or

194

coffee pots, to withstand the heat, while other pieces are nearly as delicate as porcelain.

The early patterns, besides being silvered within, are also quite plain in shape, the beautiful ornamentation with which many pieces are enriched being a later development. A choice specimen of plain silver lustre is shown in the fluted jug in Figure 220.

The tea-sets in Queen Anne patterns (see Figures 221, 222, and 223) and the two helmet teapots and the one with " pineapple " pattern shown in Figure 224 are extremely beautiful. Many such sets were cast in old silverware moulds, or modelled in flutings and beadings by hand, the numerous examples shown covering almost every variety of known pattern. In fact, they are almost handsomer than silver, since the lustre takes a deeper shade, and is broken up into higher lights than is possible with even the most highly burnished silver. Not only were there tea-sets, but cups and saucers as well. The only one I ever saw was a delicate bit with flutings on the cup, which was of an early type, since it had no handle. It was in perfect condition and sold for ten dollars.

A perfectly plain cup and saucer this time, with a handle, can be seen in Figure 225. It is a beautiful and perfect piece, and with the other articles in the photograph belongs to a Mexican correspondent. The two lovely candlesticks are of silver lustre also, " Cupid Bound," and are not marked in any way. They are, however, very choice, the modelling of the figure being exquisite, and they are quite perfect, except that the

195

lustre is a little mottled. In design they are quite as choice as the Wedgwood pair shown in another figure.

The largest piece of silver lustre which has come under my notice was an ewer and basin which I saw in the summer of 1903 at Salem, Massachusetts. It was of the diminutive size seen in the old blue toilet sets, — tiny things, which seem to have satisfied our Colonial ancestors in whose estimation cleanliness does not seem to have come next to godliness.

Many people desire to have one or two pieces of silver lustre, but it is by no means easy to find, though many of the teapots shown in this article belong to a fortunate collector who has two thousand other teapots of every variety of pottery and porcelain to keep them company.

At the sale, in March, 1903, of the late Mr. Burritt's collection of pottery and porcelain when such phenomenal prices were obtained for "Old Blue," there were a few pieces of lustre sold also. The prices given for them seem large, but there were plenty of people willing and eager to take them at these figures. There were but two separate silver lustre teapots similar to the tall ones shown in this article. One of them, fluted, sold for $20. The other, plain, brought $18. A tea-set in fluted pattern, consisting of teapot, sugarbowl, and cream jug, brought $60. A silver lustre goblet sold for $11, a pepper box for $12, and a salt cellar, silver without and copper lustre within, cost the purchaser $14.

It must be borne in mind that these prices are un-

usual; no dealer will ever give them. Yet silver lustre
seems to stand apart in value, for I have known a very
choice teapot which had lost its spout to have the missing member replaced by one of plated silver and then
sell for $15.

So far we have dealt only with plain silver lustre, or
that cast in moulds.

There is another form of decoration for this variety
of lustre which is uncommon and very beautiful. An
example is given in Figure 226. I call this the second
period, since the plain ware was evidently the first expression of the potter's ability to use this metal. All
the shapes in which lustre ware was made — pepper
pots, tea-sets, jugs, bowls, two-handled cups, and cups
and saucers — are to be found in this decorated ware,
which is called " resist " from the method of manufacture. Birds and flowers are the subjects oftenest
chosen, the patterns often being exceedingly intricate
and elaborate.

The article to be decorated was first dipped into or
covered with a white or cream-coloured slip, and upon
this the pattern was painted with an adhesive mixture
which " resisted " the silver lustre when the pottery was
dipped into it. All the surface not previously covered
with this resistant mixture became covered with the
lustre. The second firing (the first was to harden the
covering of white slip) burnt away the resist mixture
and fixed the silver lustre, and the pattern stands out
in white.

Very rarely in this country, and not often in England, is this silver " resist " decoration found in which the pattern shows canary-coloured instead of white. Such pieces command very high prices. At the Burritt sale, previously quoted, a silver lustre pitcher with " resist " pattern in white brought $47.50, the pitcher being nine inches high. The one pictured in Figure 226 is six inches tall, and although part of a collection in this country, was found in England.

What remains of a very beautiful tea-set of this resist ware is shown in Figure 227. It was part of a bridal outfit in 1825. None of the pieces are marked, but the ornamentation on the top of the teapot and sugar-box and the beauty of the " honeysuckle pattern " on the body of the pieces, all show it came from some high grade pottery. It is on white china, too, and the bottom of the saucer is left plain. The plate is one of a pair and is an extremely choice one. This, as with so many other antique treasures, may be found in New England, and, happily, is not for sale.

The last stage of silver lustre is shown in Figure 228, which gives a cake or fruit basket of gray pottery ornamented with a graceful pattern covered with the lustre. The combination of the gray and silver is very pretty, while the dancing figures modelled on the panels of the vases are graceful and full of motion. These pieces are probably between fifty and sixty years old, although ware like this was made some years earlier also.

A china merchant tells me that he used to sell pieces like this when he was first in business, about 1860. He

198

Fig. 222   TEA-SET, SILVER LUSTRE

Fig. 223   TEA-SET, SILVER LUSTRE

Fig. 224 Teapots, Silver Lustre

Fig. 225 Cup, Saucer, and Candlestick

Fig. 226 SILVER LUSTRE "RESIST"

Fig. 227 SILVER LUSTRE "RESIST"

Fig. 228 GRAY POTTERY AND SILVER LUSTRE

Fig. 229 WEDGWOOD, SILVER LUSTRE

Fig. 230 a   COLLECTION OF SILVER LUSTRE

Fig. 230 b. COLLECTION OF SILVER LUSTRE

Fig. 231 ROSE OR GOLD LUSTRE JUG

Fig. 232 SUNDERLAND JUGS

Fig. 233 WEAR BRIDGE AND LUSTRE JUGS

Fig. 234   ANOTHER WEAR BRIDGE JUG

Fig. 235   MONUMENT JUG

had to work them off as best he could, since they were
"old stock." The basket shown is nine inches high and
eleven across the top. The lines showing dark on the
base and the leaves and vines about the top are of the
silver lustre, while the pendant bunches of grapes are
covered with the brown enamel. To-day the basket is
valued at $15. The day it was new it could be bought
for one-fifth of that sum.

In Figure 229 is given a pair of candlesticks by
Wedgwood, representing figures of Tritons. Many
groups, busts of children, griffins, and figures such as
the candlesticks, came from Wedgwood's potteries,
quite a large proportion of them being modelled by the
hand of the master himself. There is a note among
his records of a payment made to William Bacon, one
of the artists in his employ, for modelling a pair of
Tritons in "broun earth." These candlesticks are such
a pair, and in common with many other objects from
the Wedgwood works were lustred. 1791 is given in
Miss Metayard's "Life of Wedgwood" as the date
when silver lustre was first used in his potteries, and
these Tritons are undoubtedly "Old Wedgwood," —
i. e., made before 1795, when Josiah Wedgwood died.
They are a portion of the fine collection of pottery and
porcelain which is on exhibition at the Boston Museum
of Fine Arts.

There is a material known as "lead glass" which
bears a resemblance to silver lustre, and which has been
known to deceive the unwary. This lead glass is made
to-day, and one of its uses is as a reflector behind

bracket kerosene lamps. I have seen goblets of it, shaped like the old-fashioned communion cups, in several New England towns, and have never been able to trace their history, although their owners always assured me that they were at least one or two hundred years old!

For about seventy years — that is, since about 1830 — no important examples, nor any large quantity of silver lustre was made. Within the last three or four years, since the demand for such pieces has become marked, dishonest dealers have been found to both make and sell such forged examples. Even the novice can scarcely be deceived by these modern specimens. The colour of the lustre is dull and cloudy and darker than the bright white lustre of the old ware. Shapes are poor and no care is taken to render the specimens choice. Toby jugs, which are occasionally fitted with lids for teapots, large bowls, and goblets, and a crude pepper box in the form of a man in a cocked hat are the chief modern pieces. It is impossible to tell where this inferior modern stuff is made, but Belgium is said to be responsible for some of it. With a little care no one need be deceived by it.

Since the above was written I have seen other specimens of modern silver lustre which are being made in England. Among these new pieces may be found gourd and melon shaped teapots, and tea-sets with white china body and with spiral fluting. W. W. Slee of Leeds, who has in his employ a potter who used to work at the Old Leeds Pottery, is successfully turning

200

out tea-sets, candlesticks, tobacco jars, and small figures. Most of these are from the old Leeds models and can easily deceive the unwary. The Wedgwood firm is also experimenting in this ware, and some of Mr. Slee's specimens in lightness surpass even the old ware. Experience alone can guide the collector, and if the same shape in good condition is found in a number of shops, it would be best to avoid it, as presumably modern.

A very choice collection of silver lustre, chiefly tea and coffee pots, is shown in Figure 230. They are only a portion of what this fortunate collector owns.

The third and last metallic lustre to be considered has been made, so far as can be ascertained, in England only. It is the gold lustre, more commonly known as "rose spotted," or "Sunderland lustre," and it is quite as rare and costly as the silver lustre. The effect is obtained by precipitating gold and then applying it to the pottery either in a pattern or in spots and blotches, which vary in one from a rose colour to a purplish tint, caused by the lustre being laid on thick or diluted.

In Figure 231 is given a large gallon-sized rose-spotted jug, which relies on its good form and the delightful play of colour to make it pleasing. When I first saw this jug what a sad wreck it was! It did not have even the rudiments of a handle.

The collector who owns it now discovered it in Maine in a farmhouse, where in its dilapidated condition it had been consigned to the top shelf in the buttery.

201

When it was brought down the collector questioned what had become of the handle, and was answered, " It was thrown out." She spent an hour grubbing in dust and ashes trying to find it, but had to come away with the pitcher only. The present handle is a triumph of the restorer's art, and leads me to say that the despair of the collector of jugs is that person who insists on lifting these treasures by the handle. The person who " knows " always lifts a jug by placing one hand in the mouth of the jug and supporting the base with the other hand. This procedure shows the collector that he has nothing to fear, and is almost as welcome a sign as the " grip " among Masons.

The second jug in Figure 231 is copper lustre, about fifty years old, and of German make. Notice how entirely it differs in shape, in style of handle, and base from any of the English pieces shown. It is of a beautiful deep coppery colour, undecorated, relying on its fine glaze for ornament.

Figure 232 shows a group of Sunderland pieces, all but one in proof condition, — that is, absolutely perfect, — and all of them are interesting. The largest of the four is a gallon-size cider jug, with a view in colours of Twymouth Haven on the side shown. On the opposite side is a ship, flanked by a sailor and a female figure, while below is the following verse:

" The sailor tossed on stormy seas,
   Though far his bark may roam,
Still hears a voice in every breeze
   That wakens thoughts of home ;

202

He thinks upon his distant friends,
His wife, his humble cot ;
And from his inmost heart ascends
The prayer : ' Forget me not ! ' "

The other pitcher has a picture in colours called the
" Sailor's Farewell," with a verse which runs:

" Sweet, oh ! sweet, is that sensation,
Where two hearts in union meet,
But the pain of separation
Mingles bitter with the sweet."

I have found this sentimental verse on Sunderland
ware only, but it does duty on punch-bowls as well as
pitchers.

The little jug on feet is one of those specimens cast
in a silverware mould and then lustred. It is made of
coarse pottery, as a small chip on one foot shows.

Sunderland and Newcastle are usually classed together, and the earliest pot works at these places were
opened between 1730 and 1740.

About 1755 Mr. Byers established works at New-
castle, and in 1762 Messrs. Christopher Thompson and
John Maling erected potteries near Sunderland at
North Hylton.

In 1817 Messrs. Dawson, and also Messrs. Phillips,
opened factories at Hylton-on-Tyne, and at Sunderland and Southwick Messrs. Scott and Company built
potteries in 1789, while the Moores built there in 1803.
Early in the nineteenth century Dixon, Austin and
Company had potteries in the neighbourhood of Sunderland. The pieces made at Newcastle often bear the

names of Sewell and Donkin, or of Thomas Fell and Company.

The Newcastle and Sunderland pottery somewhat resembles Staffordshire ware, but is coarser and not so carefully finished. It has a decidedly yellowish colour, and nearly all of the subjects used for decoration have a nautical flavour, showing that they were chiefly used by sailors. There is something breezy, if rather coarse, about the drinking vessels of this ware, and we can imagine the sailors home from a cruise drinking from them and roaring out their choruses, and looking down into the mugs, so many of which had in their interiors a very naturalistic frog.

The most famous pattern ever made at these potteries was the great bridge over the Wear, begun in 1793 and finished in 1796. One of these jugs is shown in Figure 233. The other jug shown in this picture is the handsomest rose lustre jug I have ever seen. Even though the body of the pitcher is somewhat discoloured by hard usage, the picture of the ruin comes out in great beauty, the shades varying from a deep crimson to a pale pink, while over the whole plays that lustrous iridescence characteristic of gold lustre. On many jugs the patterns used were grotesque, crude in colour, and badly drawn. This design is quite charming.

Another arrangement of the Wear Bridge pattern is shown in Figure 234. This has the Bridge under the lip also, but opposite to the usual verse is a mariner's compass, flags, and nautical emblems. This is

204

also a gallon pitcher, and has considerable lustre decoration on it.

There is another class of pitchers and punch-bowls which, while they hardly come under the designation Lustre, have more or less of this decoration on them. The chief claim to interest these articles have is that many of them are more or less historic, and show scenes in our early history, or portraits of our heroes. The monument jug in Figure 235 is a sample of one style, and is a famous pitcher. It has a portrait of Washington, a design of Fame weeping beside his tomb, and several inscriptions on it. Lustre bands are at top and bottom, a pattern in lustre also surrounds the top, and even the handle has its band also. The pitchers with this design come in twelve and ten inch sizes, and are valuable specimens to own. Many variations were made of this theme; sometimes there was one portrait only, sometimes there were two, but there was always some lustre decoration.

Masonic devices were also favourite ones for jugs and mugs, some being dated as early as 1795, which, of course, adds to their value. A group of these much sought pieces is given in Figure 236, largely of Staffordshire ware, and the fine old punch-bowl in the centre has the well-known face of Franklin, surmounted by his fur cap. The English potter did not hesitate to perpetuate disastrous defeats to the British army and navy, provided these articles met with a ready sale in America, which was the best foreign market open to the potter.

205

Even when no other symbol told of our prowess the eagle screamed from many a piece, like the nice old Castleford pitcher, with pink lustre decoration, shown in Figure 237. I find many pieces with the eagle in various attitudes, sometimes grasping the thunderbolts, sometimes with the thirteen stars above or below him, but this is the only example which I have met in which he is bearing the olive branch. On the front of this jug is a beautiful monogram, also in lustre of a fine pink shade, and, judging from its excellent condition, it was carefully used. It has the pitted surface which was always to be found in Castleford ware, and a raised border surrounds the top, composed of leaves and flowers and star-like medallions.

There are hunting and guild pitchers with lustre bands on them, and frequently with borders as well, more or less ornate. On them are also scenes and devices in black or brown print, and the makers seemed to rely on the lustre bands to brighten them up.

There is much pottery and porcelain to be found here which is decorated with black or brown printed scenes, and set off with either bands of lustre or little leafy sprig decoration. Such ware is called " New Hall," and was made at Shelton, in Staffordshire, before 1825, when the works closed. Many owners of tea-sets like the cup and saucer in Figure 238 call them " New Hall " also, although the entire decoration is in lustre.

Very pretty and graceful all such sets are — plain

206

lustred decoration or with the prints. A favourite design in the printed ware is a mother reclining on a sofa and playing battledore and shuttlecock with a little girl. This picture is shown in the article on pitchers previously mentioned.

Figure 239 gives two more very handsome pitchers. The one on the left is called " Nautilus " pattern, and the design is painted on in rose lustre. The pitcher is marked " Wood," impressed. This Wood was one of the famous English potters who made so much of the " Old Blue," which is now eagerly sought. The name " Wood " alone was used as a mark between 1800 and 1818, when the sons were admitted to partnership and the signature was "E. Wood & Sons," or " E. W. & S."

The other pitcher has the main design about the body in colours, all the small details being rose lustre as well as the bands and vine designs about the top and base.

Eleven of the jugs shown belong to one collection, the indefatigable owner of which spares not herself in searching both this country and Europe. The most expensive pitcher of the eleven was the large one showing Twymouth Haven, bought in Maine, for which $6 was paid.

The cheapest was the little one on four legs shown in the same picture. This was bought for a quarter. All the others came in between these two extremes, even the beautiful silver lustre " resist " jug, with its graceful design of tulips and leaf pattern.

207

I mention these prices to encourage would-be collectors and to show how much can be done by one who has time, some money and, most important of all, " china luck " — a quality born with its possessor, next to impossible to acquire.

IX — OLD–FASHIONED TIMEPIECES

INSTRUMENTS for marking time may be included under a few great heads: sun-dials, hour-glasses, and clocks.

The origin of the earliest time-keeping device is lost in antiquity, but among the first clocks composed of an assemblage of wheels, of which there is no doubt as to age, are the clock in St. Paul's Cathedral, London, which was put up in 1286; one at Canterbury Cathedral, 1292; one at Exeter, 1300; and one in the Palace yard, London, of about the same period. All these were in England, but Froisart speak of one at Courtrai, France, which was taken to Dijon by Philip, Duke of Burgundy, in 1370.

Viollet le Duc remarks that from the twelfth to the fourteenth century no space was arranged in church towers for dial plates. Still there were clocks in many towers, but they were without dials, and only struck the hours, the act of striking often being performed by a wooden figure, several feet tall, which beat upon a metal bell.

During the fourteenth century clocks with various mechanical devices became popular; puppets were arranged to perform little scenes at the hours, like " The Mystery of the Resurrection," " Death," etc. Nor was

14

209

skill in clock-making confined to England and France. Saladin, of Egypt, in 1232 presented to Frederick II of Germany a clock run by weights and wheels, showing figures which represented the sun, moon, and other planets and the twelve signs of the Zodiac. In 1358, in the palace of Abu Hammou, Sultan of Thencen, was a clock ornamented with figures carved from solid silver.

The first of the celebrated Strasburg clocks, which were placed in the Cathedral there, was begun in 1350. From that time to the present there has been no interruption in the wonderful mechanical clocks which have been made in various countries.

One of the strangest of all clocks is the "Resurrection" clock in India. It has no dial, a gong being suspended in its place. Beneath this gong lie scattered on the ground skulls and bones enough to form twelve complete skeletons. At one o'clock the number of bones needed to form one entire skeleton come together with a snap; the skeleton springs up, seizes a mallet, and strikes the gong one blow. This done, it returns to the pile and again falls to pieces. When it is two o'clock, two skeletons strike two. At the hours of noon and midnight, the entire twelve spring up and strike, each one after the other, a blow on the gong, and then fall to pieces as before.

In the charming, old, mediæval city of Rouen in France, time seems to move more slowly than in many other places. Still, as long as one does not live there, it is sad to see the narrow streets without sidewalks,

210

traversed by a gutter in the centre, being replaced by the ordinary walks which while comfortable are far less picturesque, and necessitate the pulling down of many curious old buildings, past which, no doubt, the lovely Agnes Sorel and poor Joan of Arc once passed. In this same city, in the cathedral, is buried the heart of Richard Coeur de Lion, and some of his companions lie near him. One of the most famous streets is called Rue de la Grosse Horloge, and it is still most picturesque. The clock which gave it its name is shown in Figure 240, and is placed in a round-arched gateway surmounted by a tower, which it is said was finished in 1527, and was not the first structure which held the clock. The clock was made by Jehan de Féalins in 1389. It has been carefully looked after, and with some slight modern modifications is still an excellent timekeeper. It shows the hours, the days of the week, and the phases of the moon. The handsome dial is about six feet square, and surrounded by a circle of fine ornament. It is still the chief clock of the city, nothing modern having been allowed to usurp its place.

Even uncivilised nations have ways of telling time, some of them quite elaborate, and in the flowery islands of the South Pacific, they use means which Nature sets ready at their hands, and make a time-marker by taking the kernels from the nuts of the candle-tree and washing and stringing them on to the rib of a palm leaf. The first or top kernel is then lighted. All the kernels, being of the same size and substance, burn a certain number of minutes, and then set fire to the next one below. The

natives tie pieces of bark cloth at regular intervals along
the string to mark the division of time.

More like the hour-glass is a device which is used by
the natives of Singar, in the Malay Archipelago, who
make use of a peculiar device; two bottles are placed
neck and neck, and sand is put in one of them, which
pours itself into the other every half hour, when the
bottles are reversed. There is a line near, on which are
hung twelve rods, marked with notches from one to
twelve. A regularly appointed keeper attends to the
bottles and rods, and sounds the hour upon a gong.

Passing from these primitive constructions to some of
the wonders of modern clock-making, one may marvel
at the great clock at St. Petersburg, which has ninety-
five faces. It indicates simultaneously the time of day
at thirty places on the earth's surface, besides the movement of the earth around the sun, the phases of the
moon, the signs of the Zodiac, the passage over the
meridian of more than fifty stars of the northern hemi-
sphere, and the date, according to the Gregorian, Greek,
Hebrew, and Mussulman calendars. It is said that it
took over two years to put the works together, and get
them into running order.

Notwithstanding their bulkiness there are more collectors of clocks than one would at first imagine. It
is probable, however, that King Edward has the greatest number in any one collection, either public or private, since at Windsor alone there are over five hundred,
and he has in all about two thousand. They are all
carefully inventoried in many great volumes, which are

in the care of the Lord Chamberlain's department, and this department is also responsible for the care of the collection.

The collecting of clocks seems to be a royal hobby, since Louis XIV, Louis XVI, Queen Victoria, and King Edward all have had it. Indeed King Edward's most valuable clocks came to him by inheritance from his mother, and, perhaps, of them all the one which has the greatest "human interest" attached to it is the one which belonged to the unfortunate Anne Boleyn. This clock, which was given to her on her wedding day by Henry VIII, is a small affair, — four inches deep and ten inches high. It has passed through several hands since the beheading of poor Anne, the last to own it before Queen Victoria being that prince of collectors, Horace Walpole. It was bidden in at the sale of his effects for the queen, for about six hundred dollars. After four centuries it still goes, though she for whom it was made was permitted but four years in which to enjoy it. The weights are beautifully engraved with "H. A." with a true-lover's knot on one, and the initials only on the other. Did the Bluebeard Henry ever call Anne to mind when he heard it strike? Perhaps it was not a striking clock after all, which must have been comfortable for him. It is of the style known as "bird-cage," and stands on an ornamental shelf.

The greatest curiosity in the King's collection is at Buckingham Palace, and is a clock made by Lepine, a *protégé* of Voltaire, and is made in the shape of a

213

negress' head. In this clock the hours are shown in one of the eyes of the negress and the minutes in the other. The figure is two feet and a half high, of ormolu, richly decorated.

He has also several clocks by Lepaute, a celebrated French clockmaker, born in 1709, and died in 1789. He improved the pin-wheel escapement by putting pins on both sides of the wheel, and he was also noted for his turret clocks, of which he erected five for the Louvre alone. They were wound by means of an air-current and a fan, a method which has been recently revived. Many of his clocks were put into superb ormolu cases, and one of these is shown in Figure 241 and is dated 1760. It is seven feet twenty-six inches tall, and, besides the rich inlay and metal mounts, has on the top a charming figure, and it may be seen that the clocks of that period assumed almost the colossal proportions of the beds.

The clocks in which we are chiefly interested are those for household use, and the earliest which we had came from England. By 1600 there were clocks made for a moderate price, and for the use of the average householder. These clocks were known by the names " bird-cage," "lantern," or "bed-post" clocks. They were put on shelves or brackets attached to the wall, and were wound by pulling down the opposite ends of ropes on which the weights were hung. Some of these were striking clocks; others were furnished with an alarm, and none of them was expected to run for more than thirty hours.

214

Fig. 236 COLLECTION OF JUGS

Fig. 237   CASTLEFORD JUG

Fig. 238   "NEW HALL" WARE

Fig. 239   JUGS WITH LUSTRE DECORATION

Fig. 240 Old Clock at Rouen

Fig. 241 Clock by Lepaute   Fig. 242 "Bird-Cage" Clock

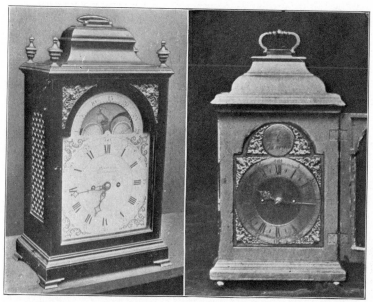

Fig. 243 BRACKET CLOCK   Fig. 244 ANOTHER BRACKET CLOCK

Fig. 245 SPANDRELS

Fig. 246
JOHN HANCOCK'S CLOCK

Fig. 247
GEORGE WASHINGTON'S CLOCK

Figs. 248–250 ENGLISH AND AMERICAN CLOCKS

Fig. 251 DWARF CLOCK   Fig. 252 CLOCK WITH WOODEN WORKS

Samuel Pepys mentions in his diary such a clock belonging to Catherine of Braganza in 1664. He says:

" Mr. Pierce showed me the Queen's (the Portuguese Princess, wife of Charles II) bedchamber . . . and her holy water at her head as she sleeps, with a clock at her bedside, wherein a lamp burns that tells her the time of the night at any time."

In fact small portable clocks were mentioned nearly two hundred years earlier than Pepys' note, and in the " Paston Letters," which are such valuable repositories, I take the following extract. The letter is from Sir John Paston, and is dated 1469:

" I praye you speke wt Harcourt off the Abbeye ffor a lytell clokke whyche I sent him by James Gressham to amend and yt ye woll get it off him an it be redy, and send it me, and as ffor mony ffor his labour, he hath another clok of myn whiche St. Thoms Lyndes, God have hys soule, gave me. He maye kepe that tyll I paye him. This clok is my Lordys Archebysshopis but late hym not wote of it."

The form was doubtless similar to the bird-cage clocks, though it is known that some of the early clocks had revolving dials. In the South Kensington Museum there is on an inlaid wooden panel the representation of a clock with a revolving ring, on which the twenty-four hours are marked, the current hour being indicated by a pointer. The date of the panel is certainly not later than 1500, and of course the date of the clock is older. In 1544 the Master Clockmakers of Paris were incorporated by statute, and, in 1627, a proposal to grant letters patent to allow French clockmakers to

215

carry on their trade in London, caused such an agitation in London, that a committee of clockmakers was formed, and a petition for a charter was presented to Charles I, which he granted on the 22d of August, 1631.

The pendulum, which was introduced about 1661, superseded the balance. The first form was known as the "bob pendulum," which by 1680 was followed by the "royal" or long pendulum. The clocks of the lantern or bird-cage variety were small, ranging in size from three and one-half inches to five inches square. One of unusual size was eight and one-half inches by sixteen inches high. The rounded top seen in Figure 242 is the bell upon which the hours are struck; and one peculiarity of these clocks is that the dial face often projects an inch or two beyond the sides of the frame. They are not uncommon in England yet, for they were made continuously till about 1825, and as the works are of brass and well made, they are excellent timekeepers. The little ornaments which stand up in front of the clock are known as "frets," and they are quite a sure indication of when the clock was made. The design of crossed dolphins came into use about 1650, and was a favourite pattern; and there were other frets, generally of geometric design, which also became well known.

Another style in use about this period was known as the "bracket" clock, and these clocks had either the handle on top, like that in Figure 243, or on the sides. Such clocks as these were luxuries, however, and cost what would be equivalent to seven hundred dollars.

There are records showing that a popular clockmaker of the period, Henry Jones, of Inner Temple Gate, London, charged £150 for a similar clock which he furnished to Charles II in 1673. This style of clock continued in use for one hundred years and more, and with them the fret, which was now placed in the corners of the dial plate, became, as in the lantern clocks, indicative of their age.

A fine example of the bracket clock is shown in Figure 244, and is owned in White Plains, New York. It shows that it is a veteran, but it still goes, and it has beautiful spandrels and an engraved face. It has been in the possession of the family for over one hundred years, and in the upper circle has, in black enamel, William Buttock, Bradford. The spandrels or brass ornaments in the corners of the face point to the first half of the eighteenth century, as being the time when it was made. The case is of mahogany and there are brass screens at the sides to permit the sound of the striking to be distinctly heard. This clock is very similar to one at Windsor Castle, made by Justin Vulliamy, who came from Switzerland and settled in London in 1730. He became noted for the beauty and accuracy of his timepieces, and was appointed clockmaker to the King during the reign of George II. The succeeding members of the family held this office in the different reigns till the death of Benjamin Lewis Vulliamy in 1854. Specimens of his work abound in the royal palaces, and many of the clocks of Queen Victoria that were in active service were by him. In the presence chamber was one of them set into

217

a splendid piece of white marble sculpture by J. Bacon, R.A., which was made in 1790. Under the clock on a marble shield is an inscription by Cowper:

" Slow comes the hour, its passing speed how great!
Waiting to seize it — Vigilantly wait."

The long-case or " grandfather " clocks were developed from the brass chamber clock with a wooden hood, which had to be entirely removed before the clock could be wound. Cockscrew or twisted pillars at each corner of the hood were characteristic of this period and that of Queen Anne, and frequently the cases were splendidly decorated with marquetry, which was the work of some of the numerous Dutch cabinet-makers at that time settled in England. Many of the early tall clocks were very narrow in the waist part, where the weights and pendulum hung, and the swing of the pendulum was allowed for by the addition of " wings " or extra width in the case at the sides.

There were many variations of the hour circles on the dial. Before the minute hand came into use there were double circles where the numerals were, dividing the hours into quarters, the half hours being indicated by an ornament of extra length, like an arrow-head or fleur-de-lis. The engraving on clock faces and on the brass plates at the back was very beautiful, and artists were frequently employed to make them. Borders, intricate rings about the winding holes, birds and flowers, were all introduced into the decoration, and the spandrels or ornaments at the corners still further ornamented them.

218

On many of the clocks of the seventeenth century the maker's name will be found engraved on the edge of the dial plate below the circle with the numerals. Later it was engraved on the dial plate between the figures V and VII. Sometimes two names are found, particularly in the earliest clocks, and in this case the name engraved in the centre of the dial surrounding the hands is the name of the maker, while the name at the foot of the dial is the name of the seller of the clock.

Some of the most famous English clockmakers were: Bartholomew Newsam, who was established in London as early as 1568; Rainulph Bull, keeper of His Majesty's great clock in 1617; Ferdinando Garrett, a working clockmaker, in 1600; William North, in 1615; Thomas Alcock, in 1661; and Daniel Ramsay, in 1610. The Clockmaker's Company was chartered in 1631, and was a trade guild for protecting the trade in London, or within ten miles thereof. Edward East, one of the most noted of English makers, was at work by 1620, and became watchmaker to Charles I. Henry Jones was at the height of his fame about 1673, and Samuel Betts about 1640. Thomas Tompion, known as the " Father of English watchmaking," had by 1658 attained much renown. He was succeeded by Daniel Quare, who had a shop at St. Martin's le Grand, London, in 1676. Then came George Graham, an apprentice of Tompion, and much beloved by him, and who succeeded to his business in 1713.

As I have said, the spandrels or corner ornaments are important indications of the age of a clock. Very early dials have a line of verse in the corners, like the following:

> " Behold this hand,
>> Observe ye motion tip;
> Man's precious hours
>> Away like these do slip."

The clock from which this rhyme was taken is dated 1681, and was made by John Ogden, Bowbrigg, England. Then came the angels' heads, which design was later elaborated; then two cupids holding a crown, which lasted through the reign of Queen Anne. After this came the Rococo during the eighteenth century, and then the period of George III, where the design became degenerate, and the spandrels were cast, without even being retouched with a chasing tool.

Drawings of spandrels are shown in the next figure, number 245, and from them the approximate date of the clock can be told.

Oak has always been a favourite material for the cases, and walnut, both inlaid and plain, was particularly favoured from about 1675 to 1725. Very elegant cases of Dutch marquetry were made as early as 1665, and specimens of Oriental lacquer were by no means unusual from 1740 onward. From 1750, when Chippendale began to work and design, mahogany, both solid and veneered, became popular, and has continued so ever since.

The clock shown in Figure 246, besides being remarkably elegant in its case of Oriental lacquer, has an interesting history as well. It was imported from London in 1738 by Thomas Hancock, and then descended by inheritance to John Hancock. It was made by Marmaduke Storr, foot of London Bridge, who was a famous maker in his day. The order reads that the clock was to be ten feet long, "the price 15 not to exceed 20 Guineas, and as it is for my own use, I beg your particular care in buying of it at the Cheapest Rate. I am advised to apply to one Mr. Marmaduke Storr, at the foot of London Bridge."

Another interesting timepiece is shown in the following Figure 247, as this clock belonged to George Washington. It was made by the well-known Frenchman, Lepine, and is a curious looking affair. It was wound at the back, for there are no keyholes on the face, and the keys may be seen lying on the stand. It was covered with a glass case, is made of brass, and has a handsome brass engraved wreath about the dial. It is now in the National Museum at Washington. It must have been a good timekeeper for one of General Washington's characteristics was promptness. He gave away more than one watch to his friends as keepsakes. One of these is now to be seen among the half-buried treasures at the New York Historical Society. The watch is of gold, with a clearly marked dial, and on the back is this inscription: " Trenton, N. J., Dec. 10, 1777. Presented to my friend Colonel Thomas Johnson, of Md. as a memento of my great esteem. Geo. Washington."

That Colonel Johnson and his descendants made good use of this gift is plainly visible from the scratched

221

condition of the dial around the keyhole; but the case is in good order, showing the inscription very plainly.

Another famous man, Napoleon Bonaparte, was almost as punctual as General Washington. It has often been told that he had the power of going to sleep at any time when it was convenient, and that he could wake at any given moment. Only recently has it been discovered that he depended on a little alarm clock. This was found among the effects of the Princess Mathilde, who died recently, and who was his niece. The clock was made by Abraham Bréguet, a Frenchman of rare attainments and inventive power, and the most famous clockmaker of his time. This clock, so evidence shows, was carried by Napoleon on his campaigns. The case is of gilded bronze, richly engraved. There are eight dials, indicating the true time, mean time, phases of the moon, seconds, minutes, hours, days and months, and date of the year.

It strikes the hours and the quarters, and has a small metallic thermometer attached to it. Bréguet also made for Napoleon a self-winding watch on the principle of the pedometer, but whether on his own invention or that of Recordon's patent is not established.

But long before this there were many watches and clocks in this country, though I doubt if anything but sun-dials, portable or stationary, and perhaps a watch or two, found their way over here in the first ship loads. A post in the ground gave the noon-mark with sufficient accuracy, and as for the hours of the rest of the day, they could be guessed nearly enough. By 1628, however, one Joseph Stratton, of the Massachusetts Colony, had both a clock and a watch; and Henry Parks, of Hartford, who died in 1640, left by will to his church a clock.

In inventories before 1677 I find many records of "striking clocks," "watches," and also "larums." These early clocks must have been of the bird-cage or lantern variety, though some large clocks seem to have found their way over here. In October, 1688, "ye 4th year of the Reigne of our Sovereign Lord, King James the second," a commission was appointed to examine into the condition of the Fort at New York. The report is long and interesting. They discover that the Fort and "Stockadoes" are in a ruinous condition and need many repairs. In a room over "ye Guard are cabbins and a standyn bed stead with two Albany beds." There is a "great old clock in ye Armourer's room." There are many other items of interest in this report, but they cannot be given here.

Joseph West, of New York, in an inventory dated May 6, 1691, leaves, among other items of value, to his "loving kinsman Edward Hastings, of Shipton, in Oxfordshire, Gentleman, my Diamond watch, one hundred pounds, and thirty French pistoles in gold."

The word "clock" was not applied as we now use it till the time of James I, but horologue was what the clock was called. "Clock" referred only to the bell upon which the hour was struck. Even at the present day a church or other large public clock is called horo-

223

logue, and in remote parts of England the name clings
to the ordinary household timepiece.

The first pendulums in long-case clocks were thirty-
nine inches long, and that style known as the "grid-
iron" is still used in many foreign regulators. This
pendulum was invented by John Harrison, about 1728,
and was composed of nine parallel rods, five of steel
and four of brass, fastened together by frames, by
which the effects of heat and cold acting on the pendulum were neutralised by the different expansion of
the two metals.

After such elaborate timepieces began to find their
way over here repairs had to be made, and by 1712
there were clockmakers prepared to either make or
keep in order any kind of clock or watch.

In old newspapers like the "Boston News Letter"
there are advertisements like this of a man who "performed all sorts of new Clocks and Watch works, viz.:
30 hour clocks, week clocks, month clocks, Spring table
clocks, chime clocks, quarter clocks, quarter chime
clocks, Terret clocks, etc." A few years later, in 1716,
there were advertised "lately come from London, a
Parcel of very Fine Clocks. They go a week and
repeat the hour when Pull'd. In Japan cases or Wall
Nutt."

The long-case clocks of early manufacture had a
square face to the dial. Then the top of the clock-case
and the top of the dial rose in an arch; and above the
dial were inserted the phases of the moon, moving
figures such as ships in motion, Father Time, etc., the

224

moving figures being preferred by the Dutch makers, who were very proficient in this style of work.

Two clocks are shown in Figures 248 and 249. The first is of English make, the second American, and both are of about the same age, being made about 1800. Figure 248 has brass works, and solid mahogany case decorated with lines of inlay. The phases of the moon and days of the month are shown above the painted face, and the clock is in fine condition and an excellent timekeeper. There is no name upon it anywhere, and its history is obscure; but some of the details are that the clock was brought from England in 1810, was owned in Hingham, Massachusetts, then changed hands and was taken to Cambridge, Massachusetts, and now belongs to a collector in Montpelier, Vermont.

Figure 249 has on its face the name Luther Smith, Keene, New Hampshire. This is no indication that he made the clock, since it was the custom, if the owner desired it, to paint his name on the face of the clock. This face is very prettily painted with flowers and medallions, and the brass hands are beautifully pierced. Like its English mate it shows the phases of the moon and days of the month. Its case, too, is solid mahogany, without inlay, however, but the brass mounts on the pillars of the case are unusually handsome, and the pillars themselves as well as those on the hood are fluted.

Another American-made clock is shown in Figure 250. The top is unusual from its plainness, the only ornamentation being the slender turned pillars. This clock is marked, " Owen, Philadelphia." The face is painted prettily, the case mahogany, some of it veneered, and the phases of the moon are shown above the dial. It is still a good timekeeper, and has a very agreeable striking tone for the hours, halves, and quarters.

A variation from the grandfather's clock was the same shape in miniature. Such a clock is shown in Figure 251. It is not four feet tall, and such a specimen in a marquetry case is not often found. It was discovered in an attic in Rhode Island, where it had lain undisturbed for forty years or more, waiting for a fortunate collector. It has a painted face and wooden works, and has no maker's name. I have never seen more than six or eight of these little grandfather clocks, and it seems strange that more old clocks did not survive, since in " Historical Collections of Connecticut " it is stated that in 1836, at Bristol, Connecticut, there were sixteen clock factories at work, making one hundred thousand clocks, with brass or wooden works, each year.

In Figure 252 is a clock with a wooden face, painted with flowers, and with wooden works also. It is wound by pulling the weights, and is even yet an excellent timekeeper. It is supposed to have been made about 1800 or during the next ten years. The fine case is mahogany with satinwood inlay, and the only blemish is that the ornaments for the top are missing.

The clockmakers of the United States have contributed many valuable inventions to the science of clockmaking, the most important being steel springs which could be produced at a low price, and thus enable the production of cheap clocks. Another invention was the pendulum covered with goldleaf, which is a necessary part of a regulator clock, and which was made by Silas B. Terry, a son of Eli Terry, of Windsor, Connecticut, who was one of the early makers of American clocks.

James Harrison was another early maker, and the first clock he made was sold January 1, 1791, for £3 12s. 8d. This was at Waterbury, Connecticut, a town which still continues to be a centre for the watch and clockmaking business. In 1783 a patent was awarded to Benjamin Hanks, of Litchfield, Connecticut, to run fourteen years, for a self-winding clock. The Eli Terry previously mentioned started at Plymouth, Connecticut, in 1793, and made his first clock with a brass dial, silver washed. His tall case clocks were very often sold without the cases, which were made by local cabinet-makers or carpenters.

East Windsor was another clockmaking town in Connecticut, and here Daniel Burnap carried on the manufacture of clocks with brass works. William Tenny also began at an early date to make clocks with brass works, and he was established at Nine Corners, Dutchess County, New York. Eli Terry's earliest clocks were made with wooden works and long cases with royal pendulums. A clock was an expensive item in those days, the prices ranging from $18 to $48 and $70. The highest priced ones had brass faces and works, and a dial for the seconds, the moon's phases, and a fine wooden case. The distribution of clocks during these stage-coach days was intrusted to pedlars, who carried them into even remote regions. This was the reason why many of them were sold without cases, as they were too bulky to carry great distances.

Some of the best known clockmakers prior to 1800 were Daniel Burnap, James Harrison, Silas Merriam, Thomas Harland, and Timothy Peck. During the next fifteen years the number of clockmakers increased rapidly, and Seth Thomas, the Willards, Silas Hoadley, Herman Clark, and Asa Hopkins were well-known manufacturers. It was Terry who invented the mantel or "short shelf clock," as it was called, in 1814. The pendulum was shortened, the weights made smaller and run on each side, and the works placed in a more compact form. At first the works of these clocks were wooden; but when rolled brass was invented, and wheels could be struck out with machinery and the teeth afterward cut, also by machine, it became less expensive to make the brass clocks than the wooden; but this was not till about 1837.

In Figure 253 is shown a very handsome mantel clock, made with brass works which run eight days, and in an unusually choice rosewood case. The two sets of doors with paintings on them is not a common feature, and with the side pillars of polished wood with their large brass tops it makes a fine example of this style of clock. The pictures, although not named, seem to be a view of Mount Vernon and the "Constitution and Guerriere," both of them favourite subjects for patriotic

Americans. One of the best known names among the clockmaking fraternity during the first half of the nineteenth century was Willard, and they manufactured a style of clock which was generally called by their name, the term "banjo" being of comparatively recent origin.

The Willards, for there were four of them at least, — Simon, Aaron, Benjamin, and Simon, junior, — were natives of New England, and Benjamin, who had workshops at Roxbury, Boston, and Grafton, took out patents for his inventions as early as 1802. Terry was a great rival of the Willards, and increased his business by using water-power, so that he flooded the market with clocks, and the price went down to $10. This was in the year 1807, when Terry made five hundred clocks. In 1814 he introduced the short shelf clock or mantel clock, of which another variety is shown in Figure 254.

In this example the wood is richly carved and has an eagle on the top, a fitting emblem to go with the portrait below, which is a much finer painting on glass than is usually met with, and to which the photograph does not do justice. Inside the case of this clock is pasted a paper which reads as follows:

PATENT CLOCKS.

Patented by Eli Terry

And made and sold by Seth Thomas,
Bristol, Conn. Warranted if well used.

There was almost always one of these papers in these mantel clocks, but few of them are dated, a great mis-

take as we think who would like so much to know just
how old our treasures are. Another style of paper runs
like this:

Patent clocks invented by Eli Terry,

Plymouth, Conn.

Warranted if well used.

N. B. — The public may be assured that this kind of clock
will run as long without repairs and be as durable and accurate
for keeping time as any kind of clock whatever.

A Willard or "banjo" clock is shown in Figure 255.
The case is mahogany with inlay of satinwood round
the door. The ornaments on top and sides are brass,
the face is covered with a convex glass, and there is but
one keyhole, these clocks generally being made without
a striking attachment.

Another and very similar clock is shown in the next
illustration, Figure 256, and this one has on the lower
part of the case the name Willard. It also has but one
winding hole, and is part of the Waters collection at
Salem, Massachusetts. There are many of these clocks
to be had; and so well were they made that even yet
they are admirable timekeepers.

The very fine clock which is shown in the next illustration, Figure 257, seems a variation of the banjo
design, and this case is also mahogany, handsomely
carved. There is no name of the maker on the clock, but
inside the door is a record of repairs. The first of these
is dated 1808, showing that the clock must have been
made some years previously. It has a striking as well

230

Fig. 253 MANTEL CLOCK   Fig. 254 MANTEL CLOCK

Fig. 255 Banjo Clock   Fig. 256 "Willard" Clock   Fig. 257 Lyre Clock

Fig. 258 Empire Clock   Fig. 259 Forestville Clock

Fig. 260 Swiss Clock

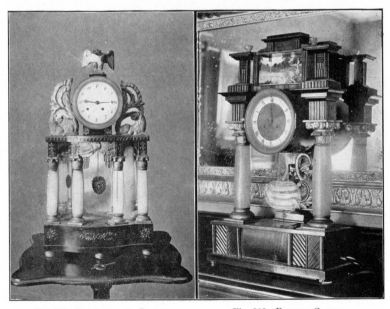

Fig. 261 Bonaparte's Clock   Fig. 262 Empire Clock

Fig. 263 Flat-top Bible Box

Fig. 264 Slant-top Bible Box

Fig. 266 SLANT-TOP DESK, WALNUT

Fig. 265 SLANT-TOP DESK

Fig. 267   GENERAL PUTNAM'S DESK

Fig. 269 DESK ON LEGS, OPEN

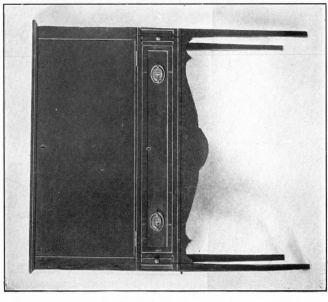

Fig. 268 DESK ON LEGS, CLOSED

as a winding keyhole. It tends somewhat towards the lyre shape which was so much affected by Sheraton in his chair backs, and may have been made about 1800.

Another clock, probably of the same period, is shown in the next Figure, 258. It has a fine mahogany case with Empire decorations on it in gilt. The large dial is clearly marked, and there is but one winding hole. It has an uncommonly long pendulum for a clock of this style, but keeps excellent time.

In Figure 259 is shown an odd clock, made by the Forestville Manufacturing Company, of Bristol, Connecticut. It has a rosewood case, and is even more " banjo " than the banjo clocks of the Willards. It has a view of the Merchants' Exchange, Philadelphia, which was probably taken from one of Child's engravings, published in 1829. The dial is very clear, and there is handsome inlay on the upper part of the case. It has brass works, an eight-day movement, and the posts which support the case are tipped with a carved acorn, making in all a very handsome and unique clock.

A quaint little clock in an inlaid case, which is about a hundred years old, is shown in Figure 260. It is of Swiss manufacture, has brass works, and keeps time perfectly. It strikes not only at the hour but at the quarter-hour divisions, all except the hours being given in two tones. Like the older bracket clocks it has little screens at the sides to allow the sound to escape, and, as may be seen, it has quite ornate hour and minute hands.

There are to be found, also, in various parts of the country, French clocks of elegant design and workmanship. Many of these are covered with glass shades to protect them from the dust, and most of them are inlaid or have elaborate carved or alabaster pillars and fine gilt mounts. A very splendid example is given in Figure 261, and the clock has an interesting history. At first sight the eagle at the top would seem to indicate that the clock was for an American, but this is not a Republican but an Imperial eagle. The clock belonged to Jerome Bonaparte, and was brought by him to this country when he came in 1803. After these many years the clock is to be found at the rooms of the Antiquarian Society in Concord, Massachusetts, where it is surrounded by other relics of equal age but more democratic extraction.

The Empire clock shown in Figure 262 is almost a finer specimen than the one which belonged to Jerome Bonaparte. It is certainly in better proportion. As you may see, this one is still filling its function, the cloud about the pendulum showing that it was in motion when the picture was being taken. The alabaster columns are very ornamental, and all the brass work is of the highest order. Sometimes the pendulums of these clocks were in the form of a many-pointed star, and in addition were finely engraved.

America, as I have said already, has done much for the improvement of timepieces. And one can but smile at our eagerness to excel as far as in us lies. We cannot have the oldest things in the world, but we can have the biggest, and we do. For many years the clock with the largest faces in the world was that in the Westminster

232

Tower, London. We were not content to have it so, and finally a clock was built in Minneapolis which exceeded the London clock in size by two inches, the dial faces of both clocks exceeding twenty feet. But even this was not enough, so a bigger one was built, and is now in the tower of the City Hall, Philadelphia. Its bell weighs more than twenty thousand pounds, and the dial is twenty-five feet in diameter, and the hour hand is nine feet long!

X—DESKS AND SECRETARIES

BEFORE the invention of printing (about the last half of the fourteenth century) books of every kind — school-books, medical and cooking receipts, as well as all public and private documents — were written by hand. The copyist was a man of importance, who had a lucrative employment. Even the monasteries had an office, called a " scriptorium," where missals, prayer-books, and other holy works were copied and illuminated; and from these works a substantial income was received, since no document or volume was approved unless it had ornamented or decorative initials and capitals. This work was done upon tables or standing-desks attached to the wall, while in private houses there were few enough of even such conveniences.

In 1459 Margaret Paston, of Norwich, England, was having her husband's room rearranged during his absence, according to his directions. She writes to him about it, saying,

" I have taken the measure in the drawte chamber there, as ye would your coffers and your cowsatewery (desk) should be set for the while, and there is no space beside the bed for to sett both your board and coffers there, and have space to go and sit beside."

234

This desk seems to have been in the nature of a table, but the common desk of an early period was a small box which locked and could be carried about when travelling. We can imagine that the earliest comers to this country did not hamper themselves much by bringing even such simple affairs as these, though, in addition to their being used for writing on, they were called on as strong boxes for papers and gold, and in many cases were furnished with a till.

The greatest treasure they were used to protect was a copy of the Bible, and they were often called "Bible boxes" from this fact. One of these old boxes, made of native oak, carved in low relief in a pattern of tulips, is shown in Figure 263; the lid, which is of deal, has but a moderate slant, and the box contains a till. It is not dated, but belongs to a period between 1650 and 1675.

Another of these rare old Bible boxes is seen in Figure 264. This has a slanting lid, is made of oak, and has rude carving on the front and base. It is dated 1651, and has the initials of its owner, A. W., on the centre of the front. The old iron hinges show on the top, and, in view of its age, the box is in an excellent state of repair. This box is twenty inches long and thirteen inches high. It once had a small shelf at the back.

The term "desk" occurs with extreme rarity in the old inventories, and even so refers to these box-like desks with either a flat or sloping top. By 1700 writing-tables were in use in Europe, and the French "scrutor," as it was most often called, began to be found over here.

235

The combination of drawers with a desk top was one of the early forms taken by this useful piece of furniture, and by as early as 1710 such desks were found here, both of domestic and foreign make.

When we take into consideration the activity of every maker and designer of furniture to publish a book containing his ideas, we are not surprised that so many pieces resembling English work are to be found here, and were the product of our native cabinet-makers. As early as 1739 works more or less valuable were being constantly presented to the public, and perhaps William Jones, when he published his "Gentleman's or Builder's Companion," in 1739, could call himself the pioneer in this line, in England.

I am tempted to give the titles of some of the most valuable of these English books since I have received inquiries where such may be found. Not in this country, except in some cases as reprints, save in the cabinet of the collector of rare works. Yet some may be stowed away, their value quite unappreciated. An undated but early volume was brought out by the Society of Upholsterers and Cabinetmakers, and they called it by the high sounding title of "One Hundred New and Genteel Designs, being all the most approved Patterns of Household Furniture in the present Taste."

Then came William Kent, who not only laid out the gardens of the nobility, but published a book in 1744 in which he discussed furniture, and gave designs for tables, chairs, candlesticks, and mirror frames, and even for styles in dress. In 1750 William Halfpenny pub-

lished his " New Designs for Chinese Temples, etc.,"
which meant summer-houses in Chinese taste, and which
book also gave his ideas on furniture.   Then appeared
Chippendale's first edition of " The Gentleman and
Cabinetmaker's Director, being a large Collection of
the Most Elegant and Useful Designs of Household
Furniture in the Gothic, Chinese, and Modern Taste."
This edition was published in 1754, and there was another edition in 1759, and a third in 1762.

Thomas Johnson, a carver, came next with designs
for picture frames, candelabra, ceilings, clock-cases,
etc., which came out first in parts, and then was bound
up.   This was in 1758.   In 1761 he published another
book, called " One Hundred and Fifty New Designs,"
many of which were wildly rococo.

Copeland and Lock brought out sets of plates and
some small publications between 1752 and 1769.   " A
New Book of Pier Frames, Ovals, Girandoles, Tables,"
was brought out in 1769 by Matthias Lock, and has in
it many of the long-billed birds which we are so prone
to call Chippendale.   Edwards and Darley made their
contribution in 1754, and Robert Mainwaring, in 1765,
published what he was pleased to call " The Cabinet
and Chairmaker's Real Friend and Companion."   Mainwaring, although his name has no importance now,
exerted quite an influence upon the cabinet-makers of
his day, and his book had a large sale.   While the charge
is brought against him that he copied from Chippendale, it might be more just to say that they both drew
from the same sources, but that Chippendale improved

237

on his models, while Mainwaring but accentuated their faults.

Ince and Mayhew, about 1770, gave to the world "The Universal System of Household Furniture," which was more florid than Chippendale's most fanciful designs. Their book contained three hundred designs. N. Wallis, 1772, published "The Complete Modern Joiner"; Thomas Crunden, 1765, "The Joyner and Cabinetmaker's Darling," 1770, "The Carpenter's Companion for Chinese Railings and Gates," 1776, "The Chimney-piece Maker's Daily Assistant."

Hepplewhite and Thomas Shearer with some others brought out in 1788, "The Cabinetmaker's London Book of Prices," and Hepplewhite and, after him, his widow brought out, "The Cabinetmaker and Upholsterer's Guide or Repository of Designs for every Article of Household Furniture." There were editions in 1788–1789 and 1794. Last of all came Thomas Sheraton, the most refined of all the great makers and designers. His books were called, "The Cabinetmaker and Upholsterer's Drawing-book" published, 1791, 1793, 1794. The "Cabinet Dictionary" came out in 1803, and the "Cabinetmaker, Upholsterer, and General Artists' Encyclopædia," from 1804 to 1807.

Books dealing with the subject of cabinet-making and joinery were published late in the eighteenth century, by William Pain. Some of them were, "The British Palladio," "The Carpenter's Pocket Dictionary," "The Carpenter's and Joiner's Repository." There were also several others.

238

Robert and James Adam also belong to this period, and though their avowed calling was that of Architecture, the " Adam Style," as it was called, had a great influence on furniture makers of the time. For their own houses and those that they remodelled, the Adams designed the furniture. This family was a great factor throughout the entire eighteenth century. The father, William Adam, designed and remodelled many Scottish mansions, for he was known by the high-sounding title of " Master Mason of Scotland." His four sons followed his profession, and of these the best known and most distinguished were Robert and James. Their most important books were " Works in Architecture by Robert and James Adam, Squires," which came out in parts from 1773 till 1778. To them we are indebted for the introduction of satinwood as a material for furniture and inlaying, and for a certain classical style of ornament which they rendered in a purer form than their contemporaries. They used in their ornaments octagons, ovals, hexagons, rounds, lozenge-shaped panels, husks, fans, sphinx, Greek and Roman vases, wreaths, honeysuckle, medallions with figures, festoons, fauns, goats, cupids, eagle-headed figures, drapery, ribbon-work, caryatides, mythological subjects, rams' heads, lions' and eagles' claws for feet, griffins, sea-horses, Greek and Roman pateræs, and draped figures. From this it will be seen how they drew on every kingdom for their purposes, and how they used not only their own finds, but adapted the finds of others.

Michael Angelo Pergolesi produced a work on " Decoration," which also showed many furniture designs, and he was distinguished for the exquisite decorations which he painted on such furniture as the Adam brothers designed. He dedicated his book in the following high-sounding terms: " To the Memory of the Late Most High and Puissant Prince, Hugh Percy, Duke of Northumberland, who was a Patron of the Arts, and to whose Virtues this work is Dedicated by His Most Grateful and Humble Servant." The book contains over seventy large pages of the most exquisite and dainty designs for ceilings, walls, chimney-pieces, furniture, frames, etc., and is a mine for those in search of beautiful ornament.

In France also many books on furniture and decoration were produced. These were brought to England, and from them the English makers drew many choice designs which they copied bodily or adapted to suit their customers. After such a list as this, it does not seem strange that we made good work. Among the illustrations in these books one is rather surprised to find, comparatively, so few desks and secretaries. Many pieces of furniture for strictly bedroom use, like dressing-tables and stands, have in them a drawer which is called a " furniture drawer," in the description. In this drawer, which was cut up into many compartments, were spaces for pens, ink, writing paper, pins, wax, wafers and all the things which went to make up the writing paraphernalia, before the days of the fountain pen. So much furniture, other than what it appeared to be, was made during the eighteenth century that in many of them could be tucked what was needful to indite a billet-doux, or receipt a due bill.

The combination of drawers and a desk top, which I have referred to before, is shown in Figure 265, and there are few such desks which do not contain somewhere one or more secret drawers or receptacles. With the advent of safe deposit companies, and strong boxes which may be rented, the necessity for places to hide away valuables becomes less each year.

The novelist delights in placing love letters in these old secret drawers, but such inflammable material was seldom placed there except by romantic souls, to whom such tokens were invaluable. In making these desks, mahogany was sometimes used, cherry was more common, and occasionally walnut desks are to be met with, but these are rare.

A very plain walnut one is given in Figure 266, and is very solid and substantial. It was made about the middle of the eighteenth century, or perhaps a little earlier, and the chair beside it is of about the same age. Another of mahogany is given (Figure 267), an interesting fact about it being the carved ball-and-claw legs. There are also a number of secret drawers, some of them being concealed behind the pigeon-holes, and some below the lower row of drawers. This desk has a further claim to our notice from the fact that it once belonged to General Israel Putnam, and is now the property of Mr. George Ropes, of Salem, Massachusetts.

By the middle of the eighteenth century reading and writing became less of an accomplishment and more of a

16

necessity, and the number of desks rapidly increased. Writing appliances were also fitted in bureaus; sometimes one drawer opened out into a desk, sometimes only a section of it let down, forming a small shelf with drawers behind. Many cabinet-makers indulged their own fancies in making desks. One of these odd shapes is shown in Figure 268, where the desk is shown closed; the whole front above the long drawer is a solid piece of wood, with the two borders at the side. When in use for writing, this top is supported by two rests which draw out for that purpose. In Figure 269 the desk is shown open; all the drawers are of curly maple, while several of them still retain the old brass knobs. The handles on the long drawer at the bottom are new and too modern in design. This drawer has a panel of the maple, and a band around it of the mahogany. The desk is at the Whipple House, at Ipswich, Massachusetts, that valuable repository of so many Colonial relics.

Very pretty little writing-tables were made for ladies' use, with tops which folded up, or opened out and were supported on rests. They had two drawers below, and looked much like the little work-tables that appeared about the same time.

In fact the branch of cabinet-making which related to ladies' desks was one of considerable interest. Sheraton made many of them, and in his books are designs for many more. A pretty and characteristic specimen of this maker is shown in Figure 270, the woods composing it are maple and satinwood. Little drawers are con-

242

cealed behind the doors, and compartments in the lower
drawers are for the necessary implements.

I have spoken of the fact that much of the furniture
of the late eighteenth century was other than what it
appeared. Under this head I give a description taken
from Sheraton's book, of a "Lady's Cabinet Dressing
Table." This piece is not inappropriate here, as it has
writing materials also in it:

"This table contains every requisite for a lady to dress at.
The style of finishing them is somewhat neat and elegant.
With respect to the manufacturing part, and what it contains,
these may be learned from the piece itself when open. When
the washing-drawer is in, a slider which is above it may be drawn
out to write on. The ink and stand are in the right-hand
drawer under the centre dressing-glass. Behind the drapery,
which is tacked to a rabbet, and fringed or gimped to cover
the nails, is a shelf on which may stand any vessel to receive
the dirty water. Above the drapery are tambour cupboards,
one at each end and one in the middle. Above the tambour at
each end are real drawers, which are fitted up to hold every
necessary article for dressing. The drawers in the cabinet part
are intended to hold all the ornaments of dress, as rings, drops,
etc. Behind the centre glass is drapery; it may be real to suit
the portion below, or it may be painted to match. . . ."

Such a little table as that given in Figure 270 is
recommended by Sheraton, as the lady writing may sit
at it near the fire, from which the upper part screens
her face. As may be seen the writing-shelf opens on
hinges, and room for the knees is afforded by the portion which is cut out. "Kidney Tables" for writing
("named on account of its resemblance to the intestine

243

parts of animals, so called," Sheraton says) were also made for writing at too, and so were some of the popular Pembroke tables, named from the lady who first desired one of this pattern made for her.

After the combination of table and desk, the next most desirable union of two articles in one, was that of desk and bookcase. All the pattern books show innumerable designs for these, from heavy and cumbrous pieces of furniture to such graceful and elegant pieces as that given in Figure 271 A. This piece belonged to Washington Allston, the well-known American painter, who died in 1843. It is a more than commonly handsome piece of furniture, decorated with both carving and inlay. The ball-and-claw feet are carved on the knees, and there is a beautiful shell in the opening of the broken-arch cornice. The glassed door is in Gothic pattern, and many are the directions given for fluting or draping the silk which it was customary to put in these doors. All the pattern books give such directions down to the most minute point, for the benefit no doubt of country cabinet-makers, and such amateurs as cared to attempt it themselves.

Sheraton used more veneer than Chippendale, since he used inlay while Chippendale used carving, and his instructions regarding the use of it are very definite. He says, " If the veneer be very cross and unpliable, as many curls of mahogany are, it is vain to attempt the hammer. It should be shrunk and tempered well with thin glue, not with water, and if necessary the caul, which is the surest and best method, should be used."

244

By 1780 there were cabinet-makers all about the country, turning out numbers of not only useful but ornamental articles. In 1774 the following advertisement appeared in the " New York Gazette and Weekly Mercury ":

MAHOGANY FURNITURE.

3 elegant desks and bookcases.
1 chest upon chest of drawers.
1 lady's dressing-chest and bookcase.
3 desks and 1 pr. card tables.
2 setts chairs.
3 Dining-tables and 5 breakfast tables.
1 clock case furnished with a good plain 8-day clock.
Sundry stands, etc.

The above articles are well made, and most of them are of wood of the first quality, and will be sold as low as any furniture of equal value in the city, by

WILLET AND BERASEY,

Cabinet and chair makers, at the sign of the clothes press, nearly opposite the Oswego Market, at the end of Maiden Lane.

There were made at this time, also, desks and bureaus with what were called block and serpentine fronts. Figure 271 B shows a fine example of a slant-top desk with a serpentine front. The block-front furniture was finished off square on the swelling part instead of rounded, but both block and serpentine drawers were cut from the solid block of wood. This fine piece of mahogany has the original brasses, only one handle being gone. It has the moulding in its simplest form about the drawers, and handsomely carved feet of the ball-and-claw pattern. It has a more quaint aspect in reality than is given by the photograph. This style of desk

245

seems to have been quite popular in New England, and in the Antiquarian Rooms, at Concord, Massachusetts, is a similar desk, made by Joseph Hosmer about 1765. It is of cherry and is in an excellent state of preservation, but is less handsome in colour than the one I show, which is in the Whipple House, at Ipswich.

I have seen also some desks of this pattern richly inlaid in satinwood, with spread eagles, and sometimes with initials or a monogram. Floral forms are used too, and the work appears to have been done here, or at any rate in England, and leaned rather to the Italian style than to the close-set Dutch patterns. In a few cases I have seen combined on the same piece both inlaid work and painting, but I considered the painting an afterthought, and that it was not put on when the piece was made. Sometimes it may have been added by the daughter of the house, fresh home from a finishing school, where " painting on tiles, in the sweetest of styles," was one of the most popular branches of " female academies."

After a time some of these desks were fitted with bookcase tops. Such a one is given in Figure 272, its unusual feature being that the doors are fitted with wooden panels instead of glass.

Another one is shown in the next figure, 273, with the desk open to show the fine workmanship. This bookcase which was made between 1730 and 1760, is eight feet six inches high, and must have been made for a house of consequence, owing to its great size. The bookcases were not dwarfed by the beds and clocks shown in previous chapters.

246

Fig. 270 Ladies' Writing-Table

Fig. 271b SLANT-TOP DESK, WITH SERPENTINE
FRONT

Fig. 271a WASHINGTON ALLSTON'S DESK

Fig. 274 Desk with Glass Doors

Fig. 273 Bookcase and Desk

Fig. 272 Bookcase and Desk

Fig. 276 Sheraton Desk

Fig. 275 Sheraton Desk

Fig. 278 SIDEBOARD-DESK

Fig. 277 BUREAU-DESK

Fig. 281 BOOKCASE-DESK

Fig. 280 SECRETARY

Fig. 279 WRITING CABINET

Fig. 282 "MASSACHUSETTS" DESK

Fig. 283 EMPIRE DESKS

A very elegant secretary, with glass doors in Gothic style, is shown in Figure 274. It is made of solid mahogany, like its fellows already shown, and in one of the secret drawers is written the following inscription:

" This secretary originally belonged to a family named Wilcox, of Worcester, England, and was brought to this country by one of the family in 1810, and was then about seventy-five years old, having been made between the years 1732 and 1738." Pasted on another drawer is still a second record of ownership: " Presented to my wife as a token of respect on my birthday of seventy years, March 16, 1881.

" J. N. Bates, M.D."

By some strange vicissitude of fate, this old desk wound up in Worcester, Massachusetts, nearly 150 years after it was made in Worcester, England.

General Washington was always on the alert to buy comforts and luxuries to make Mount Vernon more attractive. In 1774 (he was only Colonel then) he bought many goods from the splendid home of the Fairfax family on the Potomac. Owing to the decision of the family to remain in England, all their household goods at " Belvoir " were to be sold at auction. The list of what Colonel Washington bought is still preserved. There were many items, chiefly of mahogany, — beds, tables, sideboards, etc., — and among them was one mahogany desk for which he paid £16 16s., a very high price, indeed, for those days. It was at this desk, no doubt, that he wrote those long letters containing such minute directions to his factors in London, regarding the business they transacted for him, and the goods they

247

purchased for him, including his and Mrs. Washington's clothes.

In Figure 275 is shown a Sheraton desk, the lid of which is folded back and supported by rests. The three little doors at the top open, disclosing pigeon-holes and drawers, with two or three compartments artfully concealed. The foot used on this desk is of the type known as " French foot," the outward curve giving it a more graceful appearance than when it came down straight with the edge of the desk, in which case it is known by the term " bracket foot," and is seen on many different styles of pieces, such as desks, bureaus, bookcases, etc.

The desk of Salmon P. Chase, a plain piece of furniture made from mahogany, is in one of the rooms of the Treasury Department at Washington. It was at this desk that some of the details of his financial system were worked out, and here he planned his first great loan to carry on the Civil War.

There are many of these old desks scattered about the country, their chief claim to interest being that once some well-known man leaned over them. Alexander Hamilton's travelling desk, made of mahogany and measuring twelve by sixteen inches, and ten inches high, is an interesting object to all who are familiar with the history of this great man. Upon this desk was written much of his literary work, and the worn green baize with which it is lined attests to the use to which it was put. There is a drawer in one side, and several compartments for pens and ink, while upon the top is inlaid a silver plate with the name " General Alexander Ham-

248

ilton " engraved upon it. Within the top is a strip of parchment which says, " Given by Mrs. General Schuyler to her daughter, Mrs. General A. Hamilton." No doubt the convenient size was what recommended it to the General.

Nathaniel Hawthorne's desk is preserved at the Custom House, Salem, Massachusetts. A desk at which he wrote some of his inimitable romances was just a board standing out from the wall at an angle. This is still in the Tower Room at " Wayside," his home at Concord, Massachusetts.

Victor Hugo had in his Guernsey home a study built almost entirely of glass, and perched upon the roof. Like Hawthorne he, too, stood at his writing, and his desk was a mere shelf fastened by hinges to the wall. But these were mere appliances for the convenience of genius. Every-day people demanded and had something better adapted to their needs, and there were many bookcases and desks combined which were large and handsome pieces of furniture.

Many tales could be told by these desks of use, then of abandonment, and of final resuscitation. Here is one said to be true, but the ending is not as it should be. For many years Mr. Samuel Tilden had, in his office in Nassau Street, a fine old walnut desk with innumerable pigeon-holes and some secret drawers of which he never would confide the whereabouts, nor would he tell if he hunted in spare moments for others. There was nothing remarkable about the desk, except that it was a good one, and that it was adding to its

249

years of service by growing still older under the constant use of a famous man. After Mr. Tilden's death the desk, with some other pieces of his office furniture, was put in the loft of the office building and forgotten. As time went by the room in the loft was demanded, and the furniture was put in the cellar. Moving about and lack of care had not improved the looks of the desk, and though it was still staunch and strong it did not seem to be of much value, for now the roll-top desks had come to the front. One day even the room in the cellar was needed for vaults, and the furniture in the cellar, of which the desk was a part, had to be disposed of.

The janitor not knowing just what to do in the matter at last had the poor old desk broken up and fed to the furnace, watching its destruction as the old walnut flamed high in the furnace. Years passed by, and the time came when old-fashioned things and the relics of famous men were much in demand. Still another year went past, when one day a note arrived from the former private secretary of Mr. Tilden, who wrote in behalf of the family that they were anxious to secure the old walnut high-topped desk which had been used so many years by Mr. Tilden in his office. Would the janitor, so the letter ran, kindly get out the desk and ship it to them, after having it carefully crated? The family would of course pay all expenses.

For a few moments the janitor was nonplussed. Then he gathered his wits about him, and remembered that another tenant of the building had had a desk somewhat resembling that of Mr. Tilden, which in its turn had been abandoned also. This was promptly crated and sent to Mr. Tilden's relatives. It was returned within a week, for, you see, they knew the difference. With it came a letter, saying that they would give $250 for Mr. Tilden's desk. For a week that janitor dreamed of seeing $250 slowly burning up in the furnace! Then he wrote and told his tale. There was some consolation, however, for they wrote again, asking if he had anything that was Mr. Tilden's. And he sent them an old pair of boots which had really belonged to Mr. Tilden, and had in some way escaped destruction. The return mail brought the janitor $50 in exchange.

Another and rather pretty style of Sheraton desk is shown in the next Figure, 276. This has but three drawers in the lower part, though they are small ones, and pigeon-holes behind the little doors. This desk has the ivory escutcheons which always were put on the best class of furniture, and a set of rosette and ring handles. The doors and drawers are veneered, but the writing-shelf is solid mahogany.

There was another combination that seemed to please our ancestors very much, if we may judge from the different forms we find it in, and that was the bureau and desk. I give one in Figure 277. This one is made of mahogany, and is a very handsome and solid piece of furniture. When it is closed it looks like a bureau with seven drawers; but the middle drawer of the second set opens out, as you see. I have found similar desks of English, Dutch, and American make, the one

251

shown being English. I know a Dutch one that is very handsome, as it is carved and inlaid in their beautiful fashion, and it has a third use as well, for the two tall drawers are partitioned off for bottles, each one being capable of holding six. Surely one object could not be expected to fill more purposes than this, where your clothes could be kept cosily, your literary work dispatched, and a cellaret at your very elbow. This Dutch bureau has a date, a most unusual thing to find on furniture. On the back of one of the bottle drawers, and only visible when the drawer is taken out, is a bit of paper pasted, giving the name of the maker, the town in Holland where he lived, and the year he made the bureau, 1789.

I should place the bureau in Figure 277 at least ten years later, but a fine and interesting piece. Within the year I have seen five bureau desks of similar style, all gathered in central New York State. They are not common in the antique shops, which make them even more desirable.

Speaking about these deep side-drawers in both sideboards and bureaus, Sheraton says:

" The drawer on the left is generally plain, but sometimes divided into two portions, the back division being lined with baize to hold plates, having a cover hinged to enclose the whole. The front division is lined with lead, so that it may hold water to wash glasses, which may be made to take out, or have a plug-hole to let out the dirty water. The left-hand drawer is, however, sometimes made very short, to give place to a pot-cupboard behind, which opens by a door in the end of the sideboard or desk. This door is made to hide itself in the end rail as much as possible, both for look and secrecy; for which reason a turn-buckle is not used, but a thumb-spring, which catches at the bottom of the door, and has a communication through the rail, so that by touch of the finger the door flies open, owing to the resistance of a common spring fixed to a rabbet which the door falls against. This cupboard can only be placed in these pieces of furniture which are square at the ends."

Another desk, somewhat on the order of the bureau-desk, is given in Figure 278. This I should call a side-board-desk, for the deep drawer lets down with a brass arm, and discloses a desk within, with its proper complement of drawers and letter-holes. The date of this piece is doubtless about 1800, for it is a composite style, and I doubt not that it was made here. It has some very choice inlaid work, both about the mirror and the deep drawer, which the photograph does not reveal. There is good solid carving, too, but for all that the piece is not attractive. It is interesting simply as a rather unique specimen.

How much superior in elegance the next piece appears (Figure 279). This is a writing cabinet on a Sheraton model, the upper part being designed for books, and the lower containing a desk and drawers. Observe the handsome curves in the glassed doors, and the purity of the ornamentation on the top. This book-case-desk is of mahogany, and in every way an admirable example. In Figure 280 is given one of the choicest specimens of massive construction shown. I do not think it is as old as many of the serpentine-front pieces are, from the style of the interior fittings of the upper part. It is, no doubt, a product of the eighteenth century, however, and in splendid condition, the whole piece being of dark and solid mahogany, making the desk immensely heavy. The carved flames or torches on the top, the shells on the front of the desk and in the inside are finely done; and it is such a desk as you would expect to belong to one of those maritime princes whose ships roved every sea, bringing home to their owners in Salem the richest cargoes to be found. See the shelves for the great ledgers, wherein were entered the accounts of all the argosies which had come safely home; and think how many times the owner, bending over the writing-shelf, must have entered the long columns of pounds, shillings, and pence on the side of profit.

About 1800, and a little later, what was known as the Empire style became fashionable, and was copied by both English and American cabinet-makers from French models. An American treatment of this style, which was originated under the fostering genius of Napoleon, is seen in Figure 281, which shows a large and handsome mahogany desk with bookcase combined. The combination of bookcase and desk, as I have said, had long been a favourite one; and though this bookcase is quite generous in size, those many sizes smaller would often be quite large enough to contain the limited number of books which answered for a library in Colonial days.

Even the ministers had but a few volumes, and they were considered the scholars of the community. I had occasion lately to look over a collection of books which were considered fit and proper reading for both young and old, particularly on the Sabbath days, when time hung heavy on their hands, and a few of the titles will give a fair idea of the character of the library, quite typical of the period. Increase Mather's "Angelagraphia" (1696); "The Loving Invitation of Christ to the Aged, Middle-Aged, Youth and Children, from the mouth of Elizabeth Osborn, only Three Years and Nine Months Old"; Owen's "Indwelling Sin"; Baxter's "Call to the Unconverted"; Crawford's "Dying Shots"; Doddridge on "Regeneration," and Stoddard's "Safety of Appearing in ye Righteousness of Christ" are some of the solemn titles.

There was nothing that came under the head of "light literature."

I have spoken in the chapter on Chests and Cupboards of furniture made in particular locations, or at least found there, and have shown both the Hadley and the Connecticut chest. In Figure 282 I give a picture of what is called the "Massachusetts desk," of which, recently, I have seen several examples. It does not seem a very convenient piece of furniture with that leg in the middle, but its great length must have made it possible for two persons to sit comfortably at it. This one is of mahogany, with carved legs and gilt mounts, and four shallow but wide drawers.

A desk somewhat resembling this is in the City Hall, New York, and there are quite a number in Boston and its vicinity.

255

To return to the bookcase-desk in Figure 281. It is about eight feet high, and the Gothic treatment of the doors makes them very ornamental. One of the marked peculiarities of this style of furniture was the use of metal mounts, made usually of handsome hand-worked or cast brass, and in finer pieces, of water gilt. Our cabinet-makers never let themselves be carried away by this florid style, and contented themselves in most cases with merely making the capitals at the tops of the pillars, ornaments, and sometimes the tips of the feet of brass. You will see them in this example. The lid of the desk folds back upon itself, and above it another lid swings out, revealing pigeon-holes.

The quiet simplicity of this desk is in marked contrast to the superb pieces shown in Figure 283. Every one of the splendid gilt ornaments on these desks is worth careful study.

There was only one man in England, and none here, who could have designed such desks as these, and that was Thomas Hope, whose studies in Greek and Roman antiquities enabled him almost to vie with the ancients in the beauty and grace of his figures. His book, called " Costumes of the Ancients," brought him great fame; it was published about 1807, and remains to this day a source of inspiration to those whose taste leads them to antique models. When he designed furniture it was always after classical forms, and decorated with his incomparable figures and ornaments. While many of his designs were not comfortable to sit or recline upon, they were certainly very beautiful to the eye.

256

There are few such desks as these in this country, or in fact to be found anywhere, and I give these merely as examples of what splendid furniture did find its way over here.

There are other desks also, dainty affairs if for ladies' use, standing on tall, slender legs, with sliding or "tambour" tops, as they were called, and a wealth of little drawers and cupboards, both revealed and secret. I know of one such which has recently been brought down from many years' seclusion in the attic, furbished up, and become the proud possession of a brand-new bride. But it lacks the elegance of olden days, for the modern cabinet-maker could not repair the tambour, an arrangement of slender bits of wood which were so fixed that they were flexible — something like the modern roller-top desk.

These pieces were and always are the rare exceptions; and though they are occasionally found, they cannot be considered really representative of the furniture of our forefathers any more than the superb pieces shown in the last illustration.

It must forever remain a matter of regret that the best makers did not in some way mark their productions. Even had they done so, the study would not have proved of surprising ease, since there would always have been the fanciful maker who indulged his caprices, to cope with. With what delight we seize upon a piece which is dated, like one of the Bible boxes given early in this chapter; and with what regret we leave the unnamed and undated pieces as to whose exact time

of construction hardly two people agree. In the study
of French furniture, after the middle of the eighteenth
century, the task became far simpler, for among sump-
tuary and other useless laws time was found to make
an enactment which bade, in 1751, the *maître ébéniste*
to stamp all his work. In the great museums of France,
where many of the art treasures are gathered, there are
also examples of furniture stamped with the maker's
name; and among the choicest are writing-tables, desks,
and cabinets, all of the greatest beauty and elegance.
Nothing was spared to enhance the beauty of these
gems of art; lacquer, water-gilt, inlays of tortoise-shell
and coloured stones, — every fancy which the *ébéniste*
could summon was brought to his aid. It was the age
of polite letter-writing and of diaries, and the *memoirs*
from which we glean so much of history, and even more
entertaining gossip, was set down with a quill pen at
some of these very dainty and costly *secretaires*.

They are to be bought here now, but very few came
here a hundred years ago; so few that it was impossible to find one of which the history was authentic of
its being here when the nineteenth century opened. So
the work of Riesener and of Boulle, of Cressent and
of Caffieri has been omitted as being too scarce to be
of importance in a book which deals with those household articles which were made or sold here, and which
could be found in our homes in general.

258

XI — OLD PEWTER

THE almost complete disappearance of pewter from the field of household utensils for a space of fifty years or more, and then the attempt to revive it recently for use in country houses, forms an interesting page in the history of antiques. It brings to the front again a set of articles which were graceful in shape and delightful in colour; and which, in addition, were not so valuable as to tempt the cupidity of the burglar.

It is not possible, in the limited space here given to go very deeply into the ancient history of pewter. It was used by the Romans during their occupancy of England; and some of their old seals have been found within the past few years in certain places in England, and melted up by tinkers for solder, a desecration which it is marvellous no one attempted to stop. In fact the presence of mines of tin and of lead are held responsible for bringing to the shores of Britain the Phœnician trader, and had much to do with the Roman occupation of this island. For use at home the Romans transported vast quantities of tin from Cornwall, and France got her share as well as Holland. China, Japan, Italy, Holland, Germany, France, and England were all workers in this metal, and the Oriental treatment of it was extremely ornamental. In the " Old Pewter Book " it has been possible to show examples of these works, but in this chapter I shall confine myself chiefly to pieces made in England and a few made on the Continent.

The composition of English pewter contained different proportions of tin and other metals, the use for which the object was intended governing the amount of lead used. For instance, the highest quality of " Plate Pewter " contained no lead at all, but 100 parts of tin, 8 of antimony, and 4 of copper. On the other hand, " Ley Metal," the cheapest and commonest kind, contained 80 % of tin and 20 % of lead. All the other qualities, and there were many, lay between these two extremes. Common pewter, or " Trifle," from which small objects and toys were made, contained 82 % of tin and 18 % of antimony. The metal used for salts and ewers was composed of 90 % of tin and 10 % of lead.

Tin alone is not so durable or ductile as lead; and when the two metals are combined they will not shrink so greatly as either taken by itself. This shrinking is a quality which has to be considered when the article to be made has to be cast in a mould. The fusibility of pewter made it of great use to goldsmiths in taking the casts of medals or other small articles which they desired their customers to approve before the final casting of the object in gold, silver, or bronze.

The best quality of early pewter was made of tin, with as much brass as it could take up, the proportion being about one to four. This quality, which was known as " fine," was used for many small and choice articles, as well as chargers and church vessels. A less fine quality, in which the proportion was also four to one, consisted of tin and lead; and in this were made candlesticks, bowls, and pots. All public house vessels, such as mugs and tankards, had a still greater amount of lead in them, and were often called " black metal," since they tarnished so easily.

The method of making pewter has always been the same; and upon the nature of the object depended whether it was cast, hammered, or both, and then put upon a lathe and burnished. The first things that a would-be pewterer had to acquire was a set of moulds; and these being made of gun-metal were very costly and out of the reach of many. So, very early, the pewterers came together into guilds or companies; and they owned in common sets of moulds which were loaned to the members without charge, as was the custom in York, England, or were rented for a small charge, as was the usage in most of the English towns. Not only was gun-metal used for moulds, but plaster-of-paris, wood, iron, and sand, even, were used.

If possible the article was cast in one piece; and this was the case with such small articles as spoons, salts, porringers, and bleeding-dishes, tasters, etc. When tankards or large ewers with bulging sides were made it became necessary to cast them in pieces, solder them together, and then finish them off; but in such pieces the joints are nearly always visible. Handles of all

261

descriptions were generally soldered on, though in the case of small "eared" dishes, as the porringers were called, it was forbidden by the rules of the guild to solder them on; and those who were detected in this practice were fined and reprimanded.

Not many tools were needed in this trade, and none of them were intricate or very costly. After the moulds, in order of importance came the lathe, the motive power of which was a boy or man known as a "turn-wheel," while the parts of the lathe were a head-stock, tail-stock, and simple mandrel. "The Worshipful Company of Pewterers" in England go back as far as 1348 in their records. The French had societies even earlier, since in 1295 Lyons was famous for the quality and character of her pewter ware; and by 1300 there were many famous men at work in Paris who furnished royalty with their necessary kitchen equipment. In England there was less precious metal and more pewter even among the high and mighty in the land. In both countries the pewter workmen were divided into classes which were known as "Hollow-ware" men, who made pots and vessels for liquids, "Sad-ware" men, who made plates and chargers (large platters), and "Triflers," who made the little objects like salts, medals, beggars' tokens, and toys. Plates and saucers, to be up to the regulations of the guild, were to be hammered, and you will find the mallet marks on the under side.

The demand for pewter vessels, which crowded out those of wood and horn, and which in their turn have been displaced by pottery and porcelain, grew apace.

262

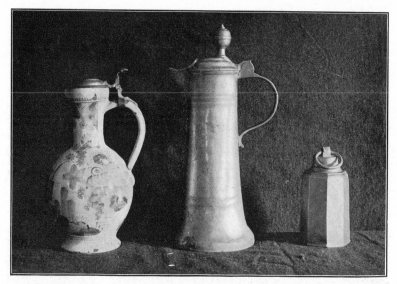

Fig. 284   PEWTER POT-LID

Fig. 285   PEWTER COLLECTION

Fig. 286   Engraved Pewter, German

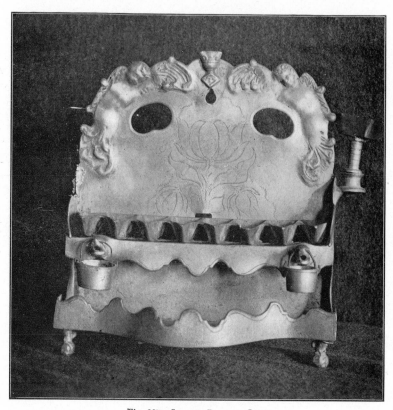

Fig. 287   Jewish Pewter Lamp

Fig. 288   HOLY-WATER CUPS

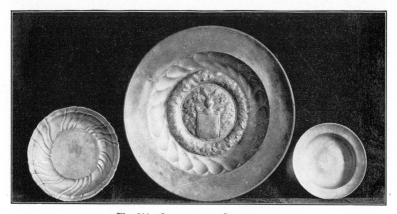

Fig. 289   ORNAMENTAL CHARGER

Fig. 290 Lead Garden Vase

Fig. 291 Mantel with Pewter Decoration

Fig. 292   EWER AND BASIN

Fig. 293   COLLECTION OF PEWTER

Fig. 294 EMERSON COFFEE URN

Fig 295 "TAPPIT-HENS"

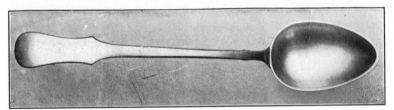

Fig. 296 PEWTER SPOON

Fig. 297 *a* MUDGE'S INHALER

Fig. 297 *b* BASE OF INHALER

Fig. 298 Group of Pewter

Fig. 299 Bowls and Boxes

As early as 1474 the marking of pewter to show it was up to the proper standard of purity began, and that which was tested and found below this was marked with a broad arrow, and consigned to the melting-pot, in which it had to be united with new metal and recast.

All the great prelates had prodigious stores of pewter, jugs, basins, tankards, measures, candlesticks, mugs, and salts. The table pewter came in what were known as " garnishes," and which consisted of " 12 platters, 12 dishes, 12 saucers; and these are either of silver fashion, or else with broad or narrow brims and bought by the pound, which is now valued at sevenpence or peradventure at eightpence." This is what Harrison wrote in 1557, concerning what was found on the tables of the middle classes. As may be inferred, pewter utensils were pretty well distributed over the kingdom where, a century before, they had been confined to the houses of the wealthy. Many regulations as to the exact size and weight of the vessels were also framed by the " Worshipful Company," and those that offended were heavily fined, in some cases being debarred from the privileges of the company. The " touch-mark," as it was called, was another method used to keep up the high quality of pewter; and in 1564 the rose and crown had become so well known and important a mark that the following rule was framed regarding it.

" Also it is agreed that euery one of the saide felowship that makith any warre shall set his owne marke thereon. And that no man shall geue for his proper marck or touch, the Rose and crown wt lettrs or otherwise, but only to whome it is geuen by the felowship. Nor that no man of the saide Craft shall geue one anothers marck nother wth lettrs nor otherwise, but euery one to geue a sondry marck such one as shalbe alowed by the maister and wardens for the tyme beinge vpon payne of forfaite and paye for euery tyme offendinge to the Crafte's box xiijs. iiijd."

The pewterers tried hard to keep all the business in their own hands and prevent the sale of goods by hawkers. Any member who sold ware to pedlars or hawkers was to be fined five pounds, a large sum in those days; and in one or two cases where a member of the guild was detected in this business his shop was closed, and he was not allowed to open it again. No other merchants were allowed to sell pewter ware in their shops, and even the goldsmiths were enjoined from having it. When silver vessels became more common the Pewterers Company petitioned the king to prevent this, and to make all taverns and ordinaries, at least, use pewter vessels only.

One great branch of the business was the putting of lids on pottery jugs; and in 1552 it was agreed that every week the jugs so lidded should be brought in for inspection, and the mark of the pewterer should be put on the inside of the lid. Later this rule was altered, and it was set down that the maker's mark should be set on the outside of the lid, together with the guild mark. Apparently the maker did not have the privilege of marking his own pots, for in 1553 it was ordered by the masters and wardens of the company that John Curtys should have " ffor markyng of every dosyn of stone potte whosesoever brought them to marck one ffarthing."

A stoneware jug with a pewter lid is shown in Figure 284; and although this one is of Delft pottery, the shape is similar to the English ones, and the tall, graceful chalice beside it is of a later period, as is the bell, which was used in church ceremonial. Other pewter lids are shown in the following Figure, 285, where, on an old mantelpiece is gathered a collection of objects suitable to their surroundings.

Almost every household has tucked away somewhere, either "up-garret" or in the buttery, one or more pieces of old pewter ware — scarred veterans it is true, but none the less interesting on that account. It seems a long way to go back to that day when Henry Hudson dropped the anchor of the Half Moon in lower New York Bay in search of the first pewter brought to this country. Perhaps 1609 is a little early; yet I have no doubt that among the stores in that ship could have been found pewter plates, and pewter tankards as well.

It is a matter of history, however, that Director-General Wouter Van Twiller reached Manhattan Island in 1633; and one of his first acts, in order to make his people contented, was to erect a great brewery, and "his colonists were never so happy as when draining their huge pewter tankards." So many other, though less durable, wares have been made for our use and convenience that pewter had rather lost caste. In Colonial days it was one of the most important household items. When the Widow Coytemore married John Winthrop in

265

the Massachusetts Colony, she brought him "household stuff" valued at £640, her share of her first husband's estate. The inventory was long, and among its items is one of £135 worth of pewter.

When Governor Bradford died, also of the Plymouth Colony, he left, as specified in the inventory of his property, fourteen pewter dishes, thirteen platters, three large and also three small plates, a candlestick, and a bottle. Peter Palfrey, of Salem, a man of substance in the town, gave in 1662 to his daughter Mary as a wedding gift two pewter platters and an iron pot. Much pewter was made in this country, and the inventory of a Boston pewterer who died in 1675 shows in his shop 2782 pounds of pewter. This with the dishes and "basons" already made was valued at £235 11s. 4d. He had also for sale "alchemy spoons, spooning pewter, tankards, milk-cans, warming-pans, kettles, skillets, frying-pans, cow-bells, and bellows."

As late as 1750 a complete outfit of pewter plates, dishes, and spoons was considered a lordly wedding gift. Fortunate was the bride who possessed them.

Most of the pewter to be found in this country is extremely plain, gaining its charm from its solid substantial lines and charming gray colour. But some of the English and much of the Continental pewter had decoration of one style or another, and one of the simplest methods may be noted on the chalice in Figure 284. You will see that there are bands of incised lines in three places on the body of the chalice, and on the front a wreath of leaves surrounding a date and initials.

266

This style of work was called "wriggled" or "jog-gled" work, and was very common on the Continent. Owing to the nature of the alloy, engraved work wears off very quickly, since it has to be very lightly done, for deeply cut work weakens the ware. The tool which is used to make patterns is in the nature of a chisel, the blades varying in length, the common size being about an inch wide.

The tool is rocked or jogged along, forming a pattern which is never of great delicacy; and, although the Dutch and German pewterers seem to have the greatest fancy for it, you will find that it has been used in all countries. The Dutch used it on church vessels, long stories from the Bible and holy narrative being illustrated in it. For such purposes came special tools with blades as fine as a thirty-second of an inch; and the pattern was made out with dots in places where it was not convenient to use the tool.

Engraved work was also put on pewter, each stroke of the tool removing some of the alloy; and on some pieces both engraving and wriggled work are combined. In Figure 286 some choice specimens of engraved work are shown, and in the cases of the beaker and pitcher there is wriggled work as well. These pieces are of German make, have elaborate coats of arms on them, and the bowl is dated 1735. All three pieces have a rose and crown on them, which emblems may be found on English, French, Dutch, German, and Scottish ware, though it is customary to assign all ware so marked to England. The difference between the engraving tool and the punch or wriggling tool can be easily told. The latter is held in an upright position and then struck with a mallet. This raises a ridge on either side of the pattern, while in engraving the pewter is removed.

When modelled and finished with engraving tools pewter may be made very rich and elegant, as may be seen from the beautiful old Jewish lamp shown in Figure 287. This lamp has eight little buckets for holding oil set on a small shelf. There were two others, larger, one of which is missing, at the sides. Observe the beauty of the figures in low relief on the top, and the form of the pomegranate flower in engraved and wriggled work on the plain space.

Two other pieces are shown with figures in the next Figure, 288, and these were also for religious purposes, being Bénitiers, or Holy-water cups. You may find cups hanging in Flemish churches now, perhaps of pewter, more likely of china, but not many will be as charmingly modelled as these. Sometimes these cups hung at wayside shrines; in the case of these shown the one object providing both cup and image, though some of them had a cross in place of the figures.

Many elegant plates or chargers for use on cupboards were cast and then sharpened up with the engraving tool. Such a charger is shown in Figure 289. Harrison writes, in his " Description of England," of the way the farmer set out his cupboard in imitation of the rich lord who had his set with silver and Venice glass. The yeoman had to be content with less, and used pewter

268

as rich as his purse would allow, polished to the brightness of the costlier metal. Sometimes this raised work was punched out from the back and filled with lead so that it would not bend; sometimes it was cast solid. Swiss Kaiserteller, as they were named, were very elegant pieces, showing figures on horseback, knights and insignia, with rich and varied borders; but such pieces are generally museum specimens.

Another use for pewter in its commoner form was for " garden ornaments," figures, vases, or urns, some of which were of very graceful and elegant shapes, and designed by such masters as the Adam Brothers, who put their skill to anything which could be made ornamental, not even the design for a reticule or a fan being too slight a thing for their notice.

Many of the splendid old gardens in Italy and England had these vases on pedestals, and one such, twenty-five inches high, after Adam Brothers' design, is shown in Figure 290.

Pewter was put to still another use by these same skilful men; and in the next Figure, 291, you may see how rich a mantelpiece of white deal may look with a decoration of pewter upon it. They used the classic shapes to which they were so wedded, and the cold gray of the pewter shows out admirably against the wood. I have never seen one of these mantels in this country, but many of them were taken out of houses about fifty years ago in England, and, luckily, some escaped the rubbish pile.

As has been mentioned already, the composition of

269

pewter varies greatly. The very finest pewter is simply tin hardened by the addition of copper and antimony. Ordinary pewter is tin alloyed with lead, which ingredient is added on account of its cheapness, and is often, therefore, present in excessive amount.

It was this lead which made pewter such a very valuable possession in Revolutionary days. All records of those hard-fought times have frequent references to the scarcity of bullets. In 1777 Madam Smith, wife of the minister at Sharon, Connecticut, invited all her friends and neighbours to come to spend the evening with her, and to bring every pewter article with them which they could possibly spare.

Before the evening had passed " several gallons of good bullets had been cheerfully run through bullet-moulds, the good ladies sacrificing without a pang the much-prized pewter. This destruction of household utensils necessitated the making of others, so there were " trencher-bees " instituted, and held from house to house for many evenings. At these the young men of the village whittled and shaped enough trenchers of maple and poplar wood to supply the housewives' needs. The women smoothed down these rough wooden vessels with broken glass, and polished them with a sand made of powdered limestone.

Figure 292 shows what was called in old lists " a bason and ewer." Our wash-stand set, while evidently much used in its day, is in a fine state of preservation. It is a good-sized pitcher for those days, holding more than a gallon, even more than the blue and white Staffordshire pitchers, which were so highly esteemed a little later in the century.

Writing about this ewer and basin some time ago, I mentioned the fact that it was the only one I had ever seen. I have since heard from the possessors of two others, one of them in the far West, who says that his was brought there many years ago by Father Ravillac, a Jesuit priest. It was marked Thomas Boardman, London. Boardman was a well-known pewterer in the last half of the eighteenth century.

Ewers this size — " guinea basons " we find them called in the pewterer's records — were a subject of much importance to the company. It was duly set down just how much they should weigh, and what quality of pewter should be used in them. But while it was possible to hold the London craft up to the mark by means of " searches " (that is, sending the officers to look for unlawful pewter) and fines, it was impossible to have the country members of the craft under control. For that reason they stinted the amount of tin, made the articles under weight, and in 1726 a letter from Philadelphia was read complaining of the bad quality of the pewter sent to the Colonies from Bristol, England.

Why there are not more of these " basons " and pitchers left it would be hard to say. Perhaps they were melted up, as were the utensils in Connecticut. It was not only the pewter in daily use which was put in the melting-pot, but every scrap which could be found.

Sir John Johnson's house, which is still standing in

the Mohawk Valley, had in 1770 a roof of lead. This was ripped off and found its way into bullets. So did the lead tablets set into monuments and gravestones. You will see some stones with the vacant spaces left in the old graveyards in and near Boston. On July 9, 1776, the equestrian statue of George III, on Bowling Green, New York City, was pulled down, sent to Connecticut and moulded, so the story runs, into forty-eight thousand bullets.

Fortunately not all the pewter was sacrificed to the god of war. Figure 293 shows a kitchen dresser set out " with shining pewter all arow." Such a complete set was the end and aim of every good housekeeper. When the pewter had been once gathered together the keeping of it bright was quite a serious matter. This duty fell to the children's share, and on Saturday mornings they were sent bright and early to the meadows for a supply of " horse-tail " or scouring-rush, the rough stems of which polished the pewter without scratching it. The mothers kept an eye to the use of much " elbow-grease," and there was no escaping for play till the task was well accomplished.

There were more articles of pewter than is generally supposed. Besides plates, platters, tankards, porringers, spoons, pitchers, and basins there were buckles for shoe and knee, coffee-urns, hot-water dishes, lamps, and candlesticks.

In Figure 294 is a variety of these articles. The coffee-urn is a solid old piece, and belonged to the grandfather of Ralph Waldo Emerson, who built

272

the "Old Manse" at Concord, Massachusetts, in 1765.

The owner of the coffee-urn was a sturdy and loyal patriot, and we love to think he had a good strong cup of hot coffee before he went out on that historic 19th of April to encourage his parishioners to fight for their liberties and homes.

The coffee-urn is a good piece in itself, for the lions' heads which hold the handles are clearly modelled. The tankard standing in the large trencher is what is known as a "tappit-hen." It is a Scotch piece, and they were generally sold three in a set. There is a very small one seen just in front of the urn. These "hens" are hard to find and rare.

Recently I have learned of two sets in this country. One of them, owned in Bangor, Maine, is shown in Figure 295. The smallest hen of all does not rightfully belong in the set, but probably from its size was used for hot milk or treacle. I was sorry to hear from the owner of this set that a portion of them had been buffed. It is a mistake to have your pewter subjected to this process, as it takes off a portion of the surface, and removes those marks of time and wear which no really antique pewter should be without. In fact, it is not pleasant to record that these sets of tappit-hens are being reproduced both in the country of their origin, Scotland, as well as in Belgium. They are being scratched and marred, and in some cases are buried for some months to obtain the proper degree of patina on them. Some are even eaten slightly with acids to give them a corroded look. There is no limit to the devices of the makers of spurious goods.

The Scotch pewterers generally marked their pieces, for all reputable makers belonged to the " Incorporation of Hammermen," which included goldsmiths, blacksmiths, saddlers, cutlers, locksmiths, lorimers, armourers, pewterers, and coppersmiths.

This guild was incorporated as early as 1483, and in its records is the following:

" December 24th, 1681.

It is ordained by consent to ye hail brethren, that each member shall have one stamp of their owne and present ye same yor to ye house betwixt this and the 2d of February, to ye effect, everie one's work may be known, and that under ye pain of Three Pounds Scots per piece. Whereupon this act is made."

The thistle is the distinguishing mark of Scotch pewter, which has in addition the smaller marks, like hall-marks, and sometimes the maker's name besides. Notwithstanding the fine of " Three Pounds Scots," much pewter is entirely unmarked, and one has to rely largely on its characteristic shape to identify it.

The English tankard in the same Figure, 294, is the shape with which we are most familiar. The lid is cone-shaped, showing that it was not one of the very early pieces, in which case it would have been flat.

The thick dish with handles is a nice piece. It is to be filled with hot water to keep a meal warm. A little slide in the top of the dish can be taken out, and slipped back when the under part is filled. A pewter spoon lies beside it, and a gruel basin to the right. One of the

274

housekeeper's yearly duties was to mould a fresh supply of spoons. They were made of soft metal, and consequently were easily broken or bent. Spoon moulds were metal affairs and not owned by every family. If one was possessed by a village the hardy pioneers thought it was ample. In a certain Massachusetts village a family whose name began with L, to add a touch of elegance to their table furniture, had the spoon mould made with this initial in the die. It did very well for them, but the whole village also had their spoons marked " L," for they promptly borrowed the new mould the first time they needed to make " a running." Consider the confusion which must have ensued at every sewing-bee or husking when individual possessions were to be sorted out!

A pewter spoon is given in Figure 296 and is a fine one. It is not home-made, nor very old, being made by Reed and Barton, a firm of New York silversmiths, in 1823. Few old spoons are to be found, for they were so easily bent, at least the home-made ones, that they were among the first things cast into the melting-pot to be run over. I have some spoons, notably one of Belgian make, which is remarkably stiff in the handle, but this is an unusually fine specimen. An amateur, who is a busy literary man, writes me that he has been amusing himself with running pewter spoons in an old mould which somebody gave him. He has great difficulty in arriving at just the proper quality of metal to make them with any degree of stiffness, and some old spoons which he sacrificed had in the handles a bit of

275

iron which gave them the desired body. The formula for spooning pewter takes a large proportion of lead which is the cause of the brittleness. I have also an old home-made pewter spoon which came from Maine. I have never been able to bring myself to use it, for I am quite sure that any strain on the handle would be fatal to it.

A pewter spoon does not seem a thing which would survive centuries, even though buried in the mud of a river bed. Yet within the last year one has been recovered from the Thames, at London, in a quite perfect condition. The handle of the spoon bears on the end the head of a woman with the head-dress which was worn in the time of Henry V, that is from 1413 to 1422. Three more spoons of this period are known; one is in the British Museum. The bowl is what was called the "plover's egg" shape, larger at the end than at the place where the handle joins the bowl. Nearly all pewter spoons have what is called a rat-tail running up the back to give added strength, and the top of the handles varied as did the patterns of the silver spoons of corresponding periods.

A unique piece of pewter is shown in the next Figure, 297, and bears on the front the words "Mudge's Inhaler." It is in the nature of a trick mug, for the handle is hollow with holes near the top, and if you do not put your finger over them, the liquid spills. The name of the maker is on the bottom, but inquiries at the number on Fleet Street have failed to find the date of his being there, the tax rolls for the nineteenth century not bearing

276

his name. It has had a strange history, this old mug, and at last was found on a rubbish pile by a collector who adds to his gatherings all the things of interest which he meets with in his travels. It is a good piece, and a puzzle in more ways than one.

Barnes is not a name to be found in the list of masters and wardens given by Mr. Welch in his transcription of the records of the Pewterers Company, but there were many names of workers which did not appear therein. There are often names on old pewter, and though in many cases it is nearly obliterated, there is often enough to enable one to piece it out. There was Townsend and Compton, who were at work in 1750, and the Jacksons, father and son; Lucas was another familiar name, Fly and Thompson, 1740, John and William Fasson, Henry and John Appleton, Joseph and Samuel Barker, Bennett and Chapman, Thomas Boardman, 1746, and hundreds of others. These men, besides the rose and crown, added their own names and often a large X which denoted " best quality."

Paris marks varied, sometimes an angel with the word " Paris " in a crown, more often a fleur-de-lis, and the inevitable crowned rose all are to be found. The Brussels rose is six petalled, crowned, and there is a figure of St. Michael and the Dragon in a beaded circle, and also a gothic B to be found too. Antwerp has the rose alone or crowned, and an arm and hand. There is a large amount of Belgian pewter to be found in this country, particularly near the early Dutch settlements.

In Figure 298 we show a Dutch tankard, dated

1747, and marked with the flying angel of Brussels. It is a handsome piece with an ornamental incised pattern, and a motto in Dutch on the front. An English hot-water kettle faces it, and between the two is a small English creamer with a fine band of repoussé work surrounding the top.

The little two-handled bowl is a rather unusual piece also, on account of the carved work in the bottom.

The worn old plate at the top has a personal history of its own which makes each scar and dent of extra value. It belonged to the Rev. Samuel Kirkland, who took up his residence about August 1, 1766, at Kanon-warohale, the chief village of the Oneida Indians, about twenty miles west of the Mohawk River.

Mr. Kirkland went as missionary to the Indians, and lived among and with them. He built a house for himself, " through constant and very hard labour," he writes, " digging the cellar, hewing and drawing the timber with his own hands."

He married Jerusha Bingham in September, 1769, and now deemed it expedient to enlarge his house, making it sixteen instead of ten feet square. By 1770 his salary had been raised to £130 a year, and he was able to buy a " sett " of pewter. Through all the Revolutionary troubles he stayed among the Indians, endeavouring to prevent their taking part in the war. During more than thirty years he laboured among them, his house being open to all the Indians who were constantly coming and going. It was no uncommon thing for him to feed sixty or seventy during a week, and his whole

278

Fig. 300 SALTS AND JUG

Fig. 301 CANDLE MOULDS

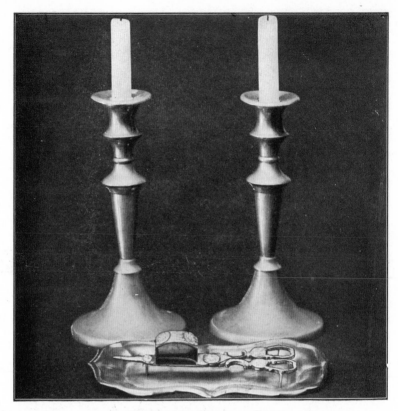

Fig. 302 Snuffers, Tray, and Sticks

Fig. 303 Pewter Lamps

Fig. 304 PEWTER LAMPS

Fig. 305 PEWTER LAMPS

Fig. 306   Tureen

Fig. 307   Plates and Platters

Fig. 309 Bureau Dressing-Table

Fig. 308 Commode, Louis XV Style

Fig. 310 Bureau Cabinet

Fig. 311 Walnut Bureaus

Fig. 312 Bureau   Fig. 313 Cherry Bureau

Fig. 315 Mahogany Bureau, Hepplewhite

Fig. 314 Maple Bureau; Hepplewhite

salary was often devoured during a year in hospitality. Many a painted and feathered savage has eaten off this plate, which is greatly cherished by one of Mr. Kirkland's descendants.

The old newspapers of Colonial times furnish a good index of what were the manners and customs of the people at that time, and what were the articles in use. By 1777 New York was filled with officers and soldiers, and apparently with a number of light-fingered gentry, as well. There are numberless advertisements of lost articles, stolen goods, and many rewards are offered and " no questions asked." This notice appears in several issues of the " New York Mercury ":

" Stolen out of a room, a small red leather trunk, with several small articles, two razors, a pewter shaving-box with soap."

I have recently heard from the owners of two pewter shaving mugs. In one case the mug has become a receptacle for buttons, while in the other it is still intact in its red leather box with all the other fittings.

In Figure 299 are two nice tasting bowls (you rarely find these called porringers in any English list) and two covered boxes. For just what purpose the latter were used it would be hard to tell, unless it was for soap. They are twisted, and so are the pieces in the next Figure (300), which are old and interesting. This twisted effect was seen on very early pieces, particularly candlesticks, and was made about that period which is called, with more or less inaccuracy, " Queen Anne." At any rate I have seen candlesticks, made about 1700,

279

in this twisted pattern, and, besides the twist, the objects themselves betray great age. The two salt cellars on either side of the jug are of the form and size common at that period, when a person's rank entitled him to sit above or below the salt.

In the records of the Pewterers Company are set down the prices for many different patterns of salts, from the "grete Staundyn Sault on Bawles" to those of smaller size and less weight. Besides all the valuable information concerning the methods of the pewterers in their work, these records tell much history, and give many glimpses into the ways of the times. For instance, all the great guilds furnished service in time of war, did duty at all great city and civic festivals, and duly are set down in these books whatever was paid, even for such things as ribbons for the hats of the members who walked in procession, when Queen Anne went to church at St. Paul's to give thanks for the victory at Ramilies.

Besides buckles and watch cases of pewter, many buttons were made, and they had to frame a rule with regard to the quality of metal put into candle moulds. In 1703 Thomas Greener "appeared upon Sumons to this Court to give account of what metal he makes Candle Moulds. And declared he made them of a mixture of Mettle something worse than pale, and that they may be better of fine. But that he has experienced that they cannot be made of Lay. Thereupon this court considering That the makeing of any new sort of Pewter Vessel or Ware of any sort of mettle than perfectly fine, or at the Assize of Lay maye be of a very dangerous consequence, and that there is great quantities of Candle Moulds now made of mettle worse than pale, though the same Moulds were made at first of fine Pewter."

In Figure 301 we show some of these old moulds, for making two, four, or eight candles. The tubing part is made of pewter, and very rough and crude they are.

Two candles made in similar moulds are shown in Figure 302. The pewter sticks which hold them have seen long service. They were brought into this country by the Hite family, who were among the first settlers in the Valley of Virginia, about the year 1730.

The snuffers and tray are of lighter and more ornamental make, and are probably of a later period. Sometimes these candlesticks are a straight column with a band of rude work around them. Queen Anne pattern has a straight stem, but it swells out into quite a bulge about the middle.

People often inquire, "How shall I clean my old pewter?" We cannot do better than recommend the good old method of scouring-rush and elbow grease. If, however, the rushes are unobtainable, there are substitutes, but there is no way to get along without abundant rubbing. While some collectors prefer to allow their pieces to stay dull and discoloured, it was certainly not the way they looked when in use and proudly displayed in livery or court cupboard, or on a fine old Dutch Kas. Neglected pewter will be found to be corroded, or covered with a coat of oxidation. The removal of this is slow, and must be accomplished by patient, hard scrubbing with a hard brush, and plenty of hot water and soap. The addition of soda, borax, or ammonia will help somewhat, but hot soap and water will do, and is less hard on the hands. When this crust of dirt is somewhat loosened, with a woollen cloth, kerosene, and any good metal polish, rub and rub, and then rub some more. When your arms are rested begin and rub again, and gradually in spots and lines the silvery surface will appear, slowly broadening as you work on. Of course, specimens which have not been cleaned in years will be the only ones requiring such labour, and when once bright can easily be kept so. A final brilliant polish can be given by whitening and a woollen cloth. Dents and bends can sometimes be removed by means of a wooden mallet and pad of leather, but one will be much more likely to damage a piece still further, for as it is a soft metal, pewter is easily knocked out of shape.

Small scratches and lines will often wear away with frequent cleanings, and any way seem a hall-mark of antiquity and respectability.

Quite a contrast to such elegance as these candlesticks in Figure 302 can be seen in the group of stout little pewter lamps next shown (Figure 303). They were made before 1763 without doubt, for at that time the flat-wicked lamp was invented, and was most popular since it gave such a superior light to the round-wicked one. All of these you see have round wicks. I do not doubt that the owner of the pair of tallest ones felt very well satisfied with them, and thought them most "gen-

282

teel." The lamp to the left has a bull's-eye of glass which concentrated the light for sewing or reading. Cannot you see the eager circle which gathered about of an evening, while the latest news of the war and of General Washington's movements were read from the broadsides which came so infrequently and were so badly printed?

Another means of procuring light was by what were called "whale-oil lamps," like the two shown in Figure 304. They were made of pewter, and sometimes of glass, but the pewter were more highly considered on account of their less perishable character. They were poor things at best, smoky and ill-smelling, and candles were used at all elegant entertainments, even if they did drip from chandelier or sconce and ruin the dresses and spot the coats of the dancers or diners. Whale oil was procurable as early as 1712, for by that date the Nantucket whalers were voyaging to distant seas in pursuit of the sperm whale. The oil boiled at sea was a pale yellow, and quite odourless. It was also the highest priced on that account, and so was not as commonly used as an inferior grade. These lamps are doubtless American made, for they are not marked, but were found in Massachusetts in a family whose oldest member could not recollect when they had not been called "old lamps."

Other humble lamps are shown in the next illustration, Figure 305, of pewter also; the swinging one was able to do duty as a hand-lamp when not wanted on the wall. The little lamp in the foreground was for bedroom

283

use, and may have been used to burn "camphine," as spirits of turpentine was called when used for lighting purposes; this gave a very white light, though extremely volatile and inflammable. It is not so very many decades since camphine was used in towns and villages; for only the other day a man in middle life told me that he remembered well being sent by his mother to buy camphine when he was a small boy, and of her particular injunctions not to spill it. He lived in Utica, New York, which considered itself quite a town. The earliest use of camphine was in 1834.

It was rather fortunate that our ancestors generally followed the custom of "early to bed and early to rise," or their eyes must have suffered from such poor and insufficient light. However, they were not bothered with a multiplicity of books, nor a dozen daily newspapers; and a single candle was enough to spin by, or to sit at rest on the settee and watch the fire crackle on the hearth. Indeed, this same candle would give light enough to compound a "night cap" of flip, to see when the loggerhead was red-hot, and that there were proper proportions of sugar and spice, pumpkin chips and beer, or whatever other personal touches went to the mixing of this favourite brew.

An unusually fine piece of pewter of German make appears at Figure 306. There has been a very large and very handsome mark on the bottom, but some parts of it have become quite obliterated. It is a soup tureen and tray, the tureen being capable of holding three or four quarts. The design on the cover, the knob, and

284

the handles are not common in this material, except in such pieces as are of the very choicest quality of plate pewter. This is a very rare and extremely choice example, and one rarely comes across a piece like it that is not a museum specimen. In fact, this specimen comes under that heading, as it belongs to that small and choice museum of antiques which is being gathered by the Misses Hewitt at Cooper Union, New York City.

Most of the early churches in this country had for their first communion sets those made of pewter, and it was generally all they could do to buy two tankards, a laver, and a round trencher. The cups were contributed by such of the congregation as were able to afford it. There are the remains of such a service at the Concord Antiquarian Society, and another at Deerfield, Massachusetts. As soon as possible the congregation obtained silver services, and the old pewter ones were turned adrift. We have heard of portions of such services, marked, turning up in a pedlar's wagon, and being rescued from oblivion by a good churchwoman of another creed.

It is rather safe to buy old pewter, if the price is moderate, for it has not been made to any extent during the last seventy years. Even the very method of mixing the metal and handling it seems quite forgotten, and cheap china, earthenware and glass have taken the place of a rich and silvery metal.

In Figure 307 is shown a set of platters and plates, the oval shape of platter to which we are accustomed coming in with chinaware.

285

The stew of meat and vegetables which composed the principal dish at the family dinner was put into one of the big trenchers, and all dipped in with their spoon or two-pronged fork (but these were a later fashion), and felt no worse for the community of interests.

The parents sat at the table, but children stood, as was considered only respectful; or, if they were much coddled, three-legged stools were provided for their use. They grew up straight backed and sturdy in those days, and woe betide the child that complained of feeling sick! A good dose of treacle and sulphur, catnip tea, or rhubarb, and an extra rub on the pewter, were the remedies applied.

Of the amount of pewter made in this country it would be hard to make an estimate. We began at it early, too, and in 1754 the London Pewterers appointed a committee to see if the exportation of moulds, tools, and utensils into " fforeign Markets " could not be prevented, since " they would soon render it impracticable for very little if any English Pewter to be vended in fforeign Markets."

Pewter was on sale in all the large cities here. About this same date Mr. Kirby, a well-known pewterer, advertises that he takes " bees-wax and old pewter in exchange for new."

Another merchant sells " Cork Rose butter, Albany planks, and pewter of the first quality."

Peter Faneuil, who gave the historic old hall of that name to Boston, Massachusetts, died in 1742. His inventory was so long and elaborate that it is classed under

286

one hundred and fifty-eight different heads. He had large quantities of brass, copper, and pewter goods, valued at over £200.

Pewter cisterns for holding water are also mentioned in these old inventories, but they are seldom met with. Boardman and Company made much pewter in New York. Fifty years before this, in 1743, John Halden advertised that he made and sold pewter ware of all kinds at Market Slip, New York. There was Robert Boyle, 1745, William Bradford, Francis Bassett, Henry Will, and Malcolm McEwen, all to be found in New York, and all ready to make pewter utensils to order or to sell you from their stock. By 1841 the last men who had retained this trade no longer advertised themselves as pewterers, but were ready to show Britannia ware of the newest patterns, and fresh from Birmingham or Sheffield.

XII — BUREAUS

IN the eighteenth century the term applied to this article of furniture when it was not called a " chest of drawers " was bureau-table or bureau-desk, or even commode-table, since commode was the name given to them in France; and in Chippendale's first edition are many illustrations of what he calls " French commode-tables," which are bureaus mounted on low cabriole legs.

All the celebrated French makers lavished their choicest materials and elegant designs on these commodes, and were not so anxious to make a piece of furniture look like something else than what it really was as were their English contemporaries. Clothes press was another name we find applied to these bureaus on legs, and little by little the term bureau grew in use till it crowded out all the other names.

In the first Figure (308) may be seen a choice example of the French commode, style Louis XVth, made of veneered woods with water-gilt ormolu mounts. In the time of the Grand Monarch, as Louis XIV loved to have himself styled, the rooms of the palaces and residences of the nobility were so lofty and vast that it required enormous pieces of furniture to fill them. During the Regency of Philippe of Orleans, the nobility

288

depleted by the extravagance of the previous reign, and wearied by the work of Le Brun and Boulle, which had become monotonous in the severity of its lines, demanded something new. Under the Regency the immense galleries disappeared, and the favourite room was the boudoir within whose modest dimensions the furniture of the previous reign could not find a place, so the call for something lighter and daintier was immediately felt. From this period dates the form of commode which exists to-day as the bureau, and though the Regency was really but a period of transition, many articles survive which for beauty of form and graceful decoration cannot be excelled.

The task of the decorative designer of this epoch was by no means an easy one. This was the period of the elegant and dainty in art as well as furniture, and Watteau, Lancret, and Pater set the fashion to which the *ébéniste* had to rise, and where he had to struggle to asert his place. One of his first efforts was to break up the stiff and stolid lines of the furniture made by his predecessors, which was necessitated by its size. The watchword was no longer massive grandeur, but grace and elegance. One of the first moves was to bend the stiff leg; and here we see the introduction into France of the cabriole leg, which appeared on chairs, sofas, and commodes. This use was not original with the Frenchman, for it had prevailed for many years in different forms in Holland, Flanders, and England. The place of the metal marquetry was supplied by that of wood, which was used of various kinds and contrasting

19

colours; and the opening of trade with China and Japan not only supplied the furniture workers with beautiful porcelain objects which could be inserted in the wood, but also with that exquisite Oriental product known as lacquer. This was used in panels and medallions in commodes and corner cabinets, and the contrast with dark-toned woods like tulip and king-wood was extremely rich. The metal mounts were made in long and sweeping lines, and set upon the furniture in such a way that they seemed an integral part of it, and did not interfere with its graceful lines and proportions.

The French *ébéniste* did not hesitate to combine many kinds of wood in the same piece, selected not only on account of their beauty, but for the way one made an admirable foil for one another. Age has given to these pieces a golden and mellow sheen, to which the perfect proportion of the piece lends but another charm. Even the changeable climate of the United States has but little effect upon these admirably made articles, and they are as perfect to-day as when they were first made. Within the last month I have seen exposed for sale in Rochester a lacquer table, red and black with cabriole legs and water-gilt mounts, which must be well over one hundred and fifty years of age, and which, except for some damage to the top, is still as beautiful as when it was made. It shines out from the dingy window, where it is placed, with a compelling lustre; and one feels almost compelled to buy it if only to give it a name, and recover it from association which must prove

290

most painful to an object which once had its place among the exalted of France.

The commode in Figure 308 has a top of marble, green and cream in colour, which seems to bring out the beautiful reddish colour of the woods. Ornate as this piece seems, it was but plain in comparison to those masterpieces of the middle and late eighteenth century in France.

In England they contented themselves with copying and adapting the French models, and in Figure 309 is a pert little bureau-dressing table on Hepplewhite's lines. It makes one almost smile, for the likeness is sufficient to make one recognise instantly the model from which he took his inspiration. The plain and elegant lines of the French piece are completely spoiled, and the knee-hole recess was a favourite at this time in many kinds of fancy tables.

The next example, Figure 310, is a museum specimen and a very handsome piece of furniture. Yet when you come to study it, even though both the lower bureau part and the upper glass fronted cabinet are inlaid with that floral design which was so common in the middle of the eighteenth century, you feel that this piece is made up of unrelated parts. The most obvious discrepancy is the relative size of the two pieces. The bottom would carry easily a cabinet top of considerably larger size, and the top of the bureau part protrudes too much to be in proper proportion. There is a certain sharpness to the carving of the cornice of the bookcase portion, and the pattern of the moulding of the latter does not match with that on the base of the piece. This putting together of two parts in this very article of furniture is a favourite device with dealers, and is one of the places where a quick observation will help you to detect the lack of symmetry which should exist between the two parts. In none of the old books by any of the English or French cabinet-makers do I find an example like this, the usage being that the sides of the top part shall come flush with the lower part, and not have that shelf-like projection which is seen in this piece. I give this by way of an example of the many fake pieces which are bought in good faith, and then presented to the student as examples worthy of study. The lower part is a good marquetry kettle-shaped bureau of Dutch make, with good handles and massive feet. The sides are of plain walnut, and the back legs a simple bracket, as we usually find in furniture of Dutch or Flemish make.

Just when the making of furniture of oak ceased and walnut was substituted it is hard to say. It is easier to put a definite date to the beginning of the mahogany period, which was about 1720. Roughly speaking, the oak period extended from the earliest times of which we have record to the later Stuart times. The walnut lasted from the later Stuart period, say 1670 to 1720. Of course there were many cases of overlap, and sometimes you will find a slant-top bureau desk, which should belong entirely to the mahogany period, made either of oak or walnut. Oak bureaus are such an anachronism that they cannot be regarded as genuine antiques,

292

although their forerunner, placed on legs with turned stretchers, is by no means unknown. Walnut bureaus with slant-tops, particularly those made of burr walnut, exhibiting a curiously knotted grain, are plenty enough; and we occasionally meet with regular bureaus of walnut also. Two are shown in Figure 311; one with a small Dutch foot and very elaborate handles, and the other with a block front. Neither of these are later probably than 1750, since the wood of which they are made and the style of handles are conclusive evidences of their age. The colour of old oak and old walnut, too, for that matter, depends largely on their treatment, and whether they have been subjected to the influence of smoke and dust. When the surface of a piece of old furniture comes to require what is called " doing over," never allow dark stains or varnish to be applied. Beeswax and turpentine with a wad of flannel are the proper articles for the amateur; and if the object on which you wish to expend your care is a table top, and if it is not excessively damaged, a few drops of linseed oil and a brick sewed up in several layers of flannel are your best materials. Drop a little of the oil on the table, then smear it over the surface with a soft rag, and then begin to rub. It is in the latter process that success lies, and not in inundations of the oil. This same treatment is the best for the veneered walnut furniture of what we call " Queen Anne " period. If your piece looks very badly, and has suffered from too frequent applications of varnish, rub it lightly with fine sandpaper, which will remove the roughness, and then

293

proceed with the linseed oil and polishing. This will eventually bring it to a better condition than the best French polishing, but it will not stand being stained with wine nor much water.

A curious instance of over-devotion to duty in this very line was brought to my attention the other day. A walnut table which had been in daily use in a dining-room for over sixty years had now passed on, through inheritance, to a young housekeeper who called in assistance to know what was the matter with it, and what could be done. It had been a good piece, built on plain and simple lines, but the top was worn in positive grooves, the softer part of the wood between the veins seeming to have been scooped out; otherwise the table was in good condition, and seemed to have had the best of care. The son of the house, whose mother had owned the table, finally, under his young wife's questions, told how its condition came about. It seems that his mother had a servant, one of the old-fashioned kind who lived long in one family, and that this girl had been taught that every day this table had to be rubbed with a waxed brush. She came into the family at the age of sixteen, and had lived with them over forty years; and being stout and carefully trained, she had literally rubbed this table to pieces in her desire to keep it always in the highest state of polish! If a cloth had been used it might have pulled through, but the brush under her vigorous hand was too much for mere wood. There was nothing for it but a new top, and now the rubbing has to begin all over, this time under less strenuous hands.

294

Too much beeswax and turpentine will produce a glassy surface, which seems to take away the feel of the wood. This is almost as much a mistake as too little polish. Potash and water will remove the surplus of coating; but then the process has to be begun again, and it takes a long time to bring it to the state of absolute perfection, that is, with neither too much nor too little polish.

Old oak has sometimes been degraded by being painted white. When this is the case it must be cleaned by scraping and potash cleaning. In the grain of the wood will probably remain some traces of the paint, giving it a silver grain, which it is nearly impossible to remove. In fact, if it is not too marked it had better be left, since at any rate it is a mark of age, and to remove it further would be beyond the scope of almost any amateur. In trying to detect old furniture from spurious imitations, if the piece is carved, pay particular attention to the state of the carving. Any piece of domestic furniture which has been in use will have the lines of the carving much worn away by the necessary dusting and the rubbing against it in passing it. There will be no hardness or sharpness, and the finer lines will be to a certain extent filled up with dirt, dust, and wax. The dents and scars are not always to be trusted, since " the foot of a master," as the French put it, could contrive to administer such signs of wear on an entirely new piece.

In many old pieces of furniture, particularly bureaus, the presence of the worm or beetle which riddles them is very unpleasant. In an old cherry bureau which I own, and which has nothing to recommend it but its capacious size, the worms are most annoying, covering with a fine dust the contents of the drawers, and working with a speed that in a single night produces quite a little pile of dust. The holes are elliptical rather than round, and the creature seems to take pleasure in making two or three of these so close together that they will sometimes merge into one large hole.

The commonest of these pests is the *Anobium domesticum,* and the larva or grub which works the greatest havoc is a trifle more than an eighth of an inch long. When the creature is in the beetle stage of its existence it is even smaller. Many times I have tried to gain a sight of these little fellows which are at work almost under my very hand; but though I sometimes hear the click of their jaws, which is called the " death-watch," I can see only the work, never the worker. They are seldom found in mahogany, seeming to prefer less dense wood, though they will occasionally be found even in that, if the article has in it an inferior piece of wood.

A fine mahogany piece is shown in the next Figure, 312, having a serpentine front cut from the solid wood, and carved ball-and-claw feet. The board top corresponds in its curves with the lines of the front,while the shell which is at the bottom is not commonly found in such a position. This bureau is made in two sections, the top part with the drawers fitting into the base with the legs. This was the way the upper part was set in the lower part of high-boys, and I am inclined to think

296

that such pieces were made at about the time the high-boys became less called for. Many of the small bureaus have handles on the side for lifting them about, and I have seen them on walnut as well as mahogany pieces. The drawers of the bureau in Figure 312 have the narrow little moulding on the bureau and not on the drawer itself. The willow brasses are of the style which was in use as early as the first half of the eighteenth century, and continued in use for many years. Unfortunately one of the handles on this piece is missing.

A small bureau shown in Figure 313 has the overlapping edge on the drawer, and is in the style used during the latter part of the eighteenth century. It is a plain piece of cherry, and very much less ornamental than the bureau shown in Figure 314. This is Hepplewhite with curly maple panels set into mahogany. There is a line of inlay of whitewood where the maple and mahogany join, and around each drawer is a single narrow moulding. The handles are of an unusual shape, and the escutcheons are of brass; and while the photograph gives the wood a stained appearance it is not so in the original, which is both choice and in the best condition. In fact it is one of the favourite pieces of a collector living in Vermont, who has a great house full of fine antiques which she has been many years in gathering. She apologised for the looks of the bureau, saying that the photograph did not tell the truth.

Both Hepplewhite and Shearer designed and made such bureaus as these, and they were successfully copied over here. They were substantial pieces of furniture, depending on the beauty of the woods put into them, and the good proportions of their lines for any beauty they might have. Only once have I come across a tall bureau like the one in Figure 315. It is not a high-boy, yet it is six feet tall, and I think was made for a special order. It is of solid mahogany except for a narrow veneered band about the drawers, also mahogany, and this band is defined by a thread-like line of whitewood. On the frame of the bureau are other lines of the inlay, and it has the graceful French foot which we always associate with the name of Hepplewhite.

The handles are round brass rosettes, very plain and solid, and altogether the piece is substantial and digni- fied. Every time I see it it seems more worthy than it did the time before, and yet for several years it has been looking for a home among articles suited to its age and merit.

On many of these bureaus were set little dressing- glasses, as they were called, set in a swinging frame, and with a few drawers below the glass to hold toilet articles. Madam Washington left, by will, to her son George, her " best dressing-glass," and at the sale of the furniture at Belvoir in 1774 he bought several glasses in gilt frames as well as dressing-glasses. At Mount Vernon now there is one of these glasses in the General's bedroom similar to the one shown in Figure 316.

This glass was said to be made about 1770, while the bureau is about the year 1810. These dressing-glasses were of many styles, and not alone wood, solid and veneered, was chosen to make them of, but Oriental lacquer ones are sometimes to be found. There are others also, painted in gold or colours on a black ground, and some are covered with beautiful inlay and are carved besides. For many years they were much used, and are mentioned, among glasses in " gold or choice mahogany frames," as on sale by 1750.

The bureau in Figure 316 is handsomely carved, with four pineapples at the tops of the posts and solid twisted pillars. The legs do not bear out the elegance of the rest of the piece, as they are but simple turned affairs, and rather detract from its appearance.

The drawers are solid mahogany with a simple moulding about them, and the rosette handles are of brass. This bureau has long been in the family which now possesses it; but there are many persons who long for such treasures and will buy them rather than not have them, though they admit that family heirlooms are the best after all. I know of a bureau like this, which was recently bought by one who has taken the disease of collecting, and who went through what might be called " experiences " in getting hold of it.

Little by little she had grown to be a collector, the first manifestations of the disease showing itself in the gathering of a few pieces of china, somewhat nondescript in character, and which came in diverse ways, some by gift and some by purchase. But the fever did not stop here; and as she had in addition the true collector's spirit and the faculty of finding "things" she went on, one step after another, till she was the proud owner of tables and chairs, desks and tabourets, lamps, girandoles, and other small articles too numerous to mention.

She laboured under disadvantages, too, for she was surrounded by a family whose chief ambition was to acquire new things, fresh of aspect and modern of form. The " antiques " which flowed into the house met with no appreciation, save from choice spirits like herself, who met and gloated over them, and wished they, too, could secure like bargains.

Then at last she had a house of her own to put them in, and those who came to scoff remained to admire, and the charm of the old furniture in its harmonious and artistic setting impressed even the Philistine whose taste had hitherto led him to admire those abominations known as " mission furniture," or the crude patterns which are foisted on a long-suffering public, many of whom, it is true, know no better than to admire.

Imagine the pleasure of our collector with all her possessions set out and well rubbed up; for after getting one of these elderly treasures the first thing to do is to put it in prime condition, and then consider how the thirst for more worlds to conquer must have devoured her. She did not depend only on her own unaided efforts to " locate finds," but had scouts from every rank of life out on her war path for her. " Butter and egg women " were questioned, the milkman was interrogated, and no chance clew was allowed to go uninvestigated.

So many pieces were hers at last, that the only thing she really " must have " was a bureau, and the outlying

districts were laid under contribution to supply one.
At last, after months of patient waiting, one was heard
of through one of the scouts, — its carved feet and
posts duly described, — and our collector felt that have
it she must, though she had not seen it. To tell the
truth, it lay in the country, seven miles from her home,
and as there were other "fiends" in the place where
she lived ready to snap up any trifles which became
noised about, she concluded to go and get it. Upon
due reflection it seemed best to go in some vehicle which
would bring back the bureau; so in her enthusiasm she
started for that drive of fourteen miles, seven out and
seven back, in a springless wagon, her only seat being
a board set on the sides. The littlest of her dogs was
taken along for company and to keep him out of mis-
chief, and on a bright autumn morning she started.

As they neared the house where the treasure was the
collector's heart rose in her mouth.

"What's this," she asked of the driver; " a funeral? "

" No," said he; " don't think so."

" Oh, can it be an auction? " she cried, acute despair
in her mind as visions of the bureau being snapped up
by some one else rose before her imagination.

" No, don't seem to be that neither," drawled the
driver, who could not be expected to be so keen on the
scent.

When she got into the yard this is what resolved itself
before her eyes: an old lady in her Sunday best sat in
a large arm-chair. Near her was a cow with the milking-
stool and a milk pail, a man holding up her head, while

301

at a little distance sat an artist painting the scene. The rest of the family, and such of the neighbours as could leave their chores, stood around in an admiring circle.

"Ain't it lovely?" asked one, as our collector drew near. "Ma is having her portrait painted with the cow. Her cow died about a week back, and it seems as though Ma could n't get along without some picture of her, so we borrowed a cow from one o' the neighbours, and he 's a paintin' it just lovely!"

At this moment, from the group gathered around the artist, rose sounds of eager discussion.

"No," said one, "I tell ye that 's all wrong. She did n't have no spot there, it was lower on the flank."

"You 're wrong yourself, Abram; 't was on the other side that spot was." And it was then explained to our collector that the defunct cow was a black and white spotted one, while the borrowed one, which was standing as model, was of the "plain-red" variety, and the artist was putting in the spots according to the memories of the family, which did not agree on the location of a single one of them.

All this time our collector was on needles and pins to see the bureau, and at last diverted enough attention to herself to get one member of the family to detach herself to show it to her. It was down in the cellar, and when she saw it her heart swelled. It was mahogany, sure enough, with carved posts, and carved feet too, though the latter had been unscrewed to allow it to be put in the cellar. She made an offer which was accepted, and the heavy bureau was brought up and was being loaded into the wagon when it caught the artist's eye. "What," he cried, "you will sell that for ——— (naming the sum)? Why, I'd give you $——— (naming a dollar more) for it."

Consider what a moment of agony for our collector!

She assisted as best she could, by pushing the drawers into the wagon, seizing the dog and climbing in also, and bidding her Jehu in a hurried voice to start right away. She thought her prize was to be wrested from her, and did not feel easy until she was well out of sight of the farmhouse, the artist, and all the rest.

What though the ride home was long and hot? What though the lack of springs became every moment more apparent to her tired frame, and that the dog was restive, and that she was sorry that she had started without a hat? To banish all these miseries it was but necessary to glance at the prize before her, to stroke its satin sides, and to consider where it would show to the best advantage when, rubbed and restored, it should rise in its old-time beauty. The village street which led to her home was long and straight; and as she rumbled down it in the bright afternoon she was espied by a party of her friends assembled to play bridge, and among them were several rival collectors who rushed out to see what she had secured.

Do you think she was amply repaid for her pains when she displayed her treasure? If you don't, then you do not know what the pleasures of collecting are, and had better stick to your "parlour suites," and get your household goods by the half-dozen from the nearest factory.

A rather unique piece, to which it is difficult to assign a period, is shown in Figure 317. It is of solid mahogany, richly carved with the full-length figures of two of the apostles. These figures seem to take the place of the usual carved pillars, but you will notice on the base of each figure a small pointed wooden knob. This pulls out, and when it is removed the figure on its base swings back, revealing two narrow but deep cupboards. The bureau is said to have come from a monastery, and the cupboards were used for holding the wine used on the altar. The carving is sharp and little worn, but the handles are of an early pattern, and the recessed Gothic panel in the upper drawer is unusual. In deciding the age of a piece of furniture it is always necessary to take into consideration for what purpose it has been used, and its situation. Churches and cathedrals, though few buildings have suffered more from the depredations of the ignorant and the profane as well as the innovators lacking taste, often contain other furniture besides the chests, chairs, and tables which we expect to find in them. Articles which have stood for many years in such places are much less worn and defaced than those of equal age which have been in domestic use, though, unfortunately, there are doubtful pieces in sacred edifices as well as everywhere else.

You cannot base your deductions as to age upon the wood used by cabinet-makers as the base to which they applied veneer, for a chest of drawers may be of walnut

304

veneered on oak, except the fronts of the drawers, which would be probably on some lighter wood. In old oak and early walnut furniture the parts will fit much less accurately than in furniture of a later period, when the cabinet-makers used mahogany and made from seasoned wood the choice pieces which are so admirable even to-day.

Spanish mahogany is the choicest variety of this fine wood, Honduras mahogany or baywood being distinctly inferior in colour and weight.

The subject of handles has been gone into at some length in the "Old Furniture Book," and they will have to be mentioned here very briefly. Iron was the metal used for the oaken furniture, the locks and hinges often being elaborately wrought. When mahogany came on the field brass was used for handles and escutcheons. There are chests and cupboards dating to the fifteenth century still existing, and these show handles of iron, in pattern a ring dropping from a flat wrought rosette or a round plate. Drop or bail handles, smaller at the top than at the bottom, are found on furniture of the next period, and these are also of iron. With the opening of the eighteenth century a solid pear-shaped drop takes the place of the bail handle of iron, and is most frequently of brass. As the century advances the bail handle becomes the ordinary one in use, the metal plate from which it hangs being first incised, with irregular outline, then pierced; while from the Chippendale period it was wrought, or pierced with more or less elaboration, having regard to the piece

20

upon which it was to be placed. With the advent of Hepplewhite and Sheraton the plate from which the handle hung took a round or oval form with a bail handle. The plate was decorated with a beehive, stars, a lion, or various devices, and they also used the lion's head with a ring hanging from its mouth. Glass handles came in after the beginning of the nineteenth century, and to my taste are always a disfigurement to a rich piece of mahogany. Battersea enamel knobs with heads or scenes upon them were occasional, but are now few and far between, and it is hard to find enough to fit out a bureau. I do know of six, all bearing portraits of American heroes, which are fitted on the three drawers of a charming little mahogany writing-table.

A bureau of mahogany with a tall swinging glass is shown in the next figure, 318. It is not a common pattern, and has fine carved pillars and a cylinder front drawer. The front feet are carved to match the pillars, but the sides of the mirror and the posts which hold it are quite plain. It would seem that the mirror was a later addition, except for the fact that it is set in the top of the dressing drawers, and screwed in.

In Figure 319 is a commodious bureau-desk with the central portion of what is usually the top drawer letting down on a brass quadrant, and forming a writing-desk. The two deep drawers at the side are fitted for wine, and so wide is the top that this object would seem to be almost as suitable for a sideboard as a desk or a bureau. It is partly veneered, and shows a deep, rich, reddish-brown colour with those fine whirl-

306

ing veins which are so popular. It was probably made about the time of the other Empire furniture, say from 1800 to 1820. Its history is not known, but it was rescued and restored, and sent up from the South, where so many fine pieces of furniture are still to be had. I am constantly receiving letters from all the Southern States, telling of antiques of one kind and another which are owned there. Some of them are amusing, some are pathetic. One of the former was from a woman whose husband was evidently well-to-do, who wrote me and sent me photographs of some really splendid things. There were elegantly carved chairs in Chippendale's ribbon-work pattern, carved four-poster beds, a table of solid mahogany with claw feet, and some " old blue " platters with those fine Cambridge views on them which would bring distraction to the ordinary collector. For years these things (which had belonged to her husband's family) had sought an inglorious refuge in the attic, but had recently, owing to articles on the subject meeting her eye, been brought down, and set out in the parlour. No, she would not sell, though large prices were offered her. Fortunately she found out in time what her treasures were worth.

One of the many pathetic letters was from an old lady of eighty, who asked my assistance in selling two linen sheets, two pillow-cases, and an old hair trunk! It is consoling when your readers have faith in your ability to serve them; but sometimes too much faith is almost as bad as too little!

The last bureau of all, 320, is also a derelict from

307

the South. It has carved and incised work on it, and glass knobs. These are of the opalescent variety, which are even more staring than the plain white ones. This bureau was intended to have a little dressing-glass stand upon it, and was made in the opening years of the nineteenth century. It is in excellent condition, and is almost large enough to keep the belongings of a whole family safely. This and the one preceding it are some of the last utterances of what might be called the American mahogany period. Then came the black-walnut age, which had nothing to recommend it, and which was responsible for the wholesale destruction of one of our finest native trees. Nobody displays black walnut furniture now who can get any thing else to take its place. Looking at the patterns in which this furniture was made, the unmeaning carvings with which it was plastered, and the bad lines and proportions, one can be quite sure that there will be no revival of it, as there has been of mahogany, and the best thing to do with it is to " pass it along."

XIII — COTTAGE ORNAMENTS

THERE are collectors, or perhaps I should say there are persons, who would be glad to be collectors if they could find some class of objects which would not take too much space to house, nor too much money to buy. They would not mind if the acquisition of their treasures was slow and difficult if, when found, each object was a joy and a delight.

" Cottage Ornaments," as they were called, fills such a want; and as many of them have histories, or were made in connection with some event of importance in England, there is much agreeable study connected with an intelligent grasp of the subject.

These small ornaments were made by the early potters to serve as mantel decorations; and while figures of great worth and beauty were put out by such famous potteries as Bow, Derby, Chelsea, Plymouth, and from the German, French, and Copenhagen factories as well, it is with the Staffordshire products chiefly that I propose to deal.

These earthenware figures were made not alone in Staffordshire, but at Leeds, Bristol, Fulham, Liverpool, Newcastle, and Sunderland, Swansea, Caughley, and several other places; but they are all classed under

the head of Staffordshire. As they are generally quaint
in their old-fashioned style and strong colouring, they
are interesting as giving pictures of the costume, manners, and customs of the time when they were put out.

Many of them deal with homely, every-day subjects;
and when in pairs it was the fashion to have a man and
a woman as may be seen in the pretty dairyman and
milkmaid which are given in Figure 321. These are
of the old creamy colour which is so characteristic of
bone paste, and, as is also common with this class
of figures in a cheaper grade, there is a sparing use of
colour in the figures themselves, although the bases are
made to represent green grass and a brook which runs
blue water. The milkmaid has a pretty little pattern
on the bottom of her petticoat, in that rich, dark shade
of blue which is ever such a favourite with the potters,
and the hair of both is brown. As you hold in your
hands the satiny paste, note its extreme lightness, and
feel how smooth the bottom is worn with frequent
movings when the shelf was dusted, you do not mind
that there is not much colour, and thank your stars that
you happened along in time to secure it, and that it
was absolutely perfect.

In answer to correspondents in both this country and
England as to what is my special hobby, I will now
admit that it is Staffordshire Ornaments, and when you
have had the pleasure of gathering a dozen or two of
these treasures you will admit that the hobby is one
which is full of pleasurable surprises.

The earliest of these figures, and a kind which it is

Fig. 318 Bureau

Fig. 317 Carved Bureau

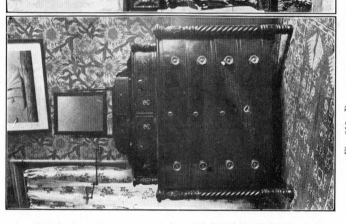

Fig. 316 Bureau

Fig. 320   Mahogany Bureau

Fig. 319   Bureau-Desk

Fig. 321 DAIRYMAN AND MILKMAID

Fig. 322 ADMIRAL NAPIER

Fig. 323 GROUP OF STAFFORDSHIRE FIGURES

Fig. 324 CROWN-DERBY AND STAFFORDSHIRE

Fig. 325 "COTTAGE ORNAMENTS"

Fig. 326   Two-Figure Group

Fig. 327   "Cottage Ornaments"

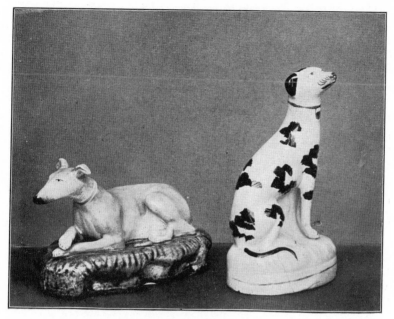

Fig. 328 STAFFORDSHIRE DOGS

Fig. 329 "COTTAGE ORNAMENTS"

Fig. 330 "Cottage Ornaments"

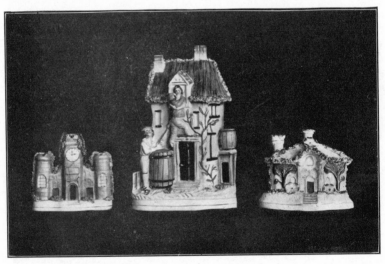

Fig. 331 Staffordshire Houses

almost impossible to find in this country, were made of a coarse pottery and covered with slip and then decorated. Indeed it is hard to secure such even in England, for while it is true that this branch of pottery has not attracted many private collectors till recently, it has been in demand by museums, and it is generally in repositories such as these that you run across these queer old pieces. To tell the truth many of them are too grotesque to be attractive, particularly the cats and owls which were such favourites.

The salt glaze are as rare as the slip figures, but there are many museum figures which may be studied. I have seen them with both single and double figures, a favourite type being two lovers sitting under a tree and holding hands. These salt glaze figures have no colour, and have the curiously pitted surface like an orange peel, which is a marked feature of this ware. There are several collections of salt glaze figures in England, those of Mr. Willet and Dr. Sidebotham being peculiarly full of interesting specimens. These figures are generally small, colourless as has been stated, except the eyes, which are represented by round bead-like dots of black or brown, giving a very startling effect. Many of the salt glaze figures are charming, since they are usually modelled by hand, the prettiest which I have seen being the seated figure of a boy, drawing a thorn from his foot. The figure is quite perfect, though tiny, as it is only three and seven-eighths inches high.

Marbled figures, called " Astbury marbled figures," are quite as rare as the salt glaze, particularly in this

country. They were produced frequently in two-col-
oured clays, with the same beady eyes as the salt glaze
ones, but they have a softness of colouring and a
smoothness of feel to the touch that is most attractive.
These figures were first made in about 1743 by the
elder Astbury, and then by his son Thomas, and probably by other potters as well.

Thomas Wheildon, who potted about 1750 and made
mottled and agate ware, also put out many different
figures, busts, officers on horseback, a man and woman
on a horse, she seated on a pillion, and many dogs. If
you find any of these figures in this country, set it
straightway in the centre of your collection, let no profane hand dust it, and keep it as long as you can. I
know one such dog, seated on a fine green cushion, but
alas he is not mine; he was far too costly for my collection. Like the other styles mentioned, these mottled
figures were made at other potteries, and their harmony
of colouring, soft browns and yellows, always made
them attractive. Busts of Milton, fourteen inches high,
the "Market Girl," Alderman Beckford, and several
groups are all fine and eagerly sought by collectors.

In order to give some idea of what prices the choicer
figures from the celebrated old potteries are worth, I
will give a few figures showing the prices which they
have brought at auction sale within the last few months
at London. "A Chelsea figure of Lord Cambden, £30.
A pair of figures, Derby, shepherd and shepherdess,
£63." In February, 1904, the collection of a Mr. Kidd,
who had been collecting for fifty years, came under

the hammer in London. Among many hundreds of examples I take the following: " Seated figure of a lady holding a basket in her lap, two lambs at her feet, richly decorated scroll, Chelsea, nine inches high, £21." " Pair of statuettes, shepherdess and shepherd, richly coloured, Chelsea, eleven inches high, £38 17s."

The Staffordshire figures run much lower, of course, the range of prices within my own experience going from thirty-five cents for a tiny group of two children, to seventy-five dollars for a six inch bust of Shakespeare, one of the rare and fine ones by Wood, beautifully modelled and coloured, and in perfect condition.

The choicer china and porcelain figures are no more artistic and pretty than the pottery ones from Staffordshire. The mode of manufacture was the same, for when the figure came from the mould in the fresh paste, it went into the hands of the " repairer " as he was called, the head was stuck on, as were the legs, arms, dogs, lambs, vases, and other accessories, the lines of the drapery were sharpened up, the colouring applied which covered many defects, and then the object was glazed. This glazing destroyed many of the finer lines by filling them up, and in many of the examples which I have it can be seen that only certain colours were applied under glaze, — vivid orange, apple-green, pink, all of them favourite colours, being applied over glaze. Sir Charles Napier shows plainly that he was cast in a mould, for the lines of the edges show clearly (see Figure 322). The oldest figures are hollow throughout and are open at the base; those that have a closed base

313

always have a hole in them somewhere. Sir Charles has it in the middle of his back.

That collector of Staffordshire who aims to have his collection as choice as possible, will tell you that these figures are roughly divided into two periods, the Early and the Victorian. He speaks with much contempt of the latter. The Early pieces were made by such potters as the Woods, Ralph, Aaron and Enoch, Wood and Caldwell, Neal, Voyez, who at one time worked for Wedgwood, Wedgwood himself, Wheildon, Walton, Adams, Lakin and Poole, Wilson, Bott and Co., Turner, Edge and Grocott, Hall, Salt and I. Dale, and many others. Besides the pastoral groups which were made, there were many religious and classical as well as domestic subjects. The marked specimens are exceedingly rare, since it seems to have been the general custom not to mark them.

"The Flight into Egypt" was a great favourite. One example of it is given in Figure 323, top row at the right. Pray observe the rotundity of the figure of Joseph, and the abundant cut of his trousers! The English potter was nothing if not fanciful in his portrayals. Falstaff was another popular figure. He is in this same figure opposite " The Flight," and below him on the left is one of those classical figures so much in demand during the last years of the eighteenth and opening decades of the nineteenth centuries. The central group at the bottom of this picture is not Staffordshire properly, but Bristol, and exceedingly charming and dainty it is.

314

High class figures were often copied in Staffordshire. Compare the Falstaff in Figure 324 with the one just seen. The latter is Crown-Derby, and worth in pounds what the other is in pence. This is but one of the many instances to be found. In this same picture the middle figure is a well-known old one, called "The Hunter." It is one of a pair, is hollow and marked "Walton," one of the eighteenth century makers, who was known for his excellent work. The third figure is also charming. "Andromache weeping over the ashes of Hector." This subject was treated by the works at Leeds as well as by the Crown-Derby porcelain works. All these three pieces are exceptionally fine as might be expected, for they belong in Salem, Massachusetts, that repository for so much that is rich and rare.

In Figure 325 are a number of subjects, and two of the portrait busts. The large figure in the centre was for a bunch of flowers or dried grasses, and there were many double figures or single ones for this purpose. I have a group of two seated in a bower with the vase part between them. They are not very choice since they lack colour, but a nice dog makes part of the group.

A double figure group is shown in Figure 326, charming in colour, and it is too bad that his hat is chipped off, for otherwise the figures are perfect. In Figure 325 may be seen two figures with tree-like backgrounds. This class of specimen is called "boskies," from the French term *bocage*. Such backgrounds are more common among the porcelain and china figures from the

315

high class potteries than among the Staffordshire ones. Few figures with them can now be found in a perfect condition, for these twigs and sprays are so fragile that they were easily broken, as were the swords and spears with which so many of the figures were armed. Both of the Falstaffs had swords originally in the right hand.

In the next Figure (327) is shown a miscellaneous group of figures, the soldier in the centre being the oldest and best. The watch-holder to the right is now mine, and is marked on the base " Milton." Imagine that poet in a sprigged matinée dictating " Paradise Lost " to his weary daughters! The next best piece in this group is the rooster. He is old and good, and this bird has always been a favourite with the potters. Next in order of value and interest are the dogs, and the collecting of these animals alone occupies the attention of many distinguished collectors, some of them choosing only what is known as the " spotted dog." One collection already numbers two hundred and fifty pieces, each one different. The dogs shown in Figure 327 are to my taste the least interesting of all the varieties. In the next picture, Figure 328, are shown two of my own which are spirited and fine. The spotted one is by far the elder, and is perfect with the exception of a crack near the base. He is of bone paste, light and soft, and every time I look at him, particularly if it be near the full of the moon, I expect to hear him howl. He looks all ready to bay the moon. The recumbent dog is a fawn-coloured greyhound, a lovely creature lying on a dark-blue cushion, in which is a small opening for a pen, as he is an inkstand.

There are several other patterns of greyhounds, also guardians of ink, which I hope to acquire to make my collection complete. There is also a standing one with a hare in his mouth which is very nice, and one may get at least eight different patterns of greyhounds. There are also some small Pomeranians, like those to be seen in Figure 325. Indeed, the collecting of dogs is a most inviting field, for when you have the greyhounds all complete, there still remain the pointers, of which there are many patterns, before you come to the spaniel, which is in reality the " spotted dog." After you have all the dogs, whole dogs, which you can get, you can then take up the faces and masks, a branch of the subject which, though difficult, is engrossing. These heads of dogs and foxes were used as whistles, or for handles to canes and hunting crops, for paper-weights, and apparently for wall ornaments as well, since some of them are to be found life size. Sir Walter Gibney has a collection of seventy-three of these, nearly all of them of Staffordshire ware, ranging from the early mottled and agate or tortoise shell wares, to those of later times, which were coloured to life. There was hardly a firm of potters, whether of porcelain or pottery, which has not turned its hand to the making of dogs. Go where you will, at Worcester, at Bow, at Battersea, where they enamelled them, at Rockingham, at Chelsea, at Burslem, they all made dogs. Go to Holland and you will find the Dutchman had his favourites too, though he will colour them blue to keep his blue cows in company; but they are attractive for all that. Even from our own potteries

317

came dogs of many colours and sizes, but those will be mentioned later.

In Figure 329 of course the most eagerly sought figure is the Franklin, nine inches high. This is one of the old pieces and always attractive. Franklin has the credit for being more often produced in porcelain and pottery than any other one person, not even Washington excepted. His long residence abroad, his picturesque personality, particularly the fur cap which he was so fond of wearing, made him a welcome figure to the potters; and there is no drinking vessel too grand or too humble but that you may, perchance, find his face on the inside or out, nor was there any pottery too coarse for a statuette of him. The figures of the cobbler and his wife are well-known and good examples, but the " Omer Pasha," which also has on it " Success to Turkey," and the Uncle Tom and little Eva are too modern to be very valuable.

The next group (330) is from my own collection, and the figures are of varying degrees of merit. All are well coloured and most of them well modelled; but one only is old, and even that is not more than eighty years of age. This is the Cricketer, on the upper row. His head has been broken off and glued on; and when the owner sent it to me she apologised for this defect, and also for the damaged nose, by saying that for years it had been the chief treasure in a lively family of thirteen. It seems strange that any of it survived such wear and tear. The three figures in the top row are the stars of the collection: the Cricketer on account of

318

his age, the middle figure on account of the tragedy which led to her being perpetuated in pottery, and the seated figure on account of the story connected with my getting it.

The middle figure says on its base Emily Sandford, and you might not think to look at her grim expression that she had ever had a lover. She did, however, and his name was Henry Rush. He was the tenant of a house called Potash Farm, and his landlord was the owner of the Stanfield Estate, and lived in an imposing mansion called Stanfield Hall, which was a regular " moated grange." For some reason or other Rush attempted to murder his landlord, the latter's wife, and, indeed, the whole family. He did succeed in killing some of them and wounding others, and he disposed of the bodies in the moat. Emily knew all about it, and finally told the whole dreadful story; and Rush was hanged in front of Norwich Castle, his being the last public execution to take place there.

All England rang with the horror of these deeds, which took place more than fifty years ago; and a set of Staffordshire ornaments, were made, five pieces in all, consisting of Emily, Henry, Potash Farm, Stanfield Hall, and Norwich Castle. These latter three pieces were of the style of ornaments, which were used to burn pastiles or scented tablets in, the perfumed smoke coming out of the chimneys in realistic style. I show some of these houses in Figure 331. The only collector who is known to have anything approaching a complete set of the Rush pieces is Prince Frederick

319

Duleep Singh of England, who has four of the five, the Norwich Castle being wanting. In my own case, I am on the lookout for Rush himself; and when I secure him I shall be content to let the other pieces go, as the houses are bulky and not pretty in colour or form. I have never come across one of these houses in this country, though there are of course plenty of them here if one could find them. The castle with the clock is the oldest; but the middle one shows that class of ornament which appealed to peasant humour, the pitchfork being particularly in evidence. All of these three examples have little sprigs and bunches of flowers scattered about the base, and these were also put on most of the figures. Many of them are highly coloured, and they add considerably to the gay appearance of the ornaments.

Coming almost into this branch of pottery were jugs, such as is shown in the following Figure (332). It is easily recognised as a caricature of Napoleon, the hand over the breast and the uniform being perfectly distinctive. It is an old and rare piece, but is in proof condition and shows its careful handling.

So popular were the Cottage Ornaments that more than one firm of American potters endeavoured to supply the market with such a class of articles, which they managed to sell for fifteen and twenty-five cents. The ornaments made at the Novelty Works, Bennington, Vermont, were made from 1847 through the next ten years, and have now become so rare that they command extraordinary prices. They were sent about the

320

Fig. 332 Napoleon Jug

Fig. 333 Bennington Ware

Fig. 334 Bennington Ware

Fig. 335 Pennsylvania Ware

country by means of pedlars; and while the more useful
articles made in this brown mottled ware have long since
been reduced to bits by hard usage, some of the ornaments, like the dog and cow shown in Figures 333 and
334, are still treasured in remote farmhouses as well
as in the cabinet of the collector. The dog is an example
of the best class of work produced at the Bennington
works, and similar ones are also to be found in white.
I saw a pair on sale in New York this last summer.
They were of very heavy white pottery, and have weird
blue eyes, which give them a Dutch look, and make
them far less attractive than when made in the homely
but rich-tinted brown ware. The cow answered for
a cream jug as well as an ornament, the lid on her back
admitting the milk, while a hole in the mouth was used
to pour it out.

All the patterns from which these articles were made
were destroyed by fire in 1873, and since that time
their value has steadily increased. These little potteries up in the mountains of Vermont acquired a wide
fame, and potters came from all over the world to
work in a place where each man was allowed to work
out his own ideas. The mottled ware like our two
figures, to make it of value, must have stamped on it
either the circular impressed mark, " Patent Enamel,
1849," or the mark " U.S.P.," which stood for United
States Pottery. It is not safe to trust to your own
judgment about unmarked pieces unless you know
all their previous history. Be sure also that they
are in the fine shades of brown, green, and olive

21

which distinguished this ware from the English Rockingham.

There are two or three collectors who have made a special hobby of getting these Bennington pieces, some of them living in Vermont, where they had special opportunities of securing authentic specimens.

Two other ornaments, more curious than beautiful, are shown in the last Figure (335). They are the work of Pennsylvania potters about 1860, and were found near New Oxford, in that state. One of them is a bird, which might belong to any species which is fancied by the potter, who seldom lets fidelity to nature interfere with his idea of what is ornamental. But the other shows an eider famous from mythological times for her habit of stripping her own breast to provide down to line the nest for her young.

In many of the museums of this country there is an excellent opportunity to study the figures which were once so common; and before one embarks on the delightful pursuit of collecting them he should become familiar with the popular patterns, the colours which were generally used, and the general appearance of the ornaments.

INDEX

INDEX

325

INDEX

327

INDEX

328

Fig. 332 NAPOLEON JUG

Fig. 333 BENNINGTON WARE

Fig. 334 BENNINGTON WARE

Fig. 335 PENNSYLVANIA WARE